Christian Thinking

© 2016 by Chad Sychtysz

2016 Spiritbuilding Publishing. All rights reserved.
No part of this book may be reproduced in any form without
the written permission of the publisher.

Published by
Spiritbuilding Publishing
15591 N. State Rd. 9
Summitville, IN 46070

Printed in the United States of America
CHRISTIAN THINKING
By Chad Sychtysz
ISBN 978-0-9829811-9-1

Scripture taken from the NEW AMERICAN STANDARD BIBLE ®,
Copyright © 1960, 1962, 1963, 1968, 1971, 1972, 1973, 1975, 1977,
1995 by The Lockman Foundation. Used by permission.

Spiritual "equipment" for the contest of life

Acknowledgments

In essence, I have been gathering notes for this book over the course of my 20+ years as a minister of the gospel. Many points in the topics covered here are drawn from my conversations with, observations of, and insightful contributions from a number of people. Some have contributed to this book knowingly, others unknowingly; thus, some I can acknowledge by name, others must be acknowledged anonymously. In particular, I want to express my appreciation to Curtis and Patsy Cantwell for their having read through the finished manuscript (more than once) in order to clean it up and make it shine. I am (again) indebted to and appreciative of Carl "Mac" McMurray at Spiritbuilding Publishing for continuing to support my writing ministry. No single person has gone out on a limb for me more than he has. Jamey Hinds deserves my sincere thanks for taking my raw manuscript and turning it into something presentable. I am always thankful for my family's encouragement to write, including my church "family" that often endures the often-unscripted original classes and talks that inspire books like this in the first place. I especially want to thank my wife, Honey, for always being there, no matter when and no matter what.

I believe that God has blessed me with a talent to write. There are many and far better writers out there, and I am fully (and painfully) aware of this. Nonetheless, it has been a driving passion of mine to use *my* God-given gift to help people draw near to the Father and His Son, and to teach the Word of God as effectively and accurately as I am capable of doing. Therefore, I am humbly and profoundly grateful to God for blessing me, using me in His service, and allowing me to honor Him in this special way.

*This book is dedicated to Honey,
my wife and best friend.*

Table of Contents

Introduction 8

Section One: The Attitude of a Believer
- What Is Your Attitude? 14
- The Importance (and Limitations) of Knowledge 17
- Thoughts and Emotions 21
- Dwelling on Good Thoughts 26
- How Your Attitude Affects You 32
- The Risks of Thinking like a Christian 44
- Contrast of Worldly and Christian Thinking 50
- How to Develop a Godly Attitude 56
- The Need for Spiritual Growth 59
- The "Blessed" Believer 66
- The Danger of Discontentment 70

Section Two: The Perspective of a Believer
- How Do You See Things? 75
- Governed by Love and Wisdom 80
- Conservatism and Liberalism 82

Section Three: Truth and Objectivity
- What Is "Truth"? 90
- Your Truth and God's Truth 92
- Objective and Subjective Thinking 97
- God Has No Opinion of You 106
- Who Are You to Judge? 110
- What Would You Say? 112
- Perceptions and Reality 114

Section Four: Godly Love
- What Is "Godly" Love? 118
- God So Loved the World 120
- How Can a Loving God Allow...? 127
- The Evidence of God's Love 130
- Loving One Another 135

Section Five: Disciples of the Master
- What a Disciple Is (and Is Not) 140
- The New Testament Pattern 142
- "Radical" Discipleship 146
- A Christian's Vocation 153
- The Lord Who Calls Us 155
- What Christ's Lordship Requires of Us 160
- Christ the Teacher 165
- Becoming Perfectly Human 171

Section Six: Greatness through Servitude
- Disciples Are Servants, Not Spectators 176
- Slaves of Righteousness 181
- The Nature of Our Servitude 184
- Various Kinds of Service 190

Section Seven: Living with Gratitude
- The Giving of Thanks 197
- Gratitude as an Act of Worship 199
- Acknowledging the Giver of Gifts 204
- God Is Good, No Matter What 209
- Gratitude and Prayer 216

Section Eight: Change Is a Gift
- Our Typical View toward Change 220
- Gratitude versus Resistance 225
- Old Thinking, New Thinking 229
- Repentance Is All about Change 235
- The Components of Repentance 237
- Good Fruit Comes from Good Trees 239

Summary Thoughts
- Christian Thinking Leads to Christian Living 245
- Thinking of Heaven 248

Endnotes 252
Sources Used 280

Introduction

What is "Christian thinking"? Two passages immediately come to my mind. One is a bit involved:

> Now we have received, not the spirit of the world, but the Spirit who is from God, so that we may know the things freely given to us by God, which things we also speak, not in words taught by human wisdom, but in those taught by the Spirit, combining spiritual thoughts with spiritual words. But a natural man does not accept the things of the Spirit of God, for they are foolishness to him; and he cannot understand them, because they are spiritually appraised. But he who is spiritual appraises all things, yet he himself is appraised by no one. For who has known the mind of the Lord, that he will instruct Him? But we have the mind of Christ (1 Corinthians 2:12-16).

The other is much shorter: "For if anyone thinks he is something when he is nothing, he deceives himself" (Galatians 6:3). Both passages say something very significant regarding the method and content of Christian thinking. First, Christians ought to know of and be thinking about God in the manner in which He has revealed Himself in His Word as well as the internalization of the Word itself.[1] Second, a person can be seriously mistaken about what (or how) he thinks if indeed he has abandoned this first principle.

Christian thinking is not just "thinking about God," dwelling on good things, or reading the Bible. In essence, it is the process in which we give Christ *full controlling interest* over how we think and what we think about with the expressed purpose of having "the mind of Christ." If we are taught by Christ, then we will think like He wants us to think. If we are led by Him, then we will go where He wants us to go. If we truly allow Him to *train* us (as His disciples), then we will increasingly become more like Him (the Master). This is what Paul is saying in the first passage I cited.

INTRODUCTION

Having the *mind* of Christ—thinking like He has taught us to think—necessarily requires a basic understanding of that thinking process. Certainly "thinking" involves attitude, perspective, objectivity, etc. These are all subjects that I cover initially in this book. But this thinking also leads us into other dimensions of the life of a believer: love, discipleship, servitude, gratitude, and change. These are also subjects that I cover in this book. In other words, we begin with more of a conceptual approach, but we must not leave it there. Eventually—and sooner than later—all Christian thinking must manifest itself in a visible and practical manner. What holds all this together is *truth*, which is appropriately in this book's middle section.

But Paul also says something about a "natural man." This refers to the unconverted person who thinks like the world has taught him to think. He is a product of his own secular society; he has been conditioned—even indoctrinated—by the various beliefs and reasoning stratagems of unconverted and godless men and women. He *could* become a Christian and thus begin the journey toward the Light (John 3:18-21), but he remains as yet an enemy of God and "hostile" to Him (Romans 8:6-8). Instead of being illuminated with heavenly truth, his heart is flooded with the world's darkness and deception. Thus, the Spirit of God is "foolishness" to him, because he thinks himself to be wiser than God and exempt from accountability to Him. While identifying this person and his beliefs is not my main objective in this book, it is at times unavoidable. I have tried to limit such discussion to comparisons ("This is how the world thinks" vs. "This is how a Christian thinks") rather than making this a separate issue of its own. Regardless, the conclusions concerning the "natural man" will be, I believe, self-evident.

Less obvious is the "natural man" who masquerades as a Christian, but who has never really let go of his unchristian or unbiblical beliefs. He seeks association with believers but is not yet a true believer himself, since he continues to think like unbelievers. He thinks he is "something," but actually deceives himself because he measures himself by a false or corrupted standard (2 Corinthians 10:12, 18). The "spirit of the world" cannot train one to think like Christ. The carnal, self-serving, and satanic spirit that pervades the realm of all unbelievers cannot and will not draw people to God. Christians who try to balance upon a "thin line" (as they see it) between an allegiance to Christ and any allegiance to the world are deceiving themselves, because it is impossible to maintain this; "No one can serve two masters ..." (Matthew 6:24). However, it is very true that the satanic world exerts a powerful and wicked influence upon *all* Christians, and thus is something that we must strive to resist. Thus, this book is written with these two purposes in mind: first, to focus very specifically on what it means to think like Christ; and second, to expose some of the false beliefs that are antagonistic to this thinking and have corrupted the minds of believers.

The title of the book as well as its subject matter requires a specific definition of what a Christian really is (and is not). At the risk of already losing you as a reader, I am morally compelled to provide this information. You may not like what you are about to read, yet I am unable to avoid it and you would be unwise to do so. The New Testament does not recognize *as* Christians those who:

- ❏ Think they are Christians, but have not yet obeyed the method of *becoming* one as specifically instructed in the gospel of Christ.
- ❏ Have merely "asked Jesus into [their] heart" or subscribed to any other conversion method foreign to the New Testament.
- ❏ Think they are Christians by association (by being married to a Christian, having friends who are Christians, having been "born and raised in the church," etc.).
- ❏ Assume that churchgoing or church membership is interchangeable with holy fellowship with God in Christ.
- ❏ Have willfully refused to repent of any sinful behavior that they practiced before making a verbal commitment to follow Christ.
- ❏ Regard themselves as Christians "at heart," but not in actual allegiance to Christ.

INTRODUCTION

- Think being a "good person" is tantamount to being a Christian "in spirit."

I have read many books written by Christians (and those who call themselves Christians, but have succumbed to one of the errors just mentioned). A number of these spend a great deal of time talking about *being* a Christian, but provide little or no biblical information on *becoming* one. It is amazing to me that the most important aspect of one's walk with God—the genuine *beginning* of it!—is so often overlooked, while the rest of one's "walk" is then assumed to be true without any reference to the facts. Having said that, the New Testament *does* recognize as Christians[2] those who:

- Hear the gospel of Christ and believe it to be true (Romans 10:17). The New Testament does not describe a single person who became a Christian apart from hearing and then obediently accepting the terms and conditions put forward in the gospel message (1 Corinthians 15:1-2, Ephesians 1:13-14, Colossians 1:3-6, et al).
- Believe that Jesus Christ is the divine Son of God *and* the world's Redeemer—the Christ of Old Testament prophecy (Luke 24:44-48, John 20:31).
- Believe that Christ was crucified as an atoning sacrifice for their sins (1 Peter 3:18) and literally rose from the dead (Romans 10:9-10).
- Put their faith in—and thus entrust their soul to—Christ as their Savior (Hebrews 11:6).
- Obey Christ's commandments as a demonstration of faith and love in Him (John 14:15, 1 John 2:3-6).
- Take responsibility for (i.e., confess and repent of) their sins (Acts 3:19, 1 John 1:6-10).
- Are baptized into Christ: in obedience to the biblical command (Acts 2:38); to die to their "old" life (Colossians 2:11-12); to unite with Him in the likeness of His death (Romans 6:3-7, 2 Timothy 2:11); and to have their conscience cleansed (1 Peter 3:21).[3]
- Pledge their fidelity to Christ through self-denial, discipleship, and self-sacrifice (Matthew 16:24).

Christian Thinking

Not just some or most of these are required, but *all* of them. It does no good to take issue with me personally on any of these points. I did not come up with them; they are put forward in the gospel of Christ. My plea is that a person will have the faith and courage to evaluate himself in light of what is written in the Word of God rather than close his heart *to* that truth because he is upset with me.

Assuming that you are still with me ...

I realize that "Christian" is ideally a *person*, not an adjective, but sometimes it is necessary to use this word to describe what Christian's *do* rather than only who they *are*. Thus, "Christian thinking" most certainly defines the *kind* of thinking that Christians are to engage in. It is true that atheists and agnostics can think like Christians for the sake of understanding where we are coming from (if they find it necessary to do so), but these remain incidental and temporary excursions into the mind of the believer, not convictions of the heart. In the end, such people usually remain atheists and agnostics; thankfully, a few of them abandon such hopeless ideologies and become Christians. Once any person becomes a Christian, he obligates himself to Christ—not just to take on His name or support His cause, but (as Paul said) to "have the mind of Christ" (2 Corinthians 2:16).

This book is a huge expansion of a class I taught in 2013. As we went through that study, I was impressed by how much of our everyday *lifestyle* as Christians is forged by the *thinking process* that we have adopted—whether good or bad, positive or negative. This is hardly a novel observation, yet it was one that I myself had not specifically developed into a book format. Instead of merely writing it as a book, however, I wanted to keep the question-and-answer format at the end of each section to involve the reader more personally and promote dialogue within group studies.

This book is also considered "Part Two" of a "Fundamentals of Faith" teacher/tutorial program that I had written several years earlier.[4] "Part

One" of that work focused on laying the necessary groundwork for becoming a Christian, but it lacked adequate information about what to do *after* that decision. So then, it seemed good to me to tackle two objectives at once: fulfill a suitable ending to the "Fundamentals of Faith" project; and provide a readable and practical guide to "how to think like a Christian."

In writing this book, I purposely drew from a number of different sources—old and new, conservative and not-so-conservative, scholarly and simple language. My having cited from a particular author does not for a moment mean that I agree with all of that person's religious convictions, but it does not mean that I entirely disagree with them, either. I learned a long time ago to keep the wheat and pitch the chaff—or, in this case, to quote what is good and usable and simply let the rest go. It is not my intention to scrutinize the beliefs of every person whom I quote, only that I represent his (or her) words accurately and use them in a way that contributes effectively to what I am writing. I trust that other authors will do the same with my own written work.

I hope you will find this book very helpful to you personally. If you are using it as a study guide for group study, I hope it will contribute to a better understanding of Christian thinking for all of those involved. Feedback is always welcome; you can contact me directly at *chad@booksbychad.com*.

Chad Sychtysz
May, 2015

Section One: The Attitude of a Believer

What Is Your Attitude?

A fundamental component of a successful Christian life is a godly attitude. Fellowship with God—either now or in the hereafter—is impossible without it. Having said that, Christians tend to place great value on this ("Attitude is everything!") yet proportionately very little on what *formats* or *determines* attitude. There is no question that attitude is important, especially with regard to one's spiritual welfare. Yet, efforts to improve one's attitude without revealing and addressing those factors that *create* an improved attitude are pointless. This study will ultimately explore those factors. We will begin this study, however, by looking at "attitude" in a very general sense without regard to specific religious beliefs.

Attitude can be defined as "a series of thoughts that are connected to a feeling, or vice versa. It is the repetitive cycle of thinking and feeling, feeling and thinking."[5] Thus, attitude is made up of two basic parts: what you think about (i.e., your thoughts) and how you feel (i.e., your emotions). This is also referred to as your state of mind, mindset, mental disposition, heart (in a figurative sense), or personal outlook. In the ancient world, one's "attitude" referred to his physical posture as he presented himself before his god, whether standing, bowing, kneeling, or lying prostrate.[6] This idea is still embedded in the modern usage of the word: one's attitude describes, in essence, his *mental posture* toward a given person, subject, experience, or life in general. To "fall upon one's knees," for example, depicts not only one's physical posture in prayer but also the humble inclination of his heart (as in Ephesians 3:14). Likewise, to stand erect with one's neck stiffened and chin thrust upward is a physical posture that also depicts the defiance and insubordination of that person's heart (as in Acts 7:51).

"Thoughts" refer to what you put into your head *and* how you process that information (whether positively or negatively, objectively or subjectively, and/or truthfully or imaginatively). You think a certain way or about certain things because you *choose* to do so; or, because of earlier choices, you have been essentially *programmed* to do so. In most cases, it is the individual himself who programs his own thinking. Whatever a person thinks about is a window into that person's true nature or identity. A man of the world may have good thoughts from time to time, but he does not have "the mind of Christ" (1 Corinthians 2:16); a Christian may think bad thoughts from time to time, but his habit is to dwell upon the things of God (Philippians 4:8).

What a person thinks about ultimately determines the outcome (or "fruit") of his behavior and his words (Matthew 12:33-37). The one who is pure has filled his heart with pure thoughts; the one who is "defiled and unbelieving" has filled his heart with corruptive thoughts and wicked imaginations (Mark 7:20-23, Titus 1:15-16). "Internal character dictates what we ultimately choose to do. *If we have problems in our heart, no amount of trying to make right choices will produce good fruit in us.*"[7] (We will later discuss this "fruit" in detail.)

One's *general* attitude, however, has a much broader meaning and application. It is not limited to a particular time or incident, but describes one's overall disposition toward the social and political environment in which he lives, authority figures (including God), and/or the world as a whole. One's attitude is the product of (but is not entirely defined by):

- **Personal knowledge:** facts, information, education, life experiences.
- **Temperament:** what kind of personality one has generally.
- **Beliefs:** family, cultural, religious, philosophic, traditional, etc.
- **Thought content:** what a person thinks about (or, what he puts into his head).

We should not confuse attitude with one's personal mood. "Mood" refers to one's mental and emotional disposition at a given moment. This can fluctuate due to the given situation or set of circumstances in which that person finds himself. Weather, physical health, favorable (or unfavorable) circumstances, financial status, job status, etc., can all affect one's daily mood. Mood and attitude are certainly related—the one affects the other—but mood is far more incidental rather than general. A person may have a certain attitude for years; but his mood may change daily or weekly.

Some have likened attitude to a kind of map of the mind that observes and reflects the "territory" of human action. We allude to this when we use expressions like one's "frame of reference" or "way of thinking." This "frame" or "way" concerns itself not only with one's view of reality—in essence, that *person's* reality, as he thinks it exists—but also his beliefs about how things ought to be—in essence, his personal policy system for the world. The accuracy of this map, however, may vary greatly from person to person.[8]

Attitude can also be defined as a pre-determined way of thinking that dictates one's present behavior. The attitude that you program in your head *today* will dictate how you act (or react) *tomorrow*. This attitude will either work *for* or *against* you (in achieving what is in your best interest), depending on whether or not it is consistent with what is in your soul's best interest. Attitudes can also be understood as cyclic or habitual patterns of thinking that are formed over a long period of time. "Patterns of thinking are so deeply ingrained in our hearts that we hardly even notice them. We get so used to reacting a certain way that our choices become automatic, and in time we cease to see them as actual choices."[9]

The *Christian's* attitude—one expected of a follower of Christ (as opposed to that of an unbeliever)—is tempered or conditioned by his regard for his Lord rather than the details of his physical life. His devotion to Christ and high regard for the Word of God establish a mental disposition that transcends his earthly circumstances. Ideally, this attitude is in harmony with Christ: "Have this attitude in yourselves which was also in Christ Jesus..." (Philippians 2:5; see also

Romans 15:5-6 and Philippians 3:15-16).[10] It is, of course, impossible to have a godly attitude until one is fully committed to God's *truth*. It is not uncommon for religious people to focus on a "good attitude" but focus relatively little on divinely-revealed truth. We will have much to say about this in the coming chapters.

The Importance (and Limitation) of Knowledge

Knowledge always precedes learning, and learning precedes attitude and (then) trained behavior. One's attitude will be conditioned by what he knows, but it is not equal to what he knows. Knowledge is an acquaintance with facts, truths, or principles, as from study or investigation.[11] It is not a replacement for righteousness, nor does it align a person's heart with God independent of other factors. Certainly not all knowledge is profitable:

- ❑ The (pre-Christian) ancients studied all kinds of scientific, mathematic, and astronomical knowledge, but this knowledge did not bring them closer to God or deliver them from paganism and idolatry.
- ❑ The Ephesian sorcerers had all sorts of books filled with (allegedly) magical and secret information of the occult, but when they became Christians they consigned this collection of knowledge to the flames because it was now useless to them (Acts 19:18-20).
- ❑ Many men in Paul's day sought human "philosophy" [lit., the love of wisdom], but this was grossly inferior to the revealed Word (*Logos*) of God in the Person of Jesus Christ (Colossians 2:8-10; see John 1:1-3).
- ❑ Some of the Judaizing teachers of Paul's day dabbled in angelology—the study of angels and angelic mediation—but such elaborate pursuits did not give them any advantage with regard to salvation (Colossians 2:18-19).
- ❑ The elitist Gnostics [from *gnosis,* "knowledge" or "(an) understanding"] of the first century sought righteousness through

- intellectualism and the possession of (what they believed was) secret and mystical information, but this could not atone for their sins or transform their hearts.
- Jesus referred to "the deep things of Satan" in Thyatira (Revelation 2:24), but this information did not profit those who studied it—and it offered nothing in the way of spiritual salvation. In fact, it had the complete opposite effect.
- Likewise, today's secular world boasts of excelling in all sorts of knowledge, and we are allegedly living in an "Information Age." Yet, not even the accumulation of or immediate access to all of this knowledge can offer the human soul what the revealed Word of God alone is able to provide. Furthermore, despite our lightning-fast access to untold volumes of information, our society is becoming increasingly immoral and antagonistic toward God and Christians.

The Christian faith is established upon the information that God has revealed in His Word, the Bible. This information provides the basis *for* faith, but it does not actually *produce* faith. An atheist can read the same Scripture that a believer reads, yet he may remain an atheist; despite such excellent knowledge, his regard for God may not change at all. Likewise, ancient Israel heard "good news" from God (in the Law of Moses), yet many Israelites did not exercise faith *in* Him. As a result, they forfeited what was promised them (Hebrews 4:1-2).

In response to the question of *how much* knowledge is needed as a foundation for one's faith in God, there is no static or universal answer. The Book of Acts shows men and women with various levels of education all being taught the same gospel, and all who became Christians by obeying that gospel in the same way (or method). Clearly, one must have sufficient knowledge to be able to answer the basic questions concerning his convictions: 1) What do I believe? 2) Why do I believe it? 3) Is what I believe able to withstand objective criticism? 4) Does my belief system serve my very best interest, as measured over time)? and 5) Does my belief system serve the very best interests of all other people with whom I come into contact, as measured over time? John Piper has this to say:

> There is no necessary correlation between extensive learning and the right use of the mind. Many PhDs think poorly, and many people with little formal education think with great clarity and depth. I am pleading for a hearty engagement of the mind in the pursuit of God. I am not pleading mainly for more formal education. That may or may not be good in different cases. But the right use of the mind is always good no matter how much or how little education one has.[12]

Christians regularly assemble together in order to gain or refine biblical knowledge. This accumulated knowledge, however, does *nothing* for the improvement of one's attitude *or* life conduct until it is united with personal faith and (thus) put into appropriate practice. In other words, knowledge that does not bring a person closer to a known and beneficial goal is of little value to anyone, including the person who possesses it. More specifically, no one can achieve a godly attitude by knowledge alone. Furthermore, no one will find favor *with* or salvation *from* God based upon knowledge alone. Yet it remains unquestionably true that no one can be saved *by* God until he comes to *know* Him—not just know *about* Him but also to have fellowship *with* Him.

Christian Thinking

What do *you* think?

1.) How important do you believe one's mental disposition is with regard to his or her success as a Christian?

2.) If *God* is very concerned with what you *think*—i.e., what is going on in your head—then should *you also* be very concerned about this? Please discuss.

3.) If your attitude is not based solely upon an accumulation of knowledge, then what good is it to have knowledge—especially the knowledge of God's Word?

4.) Please read Colossians 1:9-12. What is the goal of knowledge?

   a. Do we act alone (in whatever we do for God), or is He involved in whatever we do for Him?

   b. How does this passage help to establish an appropriate *attitude* for Christians?

Section One: The Attitude of a Believer *(continued)*

Thoughts and Emotions

Your emotions refer to what you *feel* about something, someone, or the past. People commonly attach an emotional connection to something significant that happened to them, and either strongly desire to *re-create* this scenario (if they liked it) or *avoid* it as much as possible (if they strongly disliked it). This craving (in either direction) drives many of our human habits, addictions, fears, and repulsions. "The end product of any experience is an emotion."[13]

God gave us emotions for good reason. They are part of His own divine reflection in us (since we are made "in His image"). But we are expected to harness and channel those emotions in a proper manner, rather than allow them to dictate our lives. Ideally, then, one's emotions (feelings) ought to be subject to his or her thoughts (rational thinking process). Yet, no matter how much good knowledge one possesses or has access to, his emotions can override this knowledge base and assume control of his thinking. As a result, many people make their thoughts subject to their emotions.[14] This is backward and leads to erroneous conclusions, such as:

- "I feel good about this action, so therefore it can't be wrong"—i.e., a subjective *emotion* is driving a rational *thought process* rather than the other way around.
- "I know God says we need to become Christians [thought process], but this seems judgmental to all those good people who believe otherwise [emotion]."
- "The congregation I used to attend was so enjoyable [emotion], and I will not be happy until I find one that is exactly like it [thought process]."

Christian Thinking

- "I had a *horrible* experience with a preacher in the past [emotion], and now I regard all preachers with great suspicion [thought process]."

Emotions are intimately connected to the physical body. When you "feel" something (or, feel *for* something), you actually engage your body to respond in kind. For example, when you are angry, your blood pressure rises, face tenses, fists clench, and voice gets louder; when you are afraid, your heart beats faster, adrenalin kicks in, eyes widen, and you perspire; when you are very happy, you smile, muscles relax, you literally feel good, etc. Anger, fear, and happiness are emotions, yet they are supported by your body's corresponding reaction to (and support of) those emotions. Emotional memory (how you feel when a certain thing happens to you) is thus joined with physical response memory (what your body does when that certain thing happens to you). Those who *live* by their emotions unconsciously program their body to re-live that emotion in a physical way. In doing so, they "train the body to be the mind in order to live in a predictable future, based on the memory of the known past."[15] Thus, they miss the "present" and are not surprised by the future: to some degree, they made it happen.

Even though emotions can take control of our rational thinking process, it is the *quality* of thinking (or, what we think *about* in the first place) that triggers our emotional responses. Good emotions (such as the joy that a Christian *feels* when he overcomes a particular trial) are predicated upon an accurate knowledge of one's standing with God. This is exactly what Peter expresses: "... And though you have not seen Him [Christ], you love Him, and though you do not see Him now, but believe in Him, you greatly rejoice with joy inexpressible and full of glory, obtaining as the outcome of your faith the salvation of your souls" (1 Peter 1:8-9).[16] One who rejoices always in the Lord necessarily dwells upon "whatever is true, whatever is honorable, etc." (Philippians 4:4, 8). One who fills his head with the words, gifts, and promises of God will experience positive emotions. These emotions comprise part of what we call "attitude."

In contrast, bad *feelings* are often the result of bad *thinking*. One who fills his head with ungodly thoughts and useless knowledge will experience negative emotions and (thus) a negative or sour attitude. In light of this, when you feel "badly," instead of asking, "Who or what did this to me?" you should ask yourself, "What have I been *feeding my thoughts?*"

- Have you been associating with negative or worldly people?
- Have you been engaging in gossip, trash-talking, or other negative speech?
- Have you been watching negative or immoral TV shows or movies?
- Have you been excessively exposing yourself to violent or unchristian behavior (i.e., certain video games or movies, songs with explicit lyrics, or ungodly environments)?
- Have you been fixating upon or indulging in wicked desires?
- Are you looking for faults and imperfections in everyone (but yourself)?
- Are you angry with "the church" because of a few hypocritical Christians?
- Are you holding onto grudges and fostering resentment in your heart over what someone did to you in your past?

Emotions do not *make* us do good or bad things, but certainly our emotional state of mind can have a powerful *influence* upon our decision-making process. If you are in a good mood because of your right relationship with God, it is likely that wicked temptations will not be so attractive to you.[17] If you are in a bad mood for whatever reason, this makes it considerably easier for you to succumb to wicked temptations because your heart is already darkened from how you feel. What you choose to think about has a great impact on how you feel, and how you feel can influence the decisions you make. Thus, when reflecting upon your having given into temptation, instead of asking, "Who made me do this?" ask yourself, "What *thoughts* did I entertain before doing this thing?"

- ❏ Are you striving to do what is right, or are you just trying to be "happy" (by whatever means you choose)?
- ❏ Are you remembering your covenant with God throughout the week, or is this being buried beneath a host of negative feelings and angry thoughts?
- ❏ Do you find yourself engaging in sinful activities, sinful talk, or sinful pleasures, and then rationalizing this because you can always "ask God's forgiveness" later?
- ❏ Do you find yourself justifying your own poor decisions or irresponsible behavior, but are upset over other people who are doing these same things?
- ❏ Are you purposely (or carelessly) putting yourself in the proximity of sinful situations—and then acting "surprised" or "shocked" that you actually succumbed to temptation ("I don't know how that happened!")?
- ❏ Are you allowing yourself to be carried away by various "triggers"—things that incite ungodly desires—rather than seeking to identify and avoid these things? In other words, are you seeking emotional joy in sin rather than righteousness?

God's Word teaches that all sin *begins* in the "heart" and *then* manifests itself in visible action (Matthew 15:17-20, James 1:13-16). Temptation represents a decision time: it is the fork in the road where we must choose one direction or the other. There are only two choices: one leads toward God; the other leads away from Him. It is not a sin to be tempted; even Jesus was "...tempted in all things as we are, yet without sin" (Hebrews 4:15). When you bring temptation into your heart and *give life to it*, however, then this becomes a different matter. What was once an option has become a decision—an act of willful rebellion against God—resulting in sin. "Do not be deceived": you are personally responsible for what direction you choose and what goes into your heart. While it is true that many opportunities to sin may pass before your eyes (or, through your mind), the ones that you seize and make your own are the ones for which you will be held responsible.

The Attitude of a Believer

This has been said for good reason. You cannot use *emotions* to justify sin or define righteousness. Both sin and righteousness are objective in nature: they are actual, historical realities, not subjective feelings. In order to strive for righteousness, you must think like righteous people think and do what righteous people do, and you must also abstain from every form of evil. How you *feel* about sin or righteousness is irrelevant; what you *do* about these is of great importance. Ideally, you should feel very *good* about righteous decisions and very *bad* about sinful ones. Emotions ought to be the product of your thinking, not the substance of it.

What do *you* think?

1.) What is the problem with letting your subjective emotions dictate your rational thought process? (There is more than one answer.)

2.) Should you experience good emotions simply from having good thoughts?

   a. Where does *obedience to God* fit into this scenario?

   b. Is obedience to God achieved simply by filling your head with good thoughts or feeling good about yourself? Please explain.

3.) If your attitude is determined by what *you* think, emotions *you* choose to have, and decisions about right and wrong that *you* choose to make, then whose responsibility is it whether you have a "good attitude" or "bad attitude"?

Section One: The Attitude of a Believer
(continued)

Dwelling on Good Thoughts

Good *feelings* are (ideally) the result of godly *thinking*. But it is not necessary to "feel" good *always* just because our thoughts are in the right place. God never asked us to "feel" good, but He always requires us to *do* what is good (Proverbs 3:27, Galatians 6:9-10, et al).[18] The fact is, a person may "feel good" even after doing very bad things. A primary reason why people sin against God is because they obtain some kind of illicit emotional joy or physical pleasure from it. However, the Christian's mind must never reason this way. "Joy in the Holy Spirit" (cf. Romans 14:17) cannot possibly be achieved through wicked behavior (see Galatians 5:16-25). In order to fill your heart with the things of God, you must make a conscious decision and exert strenuous effort to "put away" or "lay aside" those things (thoughts, intentions, desires, etc.) that oppose Him (Colossians 3:8-10).

These two things—conscious decision and strenuous effort—are what *you* will have to provide in order for you to focus your attention upon God. This kind of focus is not natural to people, so you cannot assume that it will naturally happen to you (or any Christian). We all remain in a secular ("old self"-thinking) mindset until we make the necessary changes to get *out* of that mindset. The mistake of many well-intentioned but starry-eyed Christians is in thinking that they will become "spiritually-minded" simply because they *are* Christians who go to church and read the Bible. Thus, every day requires your conscious and stated commitment to God that you will devote your heart to Him throughout the day.[19]

At the same time, you should not think that your spiritual well-being *or* success is all up to you. Godly thinking is what you pursue, but it is God Himself who is both the source and object of that thinking. You are not being asked merely to read Scripture; you are expected to adopt the mind of Christ. There is no way in the world (literally!) that any of us will be able to have the mind of Christ simply by reading *about* Him in the Bible. (This is *not* to diminish the importance of Bible reading and studying in the least. We are simply recognizing the human limitation of such exercises.) In order to practice godly thinking, you must ask *God Himself* to act upon your heart in such a way that makes your reading, studying, conscious decisions, and all other sincere efforts *meaningful* and *effective*.[20] Thus, you should not say, "Lord, I will think deeply upon You and Your Word today, and this will increase my godly thinking." What you ought to say is: "Lord, I will do my part in adopting the mind of Christ; I implore You to do *Your* part in helping me to produce that 'mind,' since this is not something I can do on my own."

Someone will ask, "But what exactly will *God* do?" It is not necessary for you or me to know this. It is necessary—and sufficient—for us to believe in God's ability to perform and trust that whatever He does for us will be in our best interest.[21] We want to inform God of what's going on, but He already knows all things. We want to instruct Him, give Him options to choose from, and offer our strong suggestions, but this is unnecessary and even contradictory to our trust in Him. Christians often talk about trusting God, but we tend to "practice negotiation" instead.[22] We want to predict what He will do, evaluate what He has done, or even criticize His decision ("Why did You choose *that* and not the *other*?" or "I am disappointed with Your decision…"). Such positions manifest unbelief, not faith. "When our strongest passion is to solve our problems, we look for a *plan to follow* rather than *a person to trust*."[23] The thing about God that we should know and accept up front is this: *He* is God, and *we* are not. This simple understanding should put things in their proper perspective for us.

At the same time, there are some things we *do* know that God will do for us, because He has already told us of them. For example, we know that:

Christian Thinking

- ❑ He knows far beyond all that we know (Isaiah 55:8-9).
- ❑ He is capable of performing beyond all that we say or think (Ephesians 3:20).
- ❑ He is a shield and defender of those who are in a covenant relationship with Him (Genesis 15:1, 1 Peter 3:12-14).
- ❑ He will never tempt us to sin (James 1:13) and always provides us with a way of escape *from* temptation (1 Corinthians 10:13).
- ❑ He will never abandon us (Hebrews 13:5-6).
- ❑ He will always be faithful to us (1 Corinthians 1:9).

We should speak confidently of how God performs in the areas He has disclosed to us. Yet, even when He tells us *what* He will do, He does not always tell us *how* or *when* He will do it. This is where faith comes in.

One expression of your faith is to condition your mind with the things God has told you. "The mind is a battlefield—whoever controls the mind controls the person."[24] God is not going to re-program your thinking process against your will or without the application of your own effort. Just as you cannot step into God's shoes and do what He alone can do, He is not going to step into *your* shoes and do for you that which is well within your power. If you desire a Christ-like attitude (or desire to continue that attitude throughout your life), there are some things that you must do. No one else—not even God Himself—will do these for you, and you cannot do these for anyone else. One very important responsibility you have is to *put the things of God into your head*:

> Finally, brethren, whatever is true, whatever is honorable, whatever is right, whatever is pure, whatever is lovely, whatever is of good repute, if there is any excellence and if anything worthy of praise, dwell on these things. The things you have learned and received and heard and seen in me, practice these things, and the God of peace will be with you. (Philippians 4:8-9)

By dwelling on what is true, honorable, right, etc., you prepare your mind to carry out whatever "good works" God has planned for you to do (Matthew 5:16, Ephesians 2:10). "These things" is not a mere list of positive virtues to think about. Rather, they define the *heart of a true believer who is walking the path that leads to life*. Such a person will condition his mind to "dwell upon" whatever is consistent with that good life *and* the One with whom he longs to live forever. For example, some of these "true," "honorable," and "lovely" things to think about include:

- God Himself—His nature, holiness, majesty, sovereign authority, and divine grace.
- Jesus Christ—His worthiness, obedience, selfless sacrifice, kingship over His Father's kingdom, and headship over His church.
- The Holy Spirit of God—His wisdom, power, sanctification, guidance, and intercession for the prayers of the saints.
- The Word of God—its message, power, illumination, and prescription for holy living.
- Christ's church—her purity, beauty, piety, excellent character, and anticipation of eternal glory.
- God's mercy and grace—divine actions which provide for your forgiveness through the blood of Christ, without which you would have no hope of being saved.
- God's promises to believers—for help, guidance, strength, deliverance, ultimate vindication, and a home with Him in the hereafter.

"If there is any excellence…"—this involves a *kind* or *quality* of such thinking, not just the specific *content* or point of reference for such thoughts. In other words, we should not think poorly, begrudgingly, or bitterly about God or His world ("I resent how God has imposed His divine will upon me! But if I want to go to heaven, I have to obey Him"). Rather, we should think very well of such things. Simply put: Christians are to think excellently about excellent things.

Christian Thinking

"Practice these things"—clearly, Paul intends *not* for a mere "study" of these words or their meanings, but for us to put these thoughts into real, measurable, and habitual service. It is not uncommon for Christians (and preachers especially) to engage in word studies but fail to realize the practical (or "practice-able") implementation of such words. "These things" have no meaningful use to you if they remain only as "things" in your mind or the subject of a sermon or Bible class discussion. "These things" are consistent with the "new self"—i.e., the one who:

- Has the attitude of Christ (Philippians 2:5).
- Is working out his salvation with "fear and trembling" (2:12).
- Is seeking to live as a child of light in a darkened world (2:15).
- Is of the "true circumcision"—i.e., those who are born of God (3:3).
- Puts confidence in God and not his own human effort (for salvation) (3:3).
- Has counted all things "as loss for the sake of Christ" (3:7).
- Presses forward to "the upward call of God in Christ Jesus" (3:14).

"Let us therefore, as many as are perfect, have this attitude; and if in anything you have a different attitude, God will reveal that also to you; however, let us keep living by that same standard to which we have attained" (Philippians 3:15-16). One's *attitude* must be consistent with the *standard* by which he became a Christian in the first place: the Word of God.[25]

The Attitude of a Believer

What do *you* think?

1.) Why is it important that Christians know and respect God's position *as* God (especially in contrast to their own humble state) when determining what kind of "mind" they are going to produce?

2.) Please read Ephesians 4:20-24 and Colossians 3:9-10.

   a. Why does the "new self" necessarily require new *thinking*?

   b. Can the "old self" (of one who is not a Christian) produce the same kind of new thinking as one who is born of God? Why or why not?

3.) Please read Luke 5:36-39. What do these parables have to do with:

   a. One who tries to reconcile an *ungodly attitude* with righteous living?

   b. One who tries to reconcile an alleged *godly attitude* with unrighteous living?

   c. The incompatibility of the mind conditioned by "That's just that way I am"–thinking and the "new self" made in the image of God?

4.) What benefits are derived from dwelling upon the excellent things of God? On the other hand, what will such "dwelling" *cost* you (in terms of time, energy, sacrifice, etc.)? Is this cost worth it, based upon what you receive in return?

Section One: The Attitude of a Believer *(continued)*

How Your Attitude Affects You

Your attitude is not merely a mental disposition. It also has a direct effect upon how you see yourself, how you regard God and your relationship with Him, and how you project yourself to others. Your attitude is the governing influence for how you carry yourself in this life and how you deal with what happens to you. More specifically, your attitude affects:

- How you evaluate people, situations, or events: you "see" these based upon how you have conditioned yourself to think about them.
- How you cope with challenges, loss, or rejection: you either *learn to accept* these things or you *allow them to destroy you* based upon your attitude.
  - Starry-eyed, unrealistic optimism: "It's all good! No worries!"
  - Overconfidence: "This is difficult, but I cannot fail! I am invincible!"
  - Realistic, but with confident assurance: "This is difficult, but by God's grace I can do whatever is required of me."
  - Doubtful: "This is too difficult, and may well destroy me."
  - Hopeless: "I'm doomed."
- Your interpretation of what is happening (to you in particular).
  - Selfishly: "Why is all of this happening to *me*?"
  - Unrealistically: "I am able to control whatever is happening!"
  - Realistically (in faith): "Whatever is happening, God is in control of it all; I just need to let Him lead me through it."
  - Indifferently: "I am just coasting through life, no matter what happens."
  - Apathetically: "I don't care what happens."

The Attitude of a Believer

In the ultimate sense, a *good attitude* is inspired by, educated in, and consistent with God's Word. It is impossible to reconcile a "good attitude" with thinking or conduct that is contradictory to gospel teaching. Conversely, a *bad attitude* is one inspired by, educated in, and consistent with the world of unbelievers. It is impossible to reconcile a "bad attitude" with someone who claims to be living by faith (Romans 1:17) and walking in a manner worthy of the Lord (Ephesians 4:1, Colossians 1:10). A good attitude does not just "happen"—but neither does a bad attitude. Since attitude itself is a pre-determined (and thus pre-chosen) mental disposition, it stands to reason that whether this disposition is good or bad depends upon the quality of decisions of the one who is in control of it.

Someone will say, "But it wasn't *me* who caused my bad attitude—it was something *outside* of me." It is true that external problems can have a negative influence on our mental outlook, but the quality of that outlook itself remains within *our control* to decide. Below are numerous factors that might be considered "causes" of a bad attitude:

- Sin in our heart
- Sin in our behavior
- Sin in our relationships
- Poor decisions on our part
- Personal tragedy
- Legal action against us
- Death of a loved one
- Stress (external pressure)
- Separation or divorce
- Unkind treatment
- Conflict of allegiance
- Not getting our own way
- Humiliation by someone
- Unresolved anger
- Bodily sickness
- Rejection of our own ideas or proposals

- Drugs or alcohol
- Physical or emotional abuse
- Any unwanted change (temporary or permanent)
- Rejection of our love or personal affection
- Fight or argument
- Car accident (or other unplanned disruption)
- Personal hatred
- Being cheated or defrauded
- Loss of any kind: money, property, friends, health, etc.
- Bad weather
- Loss of job or any unwanted career change
- Failure (real or imagined)
- Any negative influence or "bad company"
- Facing our own mortality

Notice that some of these are internal (such as sin, unresolved anger, or hatred), whereas others are external (such as rejection, humiliation, or loss of job). In other words, some of these *we* caused, while others appear to be caused by someone else. Regardless, the responsibility for actually *having* a "bad attitude" lies with the person who *has* it. There is nothing in Scripture that teaches that if "bad" things happen to you, then you are *entitled* to a bad attitude, or that it is inevitable that you will have one.[26] On the contrary, the Bible teaches consistently that no matter *what* happens to us—good or bad—believers are to maintain a *good* attitude (Matthew 5:10-12, Philippians 4:11-13, 1 Peter 2:20, 3:8-14, James 1:2-4, et al). Thus, it may be your parent's fault for not loving and providing for you as they should have when you were young, but it is *your* fault if you allow that experience to sour your view of life and your trust in God. It may be another driver's fault for the traffic accident that severely damaged your car, but it is *your* fault if you allow that negative experience to ruin your contentment "in Christ." And it may be an inept doctor's fault for mishandling your medical diagnosis, but it is *your* fault if you become bitter, cynical, and vengeful because of his error.

Any sinful action on *our* part naturally corrupts our thinking, which negatively affects our attitude. You cannot harbor sin in your heart, for example, and still maintain a good (or godly) attitude. Likewise, you cannot practice sin in secret and still maintain a sincere, productive, and godly public representation of Christ. These two things—sin and godliness—contradict and are antagonistic to each other. Just as you cannot get both fresh and bitter water from the same spring (cf. James 3:11), so you cannot reconcile personal sin with a Christian attitude. A good attitude is predicated upon a *clear conscience* and a *pure heart*; a bad attitude is predicated upon your *poor reaction* to what is happening to you or *poor decisions* that you have made.

External factors (such as inclement weather or an accident that you did not cause) can certainly seem to ruin your day—or your week—but only if you let them. Paul said, "…I have learned to be content in whatever circumstances I am" (Philippians 4:11). What this means is that Paul did not allow his circumstances *themselves* to determine what kind of heart or attitude he was going to have. Paul's testimony is significant, since he endured a great deal of external troubles and injustices (see 2 Corinthians 11:23-28). He maintained a Christian attitude despite whatever people or life itself threw at him. He certainly could have chosen to have a *bad* attitude toward such negative things; regardless, he chose to have a *good* attitude. Likewise, it is our personal choice, and not the "things" themselves, that determines the quality of our attitude.

We should *not* conclude from this, however, that we are not allowed to be sad, angry, or even heartbroken over the things that happen to us. We are never given permission to sin; we do, however, have full permission to be *human*. This is especially true in the case of another person's negligent, selfish, or malicious conduct against us. Moses was "angry" toward the Israelites who ignored his instructions concerning the use of manna (Exodus 16:20); Jesus was "grieved" at the hardness of heart of His countrymen (Mark 3:5); and Paul was visibly upset over the mistreatment he received at one of his trials (Acts 23:2-3). There

Christian Thinking

is a *proper occasion* for the demonstration of our human emotions in response to personal trials, personal harm, injustices (whether against us or someone we care about), or the losses we face in this life. Being "content" in all circumstances does *not* mean we can never experience moments of *dis*-content. "Contentment" is a state of mind, predicated upon a hope that transcends any present problems or disappointments. It is not a prohibition against responding to the pain, disappointment, and losses we will face in this life.

Now notice the numerous factors that are considered "causes" of a *good* attitude:

- Being at peace with God
- Thinking about Christ
- Thinking about heaven
- A fulfilling marriage
- Obedient children
- Christian fellowship
- Giving to others
- New gifts or things
- Love given to us
- Love extended to others
- Being forgiven
- Forgiving others
- Freedom from guilt
- Good memories
- Good times with friends
- Rewarding friendships
- Resolution of problems
- Financial comfort
- Good health
- Good and sufficient food
- Positive influences
- Dwelling on what is good
- Good weather

- Favorable living conditions
- Serving others
- Commendation or praise
- Acceptance by people whom we admire
- Fairness or justice
- Freedom from oppression
- Stability in one's life

Just as a bad experience cannot literally "cause" a bad attitude, so a good experience cannot literally "cause" a good attitude. We probably all know people who are wealthy, abundantly talented, magnificently blessed, and/or in positions of great honor, yet they may be miserable, spoiled, selfish, and/or ungrateful despite all such "good" things. God gives blessings and kindness to evil people, but most people remain evil despite such kindness (Matthew 5:44-45, Luke 6:35, Romans 2:4, et al). Thus, good things *by themselves* do not create good people. In fact, such blessings may lead a person to become self-reliant and self-absorbed instead of looking up to thank the One who gave them (Luke 12:15-21, James 5:1-6).

Some "good" things are given to us by others (privileges, gifts, inheritances, etc.); others are internal decisions we have made (optimism, being charitable or forgiving, etc.). Regardless, we are each responsible for choosing to have a good attitude rather than succumbing (or defaulting) to a bad one. Specifically, a *godly* attitude is never something you stumble into accidentally or unconsciously. Rather, it is something you actively pursue through the instruction of God's Word. If you refuse this (or neglect to pursue it), you will develop an attitude that may seem "good" to you but that does not achieve the righteousness of God. Christ expects you to have an attitude modeled after His—and He provides you with everything necessary to achieve this. Thus, whether you are blessed with earthly wealth or are forced to live in humble means, you can choose to adopt an attitude that finds favor with God (1 Timothy 6:17-19, Revelation 2:9a).

Christian Thinking

Similar to how a computer programmer can set the format, attributes, definitions, and algorithms of a computer, so you have the power to *program* your mind to create either a *good* or *bad* attitude. This programming will be the result of at least:

- What you think about: you have *full control* over this.
- Your past history and life experiences: you have *limited control* over this.
- Your upbringing and education: you have *limited* to *no control* over this.
- How you see yourself personally (self-image): you have *full control* over this.
- How you value your own soul: you have *full control* over this.
- How you regard God's authority: you have *full control* over this, whether—
    - You submit to Him unconditionally ("I will do what He says no matter what").
    - You submit to Him only on your terms ("I will do what He says only when I approve of His instruction or He meets my expectations").
    - You refuse to submit to Him except when you choose to ("I refuse to do what He says—unless I am in trouble and I need Him to save me from my present crisis").
- Your knowledge of God's Word: you have *full control* over this.
    - If you are ignorant of God's Word, you can "read and understand" (cf. 2 Corinthians 1:13) what has been written and become educated.
    - It is impossible for someone *else's* knowledge to properly condition *your* attitude: this is something you must do for yourself. (They can influence *what* you learn or *how* you learn it, but they cannot learn it *for* you.)
    - Knowledge of God's word is necessary for mental illumination, spiritual maturity, and a lifestyle of service—all positive results of a godly attitude.

- ❑ Your trust in God's willingness and ability to perform. A godly attitude is one that believes that God will:
  - Protect your soul from being overwhelmed (John 10:27-29, 1 Corinthians 10:13)—*as long as* you remain faithful to Him.
  - Guarantee His promises to you (Ephesians 1:13-14, 1 Peter 1:3-4).
  - Vindicate your faith in Him (2 Thessalonians 1:6-10).
  - Reward you for your faith in Him *and* punish those who persecuted you.
  - Make right everything that is wrong—everything that could not be "fixed" (or that you could not fix) here on earth.

Notice: you have *full control* over the most important conditions for creating either a good (godly) or bad attitude; therefore—

- ❑ It is not someone else's fault if you have a bad attitude; it is *yours*.
- ❑ It is not someone else's responsibility to determine your attitude; it is *yours*.
- ❑ Your life's circumstances can only rob you of a godly attitude *if you let them*.

A healthy, godly attitude is most certainly conducive to a productive and rewarding spiritual life. Norman Vincent Peale writes:

> Think positively... and you set in motion positive forces which bring positive results to pass. Positive thoughts create around yourself an atmosphere propitious [advantageous—CMS] to the development of positive outcomes. On the contrary, think negative thoughts and you create around yourself an atmosphere propitious to the development of negative thoughts.[27]

This is good *general* advice, but it needs to be conditioned by the gospel of Christ. In other words, there is no question that positive thinking *by itself* can provide a certain amount of healing of body and mind, and in this respect it is (as they say) "good for the soul." Yet, it cannot be allowed to circumvent, duplicate, or replace one's obedience to God's Word. Dave Miller expresses the danger of this:

> Many churches are attempting to create an atmosphere of non-qualifying acceptance by avoiding anything negative and remaining strictly positive. Being "positive" is without question an essential ingredient to living a wholesome Christian existence. The person who constantly dwells on the negative and possesses a critical spirit is the person who likely has deep emotional problems and finds it difficult to get along with his fellow man. ...On the other hand, the increasing tendency of churches to base their entire thrust upon "being positive" and to seek progress and growth by maintaining a positive atmosphere needs rethinking. For if a religious group's primary appeal is its positive, even tolerant allure, it is no different from a myriad of movements that have drawn thousands to their ranks by whipping up a lot of enthusiasm and presenting an aura of exciting activity and positive progress. People are then attracted by the positive atmosphere and promise of acceptance and not by truth.[28]

We must not allow positive thinking (or any other philosophy or mental practice) to become an alternate system of justification (as in, "*You* are saved through your Christian beliefs, but *I* am saved through the power of my mind!"). The mind is indeed powerful, but it cannot cleanse the soul of sin or transform the sinful heart. Only the blood of Christ is *that* powerful—and no human effort can even come close to that kind of power.

Sometimes people talk about being in a good "place" even amid life's trials and upsets. While not everyone's perception of a good "place" is based upon a favorable standing with God, nonetheless there is something to be said for the concept itself. Think about the vertebrae in your spine: when everything is aligned and free from degeneration,

The Attitude of a Believer

your back feels fine and is fully functional. But if even one vertebra is out of place or unhealthy, you will experience pain not only in your back but also in other areas of your body that are affected by this. Likewise, when the soul is where it should be (by conforming to God's will), conflict, tension, and resistance evaporate. When there is something wrong with your soul, the pain this causes reverberates throughout the rest of your life (whether or not you realize the source of this pain).

Similarly, when people who are in your closest circle of influence are doing what they are supposed to do—when everyone is in *their* "place"—you experience peace and not turmoil. When such people themselves are distraught, filled with pain, or living in chaos, this will likely have a negative effect on you as well. While you cannot control all the people in your inner circle (so to speak), you *can*—and *must*—put a limitation on how much their trouble is going to affect you.[29] There are really only two parties with whom you need to be concerned: yourself and God. "God is faithful" to fulfill *all* of His responsibilities toward you correctly and completely (cf. 1 Corinthians 1:9); you do not need to worry about Him; He will not disappoint you.[30] All you need to be concerned with is *you* and *your* attitude. When God is in *His* good "place" (which He always is) and you are in *your* good "place" (by living in harmony with His will), everything necessary for a *good attitude* will also be in place, regardless of any other factors. You do not *need* the cooperation of your spouse, family members, co-workers, the weather, world politics, etc.—you can be at peace with God *despite* all these people or things.

A good attitude embraces "…the wisdom from above [that] is first pure, then peaceable, gentle, reasonable, full of mercy and good fruits, unwavering, [and] without hypocrisy" (James 3:17). Wisdom that is "earthly, natural, [and] demonic" produces "bitter jealousy and selfish ambition" which create "disorder and every evil thing" (cf. James 3:14-16). It is not surprising that people who listen *to* the world start thinking and behaving *like* the world. Their lives become chaotic,

Christian Thinking

morally confused, and filled with strife and unrest. The opposite is also true: people who listen to God start thinking and behaving in a godly manner. *Their* lives are filled with blessings, stability, and an anticipation of a heavenly future with the One to whom they have entrusted their souls.

What do *you* think?

1.) What are the problems with the following statements?

   a. "I *would* have a good attitude, but I am surrounded by so much negativity."

   b. "I believe it is the church's responsibility to make me feel good about myself."

   c. "I'm not happy when I come to Bible class—so I seldom come, or I choose not to come at all."

   d. "I have a right to feel angry and resentful inside—after all, look what has happened to me!"

   e. "It's easy for him to have such a cheery attitude: his life has been filled with blessings and prosperity, whereas mine has been filled with trouble and poverty."

2.) What does a person with a *bad* attitude think about, especially with regard to God, His authority, and Christians in general?

3.) What does a person with a *good* attitude think about, especially with regard to God, His authority, and Christians in general?

4.) Can you choose to dwell on godly virtues and at the same time have a negative, pessimistic, or cynical attitude?

5.) Can you simply stop thinking about "bad" things in order to produce virtuous thinking or behavior?

6.) Can *positive* thinking make you righteous? Atone for your sins? Take the place of obedience to specific commandments? Save your soul?

Section One: The Attitude of a Believer *(continued)*

The Risks of Thinking like a Christian

God is not as concerned with what happens *to* you as He is with *how you react* to what happens to you. If you are actively living your faith in Christ, this will automatically put you at odds with the world (1 John 3:13). This means that the world will not treat you better than it did prior to your conversion, but instead may hold you in contempt because of what you have chosen to believe *and* what that belief says about those who reject it (see John 3:18-21 and 15:18-20). Dietrich Bonhoeffer says: "The messengers of Jesus will be hated to the end of time. They will be blamed for all the divisions which rend cities and homes. Jesus and His disciples will be condemned on all sides for undermining family life, and for leading the nation astray; they will be called crazy fanatics and disturbers of the peace."[31] And when we identify *with* Jesus and His disciples, we also will be called these things. This is something we must accept up front, and not be "surprised" when it happens (cf. 1 Peter 4:12-16).

- ❏ In Matthew 5:38-42, Jesus does not deny (or apologize for) the fact that people will mistreat or take advantage of you because you are a Christian. His concern is: will you respond as the *world* does (in vengeful retaliation) or as a child of the *kingdom* is expected to respond?
- ❏ In Matthew 5:43-47, Jesus does not deny (or apologize for) the fact that your enemies will persecute you for your faith. His concern is: will you respond with *fear* and *doubt* or in *faith* and *perseverance*?
- ❏ In Romans 12:14-21, Paul does not deny that you will be the victim of unfairness, injustice, persecution, and other people's evil. His concern is: will you respond as one who belongs to the *world* or as a *Christian*?

- ❏ In 1 Corinthians 6:7-8, Paul does not deny that you will be wronged or defrauded. His concern is: will you respond as one who belongs to the *world* or as one who belongs to *Christ*?

Of course, many Christians want to avoid conflict (or uncomfortable situations) with those of opposing beliefs. Dr. Larry Crabb confirms this: "We tend to relate to one another with the hidden purpose of maintaining our comfort and avoiding whatever sort of interaction we find threatening."[32] This avoidance can become a mission or habitual behavior in itself. This results in:

- ❏ **Failure to share the gospel.** A Christian who values his friendship with unbelievers over his devotion to Christ will not openly discuss his beliefs for fear of losing such friendships (John 12:42-43, James 4:4).
- ❏ **An avoidance of all people but Christians.** In this case, a person so fears confrontation or reprisal from those who will oppose his beliefs that he only surrounds himself with people of *like* beliefs.
- ❏ **Compromise.** This is any attempt to marry two incompatible beliefs. One who compromises his faith believes that he can (somehow) sustain his faith in God even while living like those who do not believe in Him.
- ❏ **Hypocrisy.** This describes a person who acts like a Christian while around Christians, but acts like his non-Christian friends (or family members, co-workers, etc.) while around *them*. His motive is to gain the favor and approval of whichever group he is with.
- ❏ **Rejection of the gospel.** This may happen not because a person does not believe the gospel is *true*, but because he simply does not have the moral fiber to uphold it in the face of criticism or confrontation with others. Instead of engaging in the "good fight of faith" (cf. 1 Timothy 6:12), he simply gives up the fight altogether.

Such reactions to conflict do not serve the will of God, the best interest of the person involved, or the best interest of those who (as yet) do not believe.

Christian Thinking

The truth is: being a Christian is *hard work* and has *inherent risks*. Some people may take advantage of your kindness; others may misconstrue your motives; still others may misrepresent your character or wrongfully associate you with those who are disingenuous. For example, every time some so-called "Christian fundamentalist" makes the news because of his involvement with a prostitute, shooting at an abortion clinic, or latest (bogus) prophecy about the end of the world, the rest of us who want nothing to do with him are guilty in the public's eye. They think *all* people who call themselves "Christians" believe exactly the same things and act in exactly the same ways.

Sadly, we cannot avoid such misrepresentations and misidentifications. Just *being* a Christian has its risks; the more active we are *as* Christians, the more risks we incur. These vulnerabilities and risks may unconsciously limit what a Christian does for the Lord simply because he wants to avoid the adverse effects *of* such activity. More specifically, he may:

- Put up walls of self-defense and retreat into (virtual) isolation—from his marriage, family, church, and people in general.
- Always be running from trouble (rather than dealing with it in a responsible manner).
- Seek pleasure rather than an ever-deepening relationship with God. This can also be defined as "escapism," which manifests itself in a variety of ways: alcohol, drugs, affairs, sexual immorality, excessive attention to technology, video games, or television, shoplifting or stealing, etc.
- Seek peace at any price. In a real sense, he becomes content to be passive and mediocre.
- Demand compensation from God for what he has suffered as a result of doing His will (since God did not *prevent* this pain).
- Remain aloof, distant, disconnected, and hard to get a hold of. He will say something like, "I'm just not a people person," but what he really means is, "I'm afraid of getting hurt" or "I do not want to make myself vulnerable to others."

❑ Redefine what "active" *means* in order to accommodate his aversion to such risks and dangers ("I know I seldom share my faith with others, but I'm 'active' in other ways. God knows my heart!").

Such scenarios are part of a common but seldom-revealed problem among Christians: the sin of self-protection. On the one hand, a Christian wants what the gospel offers: forgiveness, spiritual blessings, providential care, and salvation. On the other hand, he recoils from what being a Christian brings upon him: difficulty, confrontation, being taken advantage of, being hurt, and outright persecution.

Two of the strongest human passions that exist are *love* and *desire*. These are the driving forces behind most of all human behavior. Yet, they are also the source of the greatest hurts, heartaches, and emotional pains that we are able to experience. Thus, if one has a great passion for God—he wants to love like God loves and desires Him with all of his heart—he makes himself vulnerable to the godless world that loathes that kind of love and passion. The deeper one's love for God, the more vulnerable he makes himself; the deeper one's desire for God, the greater the risks will be that others—unbelievers and passive Christians alike—will challenge that desire. What many Christians do not realize is that *self-protection* and *godly love* are opposites: they cannot coexist; we cannot practice the one (love) while clinging desperately to the other (self-protection).[33]

Self-protection robs God of what is rightfully His: respect, devotion, "good works" (Ephesians 2:10), praise, and faith in general (see Malachi 3:8-10, in principle). This also robs the Christian of the joy and benefit of fellowship with God. John Piper says: "If you're not suffering [as a Christian] in this world, it's because you're not choosing to walk to places where you have to trust God."[34] In other words, Christians who choose self-protection over suffering as a Christian will avoid doing anything that *produces* this suffering. In effect, they will avoid living as genuine Christians.

Christian Thinking

Self-protection is an evasion of one's commitment to God. In sharp contrast to this, the one who truly believes in Christ and His gospel will not be concerned with the negative *consequences* of that belief, but will do everything in his power to *live according* to it. Jesus clearly stated that whoever tries to save his own life (i.e., seek self-preservation through human effort) will lose everything. Self-protection stands in contrast to the self-denial that He requires of us. On the other hand, those who entrust their soul to Him will be protected indeed—not necessarily from the troubles of this life, but most certainly from the troubles that will come upon the ungodly in the hereafter (Matthew 16:24-25; see also 2 Timothy 1:12, 1 Peter 3:10-14, and Revelation 2:11).

Every commitment involves *loss* of some kind. As you choose one thing, you necessarily relinquish opportunity for what was *not* chosen. If you choose to be a Christian, then you must necessarily let go of the life of an unbeliever that you leave behind in that decision. If you choose Christ as your Lord, then you must leave all other allegiances behind that interfere with your allegiance to Him. "The most determinative fork in the road of your life may not be at the point where you decide whether to *start* following Jesus, but at the point where you decide to *keep* following Him when the person or people you love most in the world are going in a different direction."[35] Giving up all other choices is itself a choice, which contradicts the modern myth that you can still keep all your options on the table even after you have made a solemn commitment to only *one* option up front.[36]

What do *you* think?

1.) In 2 Corinthians 6:11-13, Paul asks, in essence, "You [Corinthians] have enjoyed *my* love for you; why are you withholding *your* love for me?" What might be some reasons for their having withheld their love (especially in light of some of the internal problems within the church in Corinth)?

   a. Can this situation describe a Christian's hesitation to show unconditional love to fellow believers today?

   b. Can this situation also describe one's reluctance to love God unconditionally?

2.) Since living "in a manner worthy of the gospel of Christ" (Philippians 1:27) makes us vulnerable to the abuse, manipulations, and exploitation of others, what should we do about this? What should we *not* do about this?

3.) Christ makes self-denial a mandatory requirement of our discipleship to Him (Matthew 16:24). Why do believers struggle so much with this? When we resist this, what does this say about our faith in God? Or, our confidence in Christ's ability to save us?

4.) Does our commitment to Christ require an *actual* loss of those things, people, or relationships in our lives that oppose Him, or only a *potential* loss of these? Please explain.

5.) Did a Christian choose to suffer for what is right when he chose to become a Christian, or are these two separate choices?

6.) Dietrich Bonhoeffer writes: "Not only do the followers of Jesus renounce their rights, they *renounce their own righteousness.*"[37] Do you agree with this view? Why or why not?

Section One: The Attitude of a Believer *(continued)*

Contrast of Worldly and Christian Thinking

Christians are not to think like the world thinks. We are to have a different outlook on life, love, success, and suffering than do unbelievers. We must not share the limited and godless perspective of those who are unconverted. Our goals are different; our purpose is different; our approach to dealing with people and problems is different. We serve a different God than the world serves; if we are faithful to what we believe, we will end up in a different kind of existence than that of non-Christians.

Christians are often accused of being "irrational" because our belief system necessarily requires human faith in order to make it work. Yet, our faith is supported by knowledge, evidence, and necessary implications. In contrast, the world's thinking and its belief system is based upon personal opinions, poor assumptions, and lack of evidence. *This* is truly irrational, since it defies all reason and is unprovable, but many people believe this way all the same. Christians serve a higher purpose than that of unbelievers: our objective and completion is beyond this earthly life. Those who are not Christians may appear to serve a "noble" or "transcendent" purpose, but it fails to prepare them for the life to come.

All of this has a direct impact upon the *attitude* we have toward ourselves, other people, our circumstances, and life in general. People whose entire existence is defined by their earthly life (status, circumstances, relationships, what happens to them, what *doesn't* happen to them, etc.) are easily bothered—even devastated or traumatized—when "life" is unkind to them. Their happiness is determined by an *outside-in* perspective: what happens *outside* of them [externally] defines the quality or stability of what is happening *inside* of them [internally]. In other words, they allow the physical world to dictate their mental and even spiritual disposition. Christians, on the other hand, have an *inside-out* perspective: when we are truly at peace with God, it really does not matter what happens (or does not happen) to us.[38] The internal or spiritual calm we have in knowing where we stand with the Lord (cf. 1 John 5:13-15) dictates our earthly outlook. If all is well between us and God, then all is well, period.

Attitude determines behavior, especially as measured over time. The behavior of a non-Christian will be (overall) markedly different than that of a genuine follower of Christ. As an exercise: for each comparison below, consider the *kind of action or behavior* you would expect to see from the thinking process of the person on the left versus the one on the right:

Irrational or Worldly Thinking	Christian Thinking
Everyone must love me in order for me to experience true happiness.	Christ's love is all I need to be happy.
Everyone must approve of me in order to validate my self-worth.	If I have God's approval, it does not matter who else does or does not approve of me (1 Corinthians 4:3-4).
Life is nearly unbearable when things do not go my way.	I can find contentment in Christ, regardless of my circumstances.
People who do not contribute to my self-esteem rob me of peace and joy.	My peace and joy are the result of a right relationship with God; no one can take this away from me.
If I have a problem that I cannot solve, I am paralyzed with fear and/or the inability to function.	God does not promise a problem-free life, nor do I need this in order to serve Him productively.
My emotional misery is caused by external factors: uncooperative people, tragic events, conflicts, etc.	My well-being rests upon God's promises which cannot fail and are not dependent upon outside factors.
I know I do bad things sometimes, but I cannot help this.	Sin is no longer my master, but Christ is. In any case. I am entirely responsible for my own actions.
It is too hard to be good; I am overwhelmed with my own failures.	Christ is my goodness. He deals with my failures through His mercy and grace.

Irrational or Worldly Thinking	Christian Thinking
People who do bad things to me (or to people I care about) need to be condemned and then punished.	I will not be controlled by someone else's bad behavior; I will let God take care of such people (Romans 12:17–21).
Avoiding responsibility and troubling situations ultimately leads to resolution (over time).	Avoiding responsibility is sinful (James 4:17) and only compounds the problem; time does not change this.
My past is the most important cause of my present feelings and behavior.	My past is in the past: I cannot change it, but neither will I be a prisoner of it. My present behavior is dictated by Christ, not by "what happened" to me.
I can achieve happiness by coasting through life without really committing to anything or anyone too deeply (to protect myself).	As a Christian, I cannot avoid my moral obligations to God, my family, my church, and those in need. Self-protection implies unbelief in God's providential care for me.
I need to live in such a way that does not hurt other people's feelings.	I need to live in such a way that is consistent with the will of God.
If I do hurt other people's feelings, then I must also be responsible for their resulting behavior.	If I am "speaking the truth in love" (Ephesians 4:15), I am not responsible for how people respond to this.
If people ask me to do something for them, it is wrong to turn them down.	If people ask me to do something for them, I must decide whether or not it is wise and appropriate to agree to it.
I promise to be true to myself.	I promise to be true to Jesus Christ.
My number one priority is to be happy—no matter what this takes.	My number one priority is to be faithful to Christ—no matter what this takes.

"Have this attitude in yourselves which was also in Christ Jesus…" (Philippians 2:5). Literally, this translates to: "Let the mind of Christ become your mind." It is not enough that you or I take on Jesus' name in calling ourselves "Christians"; we must also internalize His mission, attitude, and general behavior. "We should follow Christ's example, rather than put ourselves first. He did not think too highly of his own status to take on our humanity (2:8) with its complement of suffering and humiliation."[39] This mindset leads you to appropriate (godly) behavior, but it requires:

The Attitude of a Believer

- ❑ Your knowledge of Christ's own attitude and behavior (Ephesians 4:21, "... You have heard of Him and been taught in Him, just as truth is in Jesus").
- ❑ Your willingness to embrace His attitude and behavior as your own (1 Corinthians 2:16, "But we have the mind of Christ"; Galatians 2:20, "... it is no longer I who live, but Christ lives in me ...").
- ❑ Your actual internalization of His attitude and behavior—i.e., conformity to His pattern of life (1 John 2:3-6, "... The one who says he abides in Him ought himself to walk in the same manner as He walked").
- ❑ Your habitual practice of this behavior, regardless of circumstances or other's approval (1 Peter 4:4, "In all this, they [unbelievers] are surprised that you do not run with them in the same excesses of dissipation, and they malign you...").

Many Christians are trying to recreate the Garden of Eden experience in their lives. They want ideal and fulfilling relationships, a comfortable living space, material possessions, the perfect job, flawless friends, model children, an upbeat and gratifying church, and a life without heartache, turmoil, or struggle. This is the anticipation of the modern plastic Christian, and such people either lose their faith in pursuit of this kind of life, or they lose their faith in the utter disappointment of not having it. In either case, *they lose their faith* simply because their faith was not founded upon Christ and the attitude that He requires of His followers.

We cannot long for heaven and at the same time adopt the mindset and lifestyle of the unconverted world. This does not mean we must choose to live miserable, impoverished, and friendless lives, either. It simply means that our passion for fellowship with Christ and drawing near to God must be a *first priority*. It also means that all other priorities are subordinate to this (and thus expendable, if one is forced to choose between the two). Jim McGuiggan says wisely:

> Acceptable worship [cf. Hebrews 12:28] means ascribing worth and honor to God such as befits His status. It means doing what pleases Him in a pleasing manner. It involves an inner attitude and an outward response. The thing "done" must have His approval and the attitude in which it is done must involve seeking *His* glory and honor. Acceptable worship means: 1.) Serving God; 2.) Serving God in activities which have His approval and authorization; 3.) Serving God with an attitude of which He approves.[40]

It is clear that the believer's "service" to God far exceeds what we call "worship services" or church assemblies. *Life* worship has to do with the heart of the believer as manifested through his (or her) outward conduct. A contemporary writer, Jared Wilson, notes one of the great "ironies" of the modern Christian mindset:

> …We are very big on "making" the Christian faith practical and "relevant," yet by and large we go on living our lives as if Jesus had nothing to say about what we do and say, who we date and marry, what sort of jobs we take, what sort of families we raise, where we spend our time, and who we spend it with. We're cool with Jesus being good and nice, but we're hesitant to live as if he is omniscient as well.

A holistic approach to Christian intellect is part and parcel of our having "the mind of Christ," or our loving God with all of our minds. Too many Christians, though, seem to think that this merely means that we interrupt our "regular" thoughts of earthly things with "better" thoughts of heavenly things, that we remind ourselves, "Someday we'll be in heaven," but in a sense that mitigates the reality that Jesus is Lord *now*, and that our taking on the mind of Christ has real bearing on our lives and our thoughts about our lives now.[41]

Clearly, God's level of expectation for us is far beyond a superficial or momentary approach. This makes discipleship to Christ far more difficult than how the contemporary religious world often portrays it, but it is also far more beneficial and rewarding. God does not want us merely to have a "good attitude," but a spiritual mindset that completely trusts that *His* way is the *best* way to live.

What do *you* think?

1.) Please read 1 Peter 2:21-23. Why did Christ react in the way that He did? Why did He *not* react in the way that the world typically reacts? Are believers expected to imitate Him in this?

2.) If we have "died" with Christ (cf. 2 Timothy 2:11), then we must live "for the will of God" (cf. 1 Peter 4:1-2). But what does it mean to live for the will of God, exactly? Do we know what His will really *is*, or are we to follow our heart and hope that we are doing well?

3.) Do you think it is true that many Christians are trying to "follow" Christ while at the same time seeking to fill their lives with the pursuits and pleasures of the world?

   a. If not, then why are so many Christians today so passive or indifferent toward their commitment to Christ?

   b. If so, then what are we—those with a divided heart as well as those who observe such people—to do about this?

4.) Jared Wilson's quote in this section is a response to what he calls religious "consumerism." Do you think that this appropriately identifies the attitude of many churchgoers today? Or, do you have a different explanation? In either case, please explain.

Section One: The Attitude of a Believer *(continued)*

How to Develop a Godly Attitude

The Christian life is all about growing and maturing, and these actions necessarily require *change*. (We will explore the topic of "change" in further detail later in this study.) God *wants* you to grow and mature, and therefore He *expects* you to change—always in the right direction and for the right reason. He has given you the tools (in His Word) to do this. He has given you the people (in His church) to assist you in this. He has given you His Holy Spirit and the intercession of His Son to do this. God is completely committed to your spiritual success. The question is: first, what do *you* want? Second, what exactly needs changing—and how is this to be accomplished?

It is important to recognize up front that what you *think about* is far more important to change than how you *feel*. Yet, most people who resolve to better themselves focus on changing their emotions (feelings) rather than their thinking. Your emotions tend to follow the nature or quality of whatever it is you are putting into your head. When you allow your thinking to follow your emotions (moods, tempers, hypersensitivities, etc.), the result is a mindset that has no rational substance to it. As your mood changes, so will your thinking—and thus your behavior. This results in a "moody" or fickle Christian rather than a stable and consistent one. For example:

- If you think about *good* things, then you will likely be in a *good* mood.
- If you think about what God has done for you, how blessed you are to be a Christian, the benefits of divine grace, and heaven, it is unlikely that you will become despondent, disillusioned, or depressed—no matter what is happening to you.

- ❏ If you think about *bad* things, then you will likely be in a *bad* mood.
- ❏ If you allow a despondent, disillusioned, or depressed *mood* to dictate the content of your thoughts, it is likely that you will think about negative things that only worsen your state of mind.[42]

To change (for the better) your overall attitude, you must change your way of thinking. In effect, what you *want* must be consistent with what you claim to *believe*. If you truly profess to believe in Christ and His gospel, then you must want the same objective that He seeks—the salvation of your soul.[43] You cannot say, "I believe in Christ with all of my heart!" but be lukewarm in your practice of His gospel (cf. Revelation 3:15-16). In such case, your heart and your mouth are going in two different directions. If you wish to live as a genuine Christian, this requires at least that you:

- ❏ *Choose* to dwell on whatever is true, honorable, right, pure, lovely, etc. (Philippians 4:8).
- ❏ *Refuse* to dwell on whatever is false, dishonorable, wrong, impure, wicked, etc.—i.e., the opposite of Philippians 4:8.
- ❏ *Manifest* good thoughts in the form of good behavior (Philippians 4:9, "practice these things").
- ❏ Be determined to *live in conformity* with Christ (1 John 2:3-6, 3:3).
- ❏ Remain *faithful* to your covenant with God, just as you expect Him to be faithful to this same covenant.

Changing your thinking must lead to a change in behavior: if behavior does not change then it is because the *thinking process* has not changed. However, just because your behavior changes, there is no guarantee that your thinking has changed. In other words, this only works correctly one way. You cannot transform inward thinking with mere external modifications in behavior—this is backward and often short-lived. For example, many churches may be very outspoken with their young people about the sins of addictive behavior, drugs, alcohol, gambling, immodest clothing, worldly parties, pornography, etc., but do not necessarily promote a *biblical* and *realistic* covenant relationship with God through love and devotion to Christ. In other words, they attempt to provide direction negatively ("Do not do this!") rather than positively ("*This* is what God desires of you!"). They also assume that the human heart will automatically be led by God's Spirit through the removal or absence of "deeds of the body" (see Romans 8:12-14). No wonder many young Christians are filled with rules and prohibitions but remain spiritually disconnected from God. They were led to believe that righteousness could be obtained through good behavior alone, with little regard for an allegiance to Christ.[44]

This does not mean that upright moral behavior is unimportant. No one can put on the "new self" who continues to give life to the "old self" (cf. Ephesians 4:22-24). The "old self" does not only include what you used to *do* as an unbeliever, but how you used to *think* as one—and how you used to rely upon *yourself* rather than upon Christ for your justification. The "old self" cannot draw near to God—it never could before you were a Christian, and it cannot now. It is this "old self" thinking that needs to be identified, confronted, and removed if one is going to move forward in his relationship with God. Christians who claim to be "drawing closer" to God contradict themselves when they:

- ❑ Spend little or no time with spiritual people but spend hours every day watching television, movies, and/or video games.
- ❑ Spend a small amount of time in the Word of God, but spend hours every day on social media (such as Facebook), randomly surfing the Internet, or other time-wasting and unproductive activities.
- ❑ Watch movies filled with all sorts of satanic behavior, promiscuity, and profanity.
- ❑ Indulge in recreational activities (with their friends) that Christ would never condone.
- ❑ Harbor feelings of bitterness, resentment, and unforgiveness within their hearts.

❑ Shower their family and friends with love and devotion, but refuse to spend time with those who need to hear the gospel or Christians in need of encouragement.

Christians who live like those in the world necessarily distance themselves from God. There is no way to avoid this. James warned, "...Do you not know that friendship with the world is hostility toward God? Therefore whoever wishes to be a friend of the world makes himself an enemy of God" (James 4:4). In a more positive instruction, the apostle Paul wrote: "And do not be conformed to this world, but be transformed by the renewing of your mind, so that you may prove what the will of God is, that which is good and acceptable and perfect" (Romans 12:2). Elsewhere, he revealed, "...One thing I do: forgetting what lies behind and reaching forward to what lies ahead, I press on toward the goal for the prize of the upward call of God in Christ Jesus" (Philippians 3:13-14). In pressing *forward* in the right direction—with the right attitude—you will become less like you *used* to be and more like the Master. In other words, your fellowship with Christ will be increasingly deeper and closer than it was previously. "The goal of spiritual and emotional growth isn't becoming perfect. The goal is a deepening awareness of ourselves, our weaknesses, our sins, and our needs. It is an increasingly clearer understanding of how much we need 'so great a salvation' (Heb. 2:3). ...God wants a grown-up, not a perfectionist."[45]

The Need for Spiritual Growth

All Christians are expected to grow, yet Christ does not wait *until* we grow and mature to receive us or use us. He receives us initially as we are, at whatever level of spiritual maturity we possess. But after this, He expects us to grow in grace and knowledge (2 Peter 3:18) and "add" to our faith regularly and diligently (2 Peter 1:5-7). He is, in fact, the Source of our growth, inasmuch as we are unable to bear fruit or increase without Him (see John 15:5, Hebrews 13:20-21).

Christian Thinking

This means that *you* are not expected to grow on your own and *then* present yourself before Christ, ready for action. Such thinking does not depend upon God's grace or power, but relies instead upon human effort. Instead, it means that you are supposed to do *your* part in your spiritual transformation and allow God to do *His* part.

There is no universal rate of spiritual growth for any Christian; for this reason, we cannot impose one. Spiritual growth is seldom a speedy or easy process. Those who expect a "quick change" (especially to thinking and behavior that have been years in the making) are soon discouraged by the seeming slowness of the process. It is true, however, that some will grow faster than others—and there is nothing wrong with this by itself. For others, spiritual growth is slow and painful—and there is nothing wrong with this by itself, either. In any case, Christ's disciple must *choose* to grow and put an honest and determined effort into that growth. No one can *choose* to be "slow"; likewise, those who are growing "in leaps and bounds" may be mistaken about what they perceive is happening. (Just because one learns Bible passages more quickly and proficiently than someone else, for example, does not mean that he is "growing" faster—or that he is growing in the Lord at all.)

As a Christian, you must be honest and realistic in what to expect in your discipleship. For example, just because you have had a relatively smooth couple of years of walking in the Lord does not mean that the rest of your life will continue in this way. Likewise, just because you have struggled profusely in the last several years does not mean that your struggle will continue to be so difficult, or that you will not enjoy a great surge of growth in the near future. All the same, you do not have all the time in the world *to* grow—and you cannot afford to think you are on cruise control *or* stuck in traffic, so to speak.

You are probably familiar with some computer software programs or interactive Internet pages that have a user contract statement (an "End User License Agreement," or EULA). There will usually be a checkbox

The Attitude of a Believer

or highlighted text that instructs, "By clicking on this … you agree to the terms and conditions for use of this program, etc." In a very similar manner, your baptism into Christ was your agreement to the terms and conditions of discipleship to Him.[46] Upon that symbolic death to your old self, you *morally* and *legally* bound yourself to whatever the Master requires of you in your "newness of life" (cf. Romans 6:4). After all, He *purchased* you with His blood—a profound and priceless transaction—and now "you are not your own" (see 1 Peter 1:18-19, 1 Corinthians 6:19-20). Your life is no longer all about *you*, it is all about *Him*. "[In baptism] the breach with the world is complete. It demands and produces the death of the old man [or, "old self"; see Romans 6:3-7]. In baptism, a man dies together with his old world. … When a man is baptized into the Body of Christ not only is his personal status as regards salvation changed, but also the relationship of daily life."[47] Since you belong to Him, then it is necessary and expected that you increasingly become more like Him over a reasonable period of time. This means that you must:

- Spend less time thinking about what *you* want and what makes *you* happy. You need to set your mind on the Lord's interests and not anything inferior to this (Matthew 16:23, Ephesians 5:15-17).
- Spend less time pursuing your hobbies, recreation, and entertainment and spend more time pursuing your discipleship. "Entertainment" is all about distracting you from the difficulties, responsibilities, and mundane activities of life.[48] Discipleship is all about feeding your soul, nourishing your faith, and relishing your fellowship with the Lord, not gratifying your craving for entertainment.
- Reduce your desire for and attention to time-wasting habits, addictions, and self-indulgences and spend more time conforming to Christ. This must be replaced by spending time in prayer, studying the Word of God, in fellowship with believers, and meditating upon things that are true, honorable, right, etc. (recall Philippians 4:8-9).
- Stop making provision for the "flesh"—i.e., the earthly, self-serving, and superficial things of this world—and start spending far more

time on the things of God. If you truly plan to be with the Lord in the hereafter—the major premise of *becoming* a Christian in the first place—then it stands to reason that you will do whatever it takes to prepare for that existence. This does not mean that you cannot enjoy life or its amusements while you are in *this* life; it means that these other things must remain small and expendable in comparison to your discipleship to Christ. In order to "[fix your] hope on the living God" (1 Timothy 4:10), you must forfeit any fixation upon this earthly life.

This subject can easily be misunderstood. You should not conclude, "If I spend more time doing 'Christian' things, then I will automatically become a better disciple of the Lord." This is not necessarily true. Christ wants your *heart*, not just your time, attention, and obedience to commandments.[49] For example, just because a man owns a library of legal books does not make him a lawyer; he still needs schooling, preparation, a degree, passage of the state bar exam, etc. Most of all, he needs to develop the *mind* of a lawyer. Likewise, just because a person owns a collection of oil paints, paint brushes, canvas, and an easel does not make him an artist, and he will never paint like a *master* artist until he immerses himself in what it takes to *be* a master.

So it is with Christians: just because we have Bibles, church buildings, pews, songbooks, preachers, etc., does not mean we are "disciples"—at least, not from Christ's perspective. Just because we go through the *motions* of being disciples does not mean we are in fact disciples. "A disciple is not above his teacher, nor a slave above his master. It is enough for the disciple that he become like his teacher, and the slave like his master" (Matthew 10:24-25a). Christ does not say, "Only do what the teacher *does*" but, "Become *like* the teacher." This requires the student (disciple) to adopt the mindset, heart, and perspective of his master. In the Christian context, this means that instead of saying, "I'm doing this because Christ told me to," a disciple says, "I'm doing this because it is exactly what my Master would do, and *I want to be more like Him.*"

The Attitude of a Believer

Not only this, but the disciple does what he does for the same *reason* that would prompt his Master to do it.[50] Christ said, "I always do the things that are pleasing to Him [the Father]" (John 8:29). This ought to be your objective as well: not merely, "I always go to church," or, "I always say my prayers," but, "I always strive to please God in *whatever I do*" (see Galatians 1:10). Likewise, Christ said, "If you continue in My word, then you are truly disciples of Mine; and you will know the truth, and the truth will make you free" (John 8:31-32). He does *not* say, "If you read your Bible, etc.," but (in essence), "If you *pattern your heart and your life after Me*, you will know Me and will walk in truth." Only those who do this will be His disciples; those who refuse to do this will become something else.

In order to think *like* Christ, you must be familiar with (and truly believe) what He believed. No one can have the mind of Christ who acts according to his own mind instead. The proverb is true: "For as [a man] thinks within himself, so he is" (Proverbs 23:7a). A man who sets his mind on evil and self-ambition is filled with darkness; one who fills his heart with Christ walks in the light (Matthew 15:18-20, Luke 11:33-36, 1 John 1:5-7, et al).

Consider what Christ believed *and* what He did that was consistent with those beliefs:

- ❑ He knew He was God's Son. (Are you a "son of God'?)
- ❑ He addressed God the Father with great respect (How do you address the Father?)
- ❑ He regarded the Word of God as a binding authority (How do you regard the Word?)
- ❑ He was a prayerful Man, and believed in the power of prayer (Are you a prayerful person? Do you believe in the power of prayer?)
- ❑ He "went about doing good" to others (Acts 10:38) (Are you focused on doing good?)
- ❑ He dealt compassionately with sinners and sought to save the "lost" (Are you this way?)

Christian Thinking

- ❑ He loved fully and unconditionally (Do you love like this?).
- ❑ He always did what was in the best interest of others (Does this describe you?)
- ❑ He did not change His message to accommodate anyone (Do you change your "message" or beliefs to accommodate anyone—including yourself?)
- ❑ He knew the will of God, and He did nothing to violate this (Do you know God's will, or do you allow yourself to violate it?)
- ❑ He did not ask of others that which He was unwilling to do Himself (Do you expect others to perform in ways that you yourself refuse to do?)
- ❑ "I always do the things that are pleasing to Him [the Father]" (John 8:29) (Do you "always" strive to please the Father?)

What do *you* think?

1.) What happens when a Christian only focuses on improving his outward behavior to the neglect of his inward spiritual attitude? (There are several answers.)

2.) The gradual transformation of one's heart will require prayer, education (from God's Word), fellowship with other Christians, time, and experience. These are things the individual believer pursues. But what does God do for this person? Or, is it sufficient that He has given us His Bible—and nothing else is needed?

3.) Many Christians say, "I want to draw closer to Christ," but do not want to change their lifestyle, routine, circle of friends, or way of thinking. Given this, why will such people *never* develop a deep and intimate relationship with the Lord?

4.) What specific commitments do *all* Christians agree to when dedicating their lives to serving the Lord? Are these negotiable and conditional agreements or non-negotiable and unconditional?

   a. Is our *mental* disposition included in these commitments, or are our commitments merely external or behavioral?

   b. In becoming a Christian, do we give our *heart* to the Lord, or is it sufficient that we give our time, monetary offerings, church attendance, and good behavior? Please explain. (Consider 2 Corinthians 8:3-5 in your answer.)

5.) Did Christ give us an example to *follow* or merely an example to *admire*? Are we supposed to *adopt* His cause or is it enough that we are *convinced* by His own devotion to His cause?

Section One: The Attitude of a Believer *(continued)*

The "Blessed" Believer

Godliness is not achieved through the mere adherence to rules and laws, but through the transformation of the heart which strives to imitate Christ. Many misconstrue this to mean that "rules and laws" are therefore not necessary, but this is hardly the case. Christ Himself *proved* the necessity and importance of these in the fact of His own obedience to the commandments of God under which He was born ("the Law"—Galatians 4:4). Christ was not a law-*breaker*, but a law-*keeper*. In fact, "law" is absolutely necessary to: define what sin is; define what holiness is; teach us how to deal with sin (when we commit it); pursue holiness instead of sin.[51]

A godly attitude is not merely one that has God in the picture, according to one's own preference. Rather, it is a mental disposition *and* will of the heart. During His so-called "sermon on the mount," Christ provided a prescription—familiarly known to us as the Beatitudes [lit., happy statements] (Matthew 5:3-11)—that defines this disposition. In this prescription, Christ "is stating that though everybody may consider his followers to be most wretched and unfortunate and though they themselves are by no means always filled with optimism regarding their own condition, in the sight of heaven and by the standards of its kingdom they are happy indeed; yes, 'happy' in the most exalted sense of the term; hence, superlatively blessed."[52]

- ❏ *"Blessed are the poor in spirit, for theirs is the kingdom of heaven"* (Matthew 5:3). The "poor in spirit" are those who are humble before God, not proud, boastful, or self-reliant. It describes "those whose minds are suited to the humble station of life; 'poor' means destitute of something; poor in spirit means those who are destitute of the proud, haughty, arrogant spirit of the world."[53]

The Attitude of a Believer

- *"Blessed are those who mourn, for they shall be comforted"* (Matthew 5:4). To "mourn" in this context means to express sorrow for one's sins, but also to recognize the pain those sins have caused God (and the price He paid in order to remedy that situation). By extension, the believer also mourns for the sins that his fellow human beings have caused themselves, the world, and God—necessitating Christ's own agonizing experience on the cross.

- *"Blessed are the gentle [or, meek], for they shall inherit the earth"* (Matthew 5:5). Those who are "gentle" are those who are kind, sympathetic to the needs of others, and have a quiet disposition overall. Meekness is not weakness, but a withholding of retaliation in order to serve a higher moral purpose. "Selfish people may *possess* the earth, but it is the meek alone who inherit the real blessings of this earth and of the spiritual kingdom. The meek will enjoy the temporal blessings more than others and finally will triumph over the earth in the kingdom of God."[54]

- *"Blessed are those who hunger and thirst for righteousness, for they shall be satisfied"* (Matthew 5:6). This refers to those who crave not the things of this world, but the will of God—what *He* defines as "right" and is consistent with His holy nature. Coffman says: "The desire for righteousness is the only desire of man that can be truly and finally satisfied. Appetites of the flesh, all of them, can be satisfied only for the moment."[55] Hendriksen adds: "God never made a soul so small that the whole world will satisfy it."[56]

- *"Blessed are the merciful, for they shall receive mercy"* (Matthew 5:7). The godly attitude is keenly perceptive to the needs or sufferings of others, and demonstrates compassion toward such people. "Mercy is love for those in misery and a forgiving spirit toward the sinner. It embraces both the kindly feeling and the kindly act."[57]

- *"Blessed are the pure in heart, for they shall see God"* (Matthew 5:8). Purity is an essential virtue of the redeemed, inasmuch as God cannot have fellowship with those whose hearts are corrupted or impure. This refers to moral purity, purity of one's dealings with others, and purity of one's thoughts. "To 'see' God is to enjoy him, to enjoy his presence. ... Not only do the pure in heart see God here, but they shall see him face to face."[58]

- ❑ *"Blessed are the peacemakers, for they shall be called sons of God"* (Matthew 5:9). While actual peace requires the cooperation of all parties involved, children of the kingdom must be *pursuers* of peace ("so far as it depends on you"—cf. Romans 12:18), and not the source of strife, discord, or contention. "These are not unionistic peacemakers who combine contrary doctrines by agreeing to disagree. Truth of God comes first, peace with men second. Friends are dear, [but] the Word of our greatest Friend [is] dearest."[59]

- ❑ *"Blessed are those who have been persecuted for the sake of righteousness, for theirs is the kingdom of heaven. Blessed are you when people insult you and persecute you, and falsely say all kinds of evil against you because of Me"* (Matthew 5:10-11). These two "blessed" statements are really one and the same. The qualifiers for these statements are "for the sake of righteousness" and "because of Me." While many people in the world *suffer* for various reasons, the believer suffers specifically because he is doing what is *right* in God's sight and (concurrently) is demonstrating loyalty to Christ.

No one can be "blessed" unless he dutifully carries out God's commandments in his own life. While no one is saved *because* of commandment-keeping, it does not follow that *any* of God's commands are optional, situational, or open for private interpretation. "For this is the love of God [really, this is the evidence that we *love* like God loves], that we keep His commandments; and His commandments are not burdensome" (1 John 5:3, bracketed words are mine). Bonhoeffer expresses this succinctly: "Unless he obeys, a man cannot believe."[60] In other words, the genuine *expression* of belief is manifested in one's obedience to the One whom he says he believes. "By eliminating simple obedience on [or, for the sake of] principle, we drift into an unevangelical interpretation of the Bible."[61]

Obedience must never be viewed as a "burden," but as a route to the state of blessedness. Jesus thoroughly enjoyed obeying His Father, despite the hardships—up to and including crucifixion—that this required of Him. "For joy" He endured the torture and reproach of the cross—i.e., not the joy of literally being nailed to a cross, but the joy of obedience to His Father. "For consider Him who has endured such hostility by sinners against Himself, so that you will not grow weary and lose heart" (Hebrews 12:3). Obedience is to be carried out with joy and enthusiasm, not weariness and despondency. "Enthusiasm" is literally defined as "(the state of being) inspired by God."[62] Enthusiasm among believers is often described as "zeal" (Titus 2:14), "fervent in spirit" (Romans 12:11), or (by implication) a "contending earnestly" for something (Jude 3). A Christian's attitude must not be *passive* toward doing God's will, but *enthusiastic* or *zealous* for this (as it was with Jesus; see John 2:17, 5:30, and 8:29).

The blessed life of a believer is one of serene contentment, since he knows that he is on the path that leads to eternal life. "Contentment" is the state of mind in which one is genuinely at peace with God and himself, regardless of his earthly circumstances (Romans 5:1-2). This does not mean he is never bothered with or even upset because of what is happening to him. Certainly a car accident, diagnosis of a serious disease, or a death in the family will rattle the nerves of even the strongest believer. Yet, because his soul is in God's hands, such things are limited to this life. Contentment in God looks *beyond* this temporary life to the eternity that lies beyond it (2 Corinthians 4:16-18). Because of this perspective, Paul wrote (Philippians 4:11-13):

> Not that I speak from want, for I have learned to be content in whatever circumstances I am. I know how to get along with humble means, and I also know how to live in prosperity; in any and every circumstance I have learned the secret of being filled and going hungry, both of having abundance and suffering need. I can do all things through Him who strengthens me.

God's providence—His "provide-ability" for those who believe in Him—will carry Christians through whatever it is that they must face in this life. His providence will also prevent them from being truly overwhelmed with such things: He will not allow those who trust in Him to have to endure something that would ruin their soul (1 Corinthians 10:13). Therefore, believers can find contentment and peace in God, knowing that He is providentially guarding and preparing them for a life with Him in His heaven (2 Corinthians 5:5-9). *This* is the "blessed" life; it is this *attitude* that all believers must develop with regard to the struggles of life and discipleship to Christ.

The Danger of Discontentment

The opposite of contentment is not mere "unhappiness," but greed or covetousness, which amounts to idolatry (Ephesians 5:5, Colossians 3:5). Covetousness is one or more of the following:

- ❏ Wanting wrong things—things that are evil and therefore destructive to the soul.
- ❏ Wanting right things for the wrong reasons or motives—the "things" are not the problem here, but the illicit desire is (see James 4:3).
- ❏ Wanting right things at the wrong time—in other words, demanding that God provide these things on one's *own* schedule rather than yielding to His.
- ❏ Wanting right things but wanting them in the wrong amount—in other words, not being happy with the measure of God's blessings, but insisting that He give even more.[63]

In each of these cases, a person is not seeking God's will but his own; or, he is attempting to use God to accommodate his own selfish agenda. At the heart of all covetousness is a failure to trust in God's providence or sufficiency. For such people, "Feeling better has become more important than finding God. And worse, we assume that people who find God always feel better."[64]

Christians who are "unhappy" have not yet discovered the *secret of contentment in Christ*. They cling tenaciously to this world because they hope to find completion and fulfillment in it (see 1 John 2:15-17).[65] Those whose hearts are set upon this world will *never* be content, no matter how religious or spiritual they seem otherwise, no matter how long they have been Christians, and no matter how "faithful" they think themselves to be. The truth is: they have deceived themselves into thinking they can achieve righteousness by experiencing "spirituality." "If we believe that spirituality is the absence of sinfulness, we are out of touch with our sinfulness. If we are out of touch with our sinfulness, we are out of touch with our need to be forgiven."[66] Such is the mindset of the so-called "worldly Christian"—an oxymoron, to be sure. The truth is that genuine happiness in God is completely grounded upon one's full dependence upon Christ and his contentment with what He provides.

Worldly Happiness:	Happiness (contentment) in Christ:
Is artificial, superficial, and finite.	Is genuine, deep, and enduring.
Requires ideal circumstances or conditions.	Is not dependent upon external circumstances.
Requires full cooperation of others.	Is not dependent upon the cooperation of others.
Can be robbed by malicious people, unfavorable events, or tragedy.	Cannot be robbed by any person, thing, or event in this life.
Assumes that life is *meant* to be fulfilling—and often blames others when it is not.	Knows that life *is* fulfilling, but only when fulfillment is sought in Christ and not in the experience of life itself.
Is self-serving and presumptive in nature (see Luke 12:16-21).	Is selfless, factual, and practical in nature.
Does not prepare one for the afterlife.	Fully prepares one for the afterlife.
Completely evaporates upon one's death.	Continues beyond this life into eternity.
Results in the loss of one's soul.	Results in the salvation of one's soul.

Every form of sin grows from a common root: *dissatisfaction with God.* Those who will not believe in God are simply not content with the reasons He gives *for* believing in Him. Many atheists, for example, are not as opposed to the concept of God as they are unhappy with how this God performs or what He expects of people. Because He does not meet their expectations, they have allegedly etched Him out of existence.[67] On the other hand, Christians may also look to something or someone else beyond God for their completion, tacitly implying their dissatisfaction with what God has to offer them. This longing for something else translates to idolatry or misplaced worship. "God cannot give us a happiness and peace apart from Himself, because it is not there. There is no such thing."[68] In this sense, we see that sin is a *very personal* offense against God: the sinner is not just unhappy with what God offers him, he is unhappy with *God Himself.* Sin is thus relational infidelity, not just rules broken; likewise, righteousness is relational fidelity, not just rules obeyed.[69] It is one's regard for *God Himself* that is the pivotal decision toward the rest of one's behavior.

In contrast to the sinner's dissatisfaction with the Lord, the true believer seeks his completion in Christ and Him alone (Colossians 1:28). Having sanctified Christ as Lord in his heart (1 Peter 3:15), he entrusts his soul to His care (2 Timothy 1:12). This person does not have a collection of idols in his heart, but has removed all former idols in sole allegiance to his Lord and Savior.[70] He does not seek worldly pleasures as a means of gratification, but holy communion with God. Likewise, he does not try to package his service to God in the context of his own expectations, but strives to know and obey his Father's will. He is, in other words, not a passive observer of the Christian faith, but is an active participant in it. He is, in every respect, a disciple of the Lord.

What do *you* think?

1.) Please review again Jesus' "blessed" statements regarding those who are in the kingdom of God (Matthew 5:3-12). Are *all* of these necessary in order to achieve the "blessed" life, or is any *one* of them sufficient? Please explain.

2.) Please read Romans 10:2-4. "Zeal without knowledge" describes many today who call themselves Christians: they are big on "awe" and entertainment, but remain largely ignorant of the Word of God. Yet, others are big on Bible study and quoting Scripture, but remain largely unenthusiastic about their alleged salvation.

   a. Which is better: enthusiasm without knowledge, or knowledge without enthusiasm? Please explain.

   b. Is zeal a *requirement* of the Christian faith or something that only some people will have and others will not?

3.) Regarding "contentment":

   a. Is it necessary that God remove all of your earthly problems before you can be content in Him? Is it necessary that He remove *any* of them?

   b. Is contentment *purely* a state of mind, or is it also something that is *visibly* manifested (in any way) in a Christian's life? Please explain.

   c. If a Christian gets very angry, cries with disappointment, thoroughly enjoys an entertaining but secular movie, or is financially well-to-do, does this indicate that he is not "content" in Christ?

   d. On the other hand, can these things—anger, disappointment, earthly pleasure, and wealth—potentially rob a person of his spiritual contentment?

e. Can a person with a divided heart (or loyalty) ever be content, no matter how strongly he declares his love for the Lord (see Matthew 6:24, Galatians 1:10, and James 4:4)?

4.) What does Paul mean when he says that every Christian may be "complete in Christ" (Colossians 1:28)? When will this completion be attained?

Section Two: The Perspective of a Believer

How Do You See Things?

"Perspective" literally means "to see through." It refers to one's mental view or "take" on whatever he considers. Ideally, it is the capacity to view things as they really are or with relative importance.[71] Any given person's perspective is formed by a number of factors, including: where he was born; the political and religious views of his parents; the quality of his childhood; his extended family and friends; his education; his religious beliefs; his vocational training; his career; profound or major life experiences; etc. No person lives in a vacuum of pristine objectivity; we all have our biases, prejudices, and manners of "seeing" things in a certain way. Your own perspective often affects:

- How you see yourself in the world.
- How you see the world around you.
- How you see God and His world.
- How you see yourself in God's world.
- How you view Christianity.
- How you view other Christians.
- How you view those who are not Christians.

Perspective is not a genetic trait (like your skin color) or fixed characteristic (like a birthmark). Inasmuch as you are able to change your *mind* (and thus your *attitude*), so you are able to change how you "see" people, things, or concepts. This is as true with regard to spiritual things as it is to non-spiritual ones. Your perspective can be limited, unbalanced, or outright corrupted by at least the following:

- Failing to read God's Word.
- Failing to learn about and understand human history *in light of* God's Word.
- Rejecting all higher education because you disagree with some aspects of it.

Christian Thinking

- Surrounding yourself only with people who think or believe like you do.
- Refusing to be exposed to any view, belief, or value system other than your own.
- Evaluating the entire world according to your limited, finite, and sheltered exposure to it.
- Allowing other people to think for you.
- Not challenging familiar or comfortable beliefs (yours or anyone else's).
- Not allowing yourself to be challenged by someone (or something).

Your perspective can be corrected, broadened, and sharpened by at least the following:

- Reading God's Word.
- Learning about and understanding human history *in light of* God's Word.
- Choosing to be educated, even though you do not agree with everything you hear or read.
- Allowing yourself to be confronted with people of mixed views or beliefs.
- Being willing to listen to and weigh the merits of a view, belief, or value system different than your own against an objective and authoritative standard.
- Realizing that you may not know "the truth" as you thought you did, and that just because something is true to *you* does not mean it is necessarily *God's* truth.
- Listening to what others say, and retaining what is useful and letting go of what is not—keeping the wheat and pitching the chaff (so to speak).
- Allowing yourself to be challenged by your critics, your enemies, and even your own brethren who disagree with you: if you *are indeed* right, then you have nothing to fear; if you *are indeed* wrong, then this needs to be corrected.

The Perspective of a Believer

The Christian's perspective is markedly different from the worldview of an unbeliever. One who is not a Christian will allow his perspective to be conditioned by things that offer no direction for his life and have no value for his soul. It must be the doctrine of God that drives one's Christian perspective (and never the other way around). For example, Christians must necessarily believe that:

- God is the Creator of the world and the Giver of human life (Genesis 1 - 2).
- Jesus is the Son of God who has given His blood (life) as atonement for our sins (Hebrews 9:11-13, 1 John 2:1-2).
- The Holy Spirit is a Divine Personage of God who is capable of guiding us through this life into an eternal fellowship with God (Galatians 5:16-17).
- The Bible is the expressed revelation of God to all of humankind: it contains everything necessary for life and godliness (2 Timothy 3:16-17, 2 Peter 1:3).
- The purpose for and meaning of one's life can only be fulfilled through his or her obedience to God (Ecclesiastes 12:13-14, 1 John 5:2-3).
- Sin is not just a violation of one's conscience, but a violation of God's moral laws and His holy nature (Romans 3:23, Ephesians 2:1-3).
- The church is the sanctuary of believers in God and will be the only group of people that God saves from this world (Hebrews 12:22, Revelation 21:1-3).
- The gospel of Christ provides the terms and conditions necessary for entering into a covenant relationship with God (Hebrews 9:15).
- Jesus is the only way, truth, and life that leads to God (John 14:6); there are no exceptions to this; no amount of human effort or human religion can change this.
- This physical world is temporary; the human soul is eternal (2 Corinthians 4:18).

Christian Thinking

- This physical world will be destroyed by God's judgment against it; only those who abide in Him will be saved from this destruction (2 Peter 3:10, 1 John 2:15-17).
- In the hereafter, every person will stand before God and give an account of his or her life *and* will be rewarded or punished accordingly (2 Corinthians 5:10).
- Whoever tries to "save" his own life (in refusing God's will) will lose everything in the hereafter; whoever submits to the will of God will live with Him forever (Matthew 16:25-27).
- No one can serve two masters (Matthew 6:24).
- It is better to suffer for what is right than to suffer for one's own sins (or to attempt to avoid any kind of suffering at all) (1 Peter 4:15-16).
- It is better to walk the narrow path that leads to life than to follow the wide path that leads to destruction (Matthew 7:13-14).
- Godly love is superior to all other virtues and all other "loves" (1 Corinthians 13:1-7).

Believers are to take Jesus' commandments seriously rather than trying to psychoanalyze or reinterpret them in light of their own thinking. His will must always take precedent over our opinions, convictions, or perspectives, regardless of how strong these are or how long we have had them. If *your* "position" on a given subject (religious or otherwise) conflicts with God's truth in any way, then your position must change, not God's truth. If your present perspective contradicts God's revealed Word, then your perspective must change, not God's Word. God *purchased* you with the blood of His Son (1 Corinthians 6:19-20); this means He has a controlling interest in everything you do, think, and believe. While your private opinions and identity are important to you personally, your conformity to the heavenly standard is far more important to God. Your opinions and convictions will not save your soul, but your conformity to Christ is absolutely necessary *for* your salvation.

What do *you* think?

1.) Should your thinking and behavior be consistent with the Christian perspective (described above)? Or, is it sufficient to have the right perspective, regardless of anything else, to be pleasing to the Lord? Please explain.

2.) If perspective is something that *can* be changed, then what compels a person to change it? Why might a person *refuse* to change his perspective?

3.) Does God have a "perspective," or is this a strictly human characteristic?

4.) With regard to your own perspective, what should be the difference(s) between God's doctrine and our private convictions or opinions?

Section Two: The Perspective of a Believer *(continued)*

Governed by Love and Wisdom

In order to gain perspective, we must learn to think beyond our customary circles of thought or patterns of critiquing things. We are all creatures of habit in our ways of thinking as well as our behaviors. Yet, no one can "see" things as they really are without a broad and well-balanced perspective. (None of us can achieve perfect objectivity, but we can significantly improve the realistic and accurate appraisal of whatever it is that we are considering.) We also will not be able to gain perspective by always thinking the same way we have always thought or jumping to all-too-familiar conclusions. This means: if you keep thinking the same way over and over, "you keep creating the same reality." People tend to "slide unconsciously into the same old set of unconscious activities," including thought patterns, knee-jerk reactions, and conditioned responses.[72]

For many Christians—even those who claim to be "open-minded" and "broad-thinking"—learning a new *spiritual* perspective can be a frightening or unwelcome proposition. There are several significant reasons for this:

- ❏ It takes time, energy, and effort to think differently than one has become accustomed to thinking over the years. Any path of least resistance in one's thinking is familiar, well-worn, and relatively easy (to that person). For this reason, he is not apt to leave it unless motivated by something more powerful than his accustomed habit. Until that happens, he will remain the same kind of thinker, which means he will not grow, change, or mature.
- ❏ This learning process examines where a person is presently *and* exposes flaws and inconsistencies in his own beliefs. No one likes to admit being wrong, but people do not always consider the great

The Perspective of a Believer

(and possibly disastrous) *consequences* of being wrong. The Light of God is meant to illuminate any sins, errors of thinking, and errors of doctrine in a person's life (John 3:18-21). These things must not be permitted to remain in a *Christian's* life; they cannot be allowed to remain in *your* life. It is in one's best interest to have these exposed for what they are, and for him to adopt a new heart, new thinking, and a better understanding of God's doctrine instead. "Thinking is essential on the path to understanding. But understanding is a gift of God."[73]

❑ Many Christians (consciously or not) operate on a "fear and safety" approach to any new information rather than a "love and wisdom" approach. Such people fear any new approach to their thinking, and thus remain where they are presently because they think it is *safe*. Going anywhere else (in one's thinking, beliefs, understanding of the Bible, etc.) seems risky, dangerous, or even heretical (to some). Yet, this "fear and safety" perspective guarantees that a person will *always* remain where he is now and that he will never "[reach] forward to what lies ahead" (cf. Philippians 3:13). This is referred to as a kind of mental—and thus spiritual—gridlock. On the other hand, by allowing *love* and *wisdom* to govern the evaluation of any new information, a person will "see" beyond where he was previously and gain tremendous perspective. (It is critical, of course, that this love and wisdom are defined by God, not one's *version* of love and/or *human* wisdom.)

"Fear and safety" Thinking	"Love and wisdom" Thinking
"I cannot accept what you are saying about the gospel because it goes against everything I have come to believe."	"I want to hear whatever you can share with me about the Lord, as long as it is consistent with His revealed truth."
"I know that I am to show kindness to others, but I am afraid that some may misinterpret or take advantage of that kindness, so I pretty much just keep to myself."	"Every form of godly love and kindness has its risks, but I am willing to accept those risks. I will not be naive about any danger, but I have been called to serve, not to protect myself."

Christian Thinking

"Fear and safety" Thinking	"Love and wisdom" Thinking
"I only surround myself with people who think like me because I cannot risk being carried away by spiritual error."	"I am grounded upon the biblical instruction, and am not afraid to talk with those who do not think like me. My objective is to have them—and me—think like Christ."
"We can't change what we are doing because it would open the door to all kinds of problems."	"*Everything* we are doing as a church must be evaluated on the basis of what is *right* and what serves the *best interest* of our brethren."
[The preacher:] "When we let people start thinking for themselves, they always descend into liberalism."	[The preacher:] "We should teach the 'whole purpose of God' [cf. Acts 20:27] and provide good examples of how that teaching should be put into practice."
[The elders:] "Our church cannot adopt [a certain practice] because that's exactly what denominational churches do! We need to do everything in our power to remain distinctly separate from them."	[The elders:] "We should examine what other churches are doing because they might be doing [a certain practice] better than us. Adopting a similar practice does not at all mean that we have endorsed their belief system."

A "love and wisdom" perspective changes to some extent the nature of the enemy, so to speak. Those whom we might have strongly opposed in the past because they are so *different* than us may not seem so different after all. Not *everyone* is wrong about *everything*, and *all* people are equalized by the same *problem* (sin) and saved through the same *solution* (Christ). It is *love* that draws us to people to share the gospel with them. It is *wisdom* that teaches us how and when to do this most effectively.

Conservatism and Liberalism

As you can see from the table above, the "fear and safety" perspective creates an inhibited and excessively conservative mindset. Entire congregations can embrace this perspective, severely limiting their efforts at evangelism, church growth, biblical education, and compassion toward others. They are terrified of leaving behind the only way they have come to "see" God, His Word, moral responsibility, and the work of the church. While these ultra-conservative groups may obsess over the danger of "opening the door" to false doctrine and unbiblical practices, they fail to realize that their own stifled version of the gospel has opened the door to legalism, formalism, close-mindedness, and self-righteousness—all false teachings and unbiblical practices in themselves. Not only have they opened this other door, they have rushed headlong into the room where these things flourish.

Being "conservative" is one thing; taken to an extreme, however, it exceeds any God-given context and becomes "conservativ*ism*." An "-ism" is a man-made dogma, not a biblical doctrine. "Dogma" is merely an "established opinion," "a point of view or tenet put forth as authoritative without adequate grounds."[74] "Conservative" is derived from "conserve," which means to preserve or keep intact that which already exists. Jesus was conservative in every case in which He upheld the Word of God against every man-made teaching or tradition (Matthew 15:1-9 provides an ideal example of this). He protected or "conserved" the Law against any human threat to or detraction from it. But conservativ*ism* exceeds this noble and virtuous endeavor, and seeks to impose a *human dogma* upon what God has said, then masquerades the entire package as something "from God."

Conservativism tends to produce the following kinds of statements:

- ❑ "Our churches are the only ones with a scriptural name."
- ❑ "We alone [i.e., people like us or churches like ours] are the only ones who are following the Bible."
- ❑ "If any person does not read the Bible like *we* read it, he is in error."
- ❑ "If any person does not teach the Bible like *we* teach it, he is a false teacher."
- ❑ "Churches that do not conduct their worship services like we conduct *our* worship services are not 'sound' churches."

- "We can determine which church is 'sound' or not based upon how it compares to our method of worship, evangelism, and use of the 'Lord's treasury.'"
- "The 'brotherhood of believers' is thus defined by those people and churches that conform to our understanding of Scripture and how we practice it."
- "We are saved by grace, of course, but we must always strive to be deserving of that grace through our study of God's Word and reverent behavior."

While these (above) may not be the actual words being *said*, they certainly do capture the message that is being *broadcast* in order to define and maintain the "conservative" mindset. But such ideas are not merely conservative in nature; they constitute a dogma that is not actually supported by the gospel (but those who cling to it think that it *is*).

Likewise, being "liberal" is one thing; taken to an extreme, however, it also exceeds any God-given context and becomes "liberalism." Liberal dogma is no better than conservative dogma; they are both dogmas which originate from human motives and serve a human agenda. "Liberal"—as a standalone *word*, apart from any religious or political connotation—simply means "generous" or "free-giving."[75] Jesus was most certainly liberal in this sense of the word: He freely gave (Acts 20:35), freely taught (John 18:20), showed generous compassion (Matthew 9:35-36), and provided the "free gift" of eternal life to all believers (Romans 6:23). But "liberal" can also mean "free" from the constraints of human imposition, human traditions, and human authority. In this sense, also, Jesus was "liberal" in that He did not confine His thinking or His practices to the rigidly-held establishment of His day (i.e., that of the Jewish authorities). Likewise, Christians are taught to be "free" from the slavish impositions of men (Acts 15:10, 1 Corinthians 7:23, Galatians 2:4, and 5:1) and thus *liberal* in how we love, share, "do good" (Galatians 6:9-10), and show mercy.

"Freely you received, freely give" (Matthew 10:8) is one of the defining statements of genuine discipleship to Christ (see Luke 6:36-38). Liber*alism*, however—as a man-made "-ism"—exceeds the context in which this "freedom" is to be exercised. Liberalism assumes that we are free from *all* constraints and boundaries, including those which God has provided for us through His Word. This perspective determines a course of action through either a corrupted view of divine doctrine or a rejection of that doctrine altogether.

> Liberalism, whether in politics or religion, relies heavily upon emotion rather than intellect, reason and rational persuasion. The liberal call for change arises out of emotion, is driven by emotion, and depends upon emotion for its continued survival. Emotion is simply one more fuel source being tapped to achieve the objective of change.[76]

Such people go about "doing good" (cf. Acts 10:38) in a manner that is loosely based upon what Jesus did but that lacks the motive and integrity that Jesus had. Jesus sought always to please His Father through *obedience* to Him (John 8:29, Hebrews 5:8), not just through choosing to "do good" in whatever pleased Himself. Liberalism, however, seeks to impose a human agenda upon Christ's gospel and His church, and thus produces false teachings and unbiblical practices. "Liberal Christianity," as identified by liber*alism* masquerading *as* Christianity, is truly an oxymoron—a self-contradicting phrase.[77] Liberalism tends to produce the following kinds of statements:

- ❏ "The Bible is not to be understood as a fixed or rigid legal prescription for Christians, but serves as a moral guideline that characterizes Christ's virtuous behavior without succumbing to a legalistic value system."
- ❏ "The Bible is a fluid document that provides a template for believers, but is able to be re-interpreted according to social changes and the needs of modern people."

- ❑ "What Christians believed and practiced in the days of the apostles was conducive to the world in which they lived; as times change, so do certain beliefs and practices."
- ❑ "God does not want Christians dwelling on nitpicking details of religious orthodoxy. Everything we do is acceptable to Him as long as we emulate the love of Christ and seek to do good to all people."
- ❑ "Strict adherence to doctrine has historically been the source of much strife and many divisions among God's people. Therefore, it is better to focus on love, faith, fellowship, and compassion."
- ❑ "Fellowship with God does not require perfect obedience to God's Word; love, not obedience, is the goal of the believer."
- ❑ "Jesus was human like us, therefore we can relate to Him casually and familiarly even now, just like we do with other people."
- ❑ "Whatever I deem as 'worship' is acceptable to God as long as it is offered in His name and intended to show my appreciation for Him."

Again, these statements do not have to be uttered word-for-word in order to underscore the message and ministry of liberal-minded churches. Such groups of people are not being "liberal" with their love, mercy, and compassion, but have adopted a liberal*ism*—a dogma that serves the human agenda at the expense of what the Holy Spirit has revealed to all men through the gospel ("the truth"—see 2 Thessalonians 2:13-14). Those who refuse to honor the commandments of God also forfeit the right to be regarded as Christians, since they undermine the very basis *for* identification with Christ (Matthew 7:21-23, 1 Corinthians 14:37-38, Galatians 1:8, and 1 John 2:3-6).

So then, what are Christians to be: conservative or liberal? The answer is *both*, in the context of and according to the right proportions that Jesus Himself was both conservative and liberal. This *balanced* perspective is actually the very *best* perspective of all, since it is consistent with God's divinely-revealed instruction and modeled after God's own Son. Thus, we are to be conservative with regard to protecting, enforcing, and honoring God's Word; we are to be liberal with regard to demonstrating godly love, mercy, and faithfulness. However, we are never given permission to use either one of these perspectives in an ungodly or unbiblical manner—one that hijacks God's system and corrupts it with human motives and teachings.

Christian Thinking
What do *you* think?

1.) If you allow any of the following to dominate your perspective, how will this affect your discipleship to Christ? (Consider Matthew 16:24, Luke 14:26-27, and John 12:25 in your answer.)

   a. Your devotion to your family.
   b. Your personal safety and protection.
   c. Your income and material possessions.
   d. Your health issues and/or physical limitations.
   e. Your feelings of loneliness, sadness, or insecurity.
   f. Your feelings of bitterness, resentment, or vengeance.
   g. Your love for this world.

2.) How can Christians get "stuck" in their thinking if indeed they have already arrived at the truth? (Can one get "stuck" in truth?)

3.) If God owns you as His possession, does this mean that He owns your perspective, too? Or is this something that is excluded from what He has "bought with a price" (cf. 1 Corinthians 6:19-20)?

4.) What problems underlie "fear and safety" that make it an ungodly method for appropriate Christian conduct?

5.) Who or what defines "love and wisdom" and how it is to be manifested? In other words, can a person justify anything he wants to do as "love and wisdom"—and is he then exempted from being challenged? Please explain.

6.) Why is it so important to understand the difference between "conservative" and "liberal" in the way that Jesus put both of these perspectives into practice?

   a. What is the purpose for genuine "conservative" thinking (in the Christian context)?

   b. What is the purpose for genuine "liberal" thinking (in the Christian context)?

   c. Are we allowed to be "conservative" toward exercising godly love and compassion? Are we allowed to be "liberal" toward the inspired Word of God? Please explain.

7.) Why are "-isms" so dangerous (even though we may have used an "-ism" to define ourselves at one time)? Can you find any "-isms" in the Bible that Christians are to believe in or practice?

Section Three: Truth and Objectivity

What Is "Truth"?

"Truth" does not originate with human beings; we have no authority to speak it into existence. Truth is something that we are given or have been taught by an authority greater than ourselves. It is also something that we discover through our own pursuit of it, even though the *fullness* of truth remains elusive and incomprehensible to the human mind. This is because the only way to know *all* truth is to be either the *source* of all truth or have *omniscience*—attributes possessed only by God Himself, not mere human beings.

"Truth" is defined as that which is *absolutely correct* regardless of circumstances, as validated against a universal, authoritative, and fixed standard. It is the correct facts as they exist independent of any other factors. Specifically, "truth" is whatever is consistent with God's divine nature and revealed Word. God Himself serves as the ultimate standard by which all truth is determined. There is no higher source of authority than God to which we can appeal. Whenever we talk about what is right, fair, just, morally pure, or truthful, the discussion invokes—whether consciously or not—the divine righteousness of God. It is logically and philosophically impossible to ascertain genuine truth apart from appealing to His fixed and sovereign authority.

Those who "suppress the truth in unrighteousness" (cf. Romans 1:18) not only reject God's authority but replace Him with an inferior standard of measurement and valuation.[78] In other words, they no longer operate in the realm of "truth" and "righteousness," but descend instead into the realm of human opinion, human imagination, and idolatry in one form or another (Romans 1:18-23). Having rejected God's truth, they in fact reject God Himself.

God's truth—Truth with a capital T—existed before you were born and before any human being came to life. Since Jesus' existence did not begin with His human birth, but He has always existed with the Father, His knowledge of divine truth exceeds that of any other man (John 1:14-15, 14:6). Thus, He speaks with authority, power, and perspective that far exceed our own. This is why we would be wise to listen to Him rather than assume we know more or better than Him. What He says is absolutely true because of who He is and the superior source of His information. He does not need our consent, approval, or support to be right; His words stand alone, regardless of who does or does not believe them. Since Christ—the Son of God—possesses sovereign authority over us, we are in a subordinate position to Him and therefore have no right or ability to dictate what is absolutely true unless He reveals it.

Despite this, Christ gives every person the freedom to choose his own beliefs about what is true or not. Yet, no person's belief system is worth anything if there is no truth to it. If you cannot *prove* what you believe is true in a manner that transcends all subjective interpretations, then your beliefs are merely opinions and not facts. No belief system is automatically "true" just because a person embraces it, regardless of that person's credentials. You and I do not have the moral authority to pluck "truth" out of thin air. We ought to believe in what is true only when it is *proven* to be true, not just because we *want* it to be true. Even Jesus told His audience not to listen to Him only because of what He *said*, but also because of the *proofs* He offered to back it up. Such proofs were the miracles He performed which required otherworldly power and authority (John 5:36, 10:37-38, Hebrews 2:3-4).

God's Truth is not subject to human appraisal, human approval, or even human performance. You can choose to believe in His truth, but you cannot make your own "truth" equal to or superior to His. You do not have the authority, power, or ability to do this, much less enforce it. God *does* have this authority and power, however. In the future, He will hold all men accountable to Him as a direct result of these things (2 Corinthians 5:10, Philippians 3:9-11). Just because you *want* something to be true does not mean it *is* true; likewise, just because you can passionately defend what you believe, your personal convictions do not make something actually true if indeed it contradicts God's *revealed* truth.[79]

Your Truth and God's Truth

Sometimes a person will say, "The gospel may be true for *you*, but it is not true for *me*." Such a position does not invalidate the legitimacy of God's Word; it simply rejects it for what it truly is. Just because a person rejects God's truth does not mean that *his* "truth" is a fitting replacement for it. In fact, it manifests not only a logical error but a moral one. It is illogical because he has no legitimate support for his own "truth" except that, in the end, he wants to believe it. This is his *opinion*, not an argument; the two things are not the same. It is also a moral error because he has rejected the life-giving message of his Creator for the inferior and hopeless message of his own choosing—possibly of his own imagination. Christ's gospel is true regardless of who does or does not believe in it. It is true, period. Any rival or opposition to the gospel did not originate from God, but is the result of Satan's influence on the world (2 Corinthians 4:3-4, Ephesians 2:1-3, James 3:13-18, 1 John 5:19, et al).

Nonetheless, people will appeal to far lesser authorities than God and assume that such appeals are legitimate, binding, and workable. For example, someone may say, "My father, grandpa, good friend, preacher, rabbi, spiritual guru, or [insert: favorite respected mentor] told me that such-and-such is true—and *I believe him*." No one is attempting to deny that person's *belief* in another man; however, this does not mean that what is *being* believed is true. People believe in lies, deceptions, delusions, and misperceptions all the time as though they were "the truth." Yet, people can be mistaken, and even very sincere people can be very seriously mistaken. A person's words are not "true" just because he says they are, or because *you* say they are, or because a great number of people say they are. His words are only true if they say the same thing as what God has revealed to be true. God is the ultimate source of and standard for all truth, not men. No one has any *factual* knowledge of the unseen spiritual realm unless God (in one way or another) revealed it to him.

Many people think that they are something special—as in clever or unique—and make a distinction between themselves and the rest of the human race by what they claim to believe. Thus, they will say something like, "Well, that [gospel truth] works for you, but my situation is different." This overlooks or ignores the intention for God having revealed His truth to all people in the first place. He has not revealed His truth only for those who *want* to hear it, but because all men *need* to hear it. For this reason, He speaks to all of us in the same way:

- "... For all have sinned and fall short of the glory of God" (Romans 3:23)—not just those who accept this fact, or who want to be "religious," or Christians alone. One's personal "situation" does not change this fact. Anyone who is human, competent, and old enough to be accountable to God has sinned against Him.
- "And He Himself [Jesus Christ] is the propitiation for our sins; and not for ours only, but also for those of the whole world" (1 John 2:2). Jesus did not die only for those who want to be forgiven and saved; He died for *all* men *regardless* of how many actually obey His gospel. This is because all men *need* forgiveness in order to be with God—which is what He wants—and it is only through Christ's blood that this forgiveness is received.
- "For God so loved the world, that He gave His only begotten Son, that whoever believes in Him shall not perish, but have eternal life" (John 3:16). God loves *all* men, not just those who want to be loved, and not just those who respond rightly to His love. God offers to save *all* men from perishing, regardless of their personal "situations."
- "For the wrath of God is revealed from heaven against all ungodliness and unrighteousness of men who suppress the truth in unrighteousness..." (Romans 1:18). God's wrath is against *all* who suppress His truth—not just those who choose to believe this.

His wrath exists and will be unleashed against *all* who reject their Maker, regardless of their opinions, beliefs, or situations.

The subjective approach says (in essence), "I'm not so concerned whether or not a thing is *true*, as long as it works for *me*." The objective thinker realizes, "The reason why the gospel of Christ works for *everyone* is because it is *true* (i.e., from God)."

Recall our discussion on attitude in the beginning of this study. Many people—including Christians—put great emphasis on attitude but relatively little on truth. The fact is that one's attitude cannot be "good" unless it is founded upon and defined by an absolute truth. A person may claim that he has a "good attitude" when measured against his personal truth (or reality), but if his perception of truth contradicts God's actual truth, then his attitude is not a correct one. As an illustration, suppose you had a map that was thought to be of the State of Washington, when in fact it is a map of some fictitious land (like J.R.R. Tolkien's "Middle Earth"). The map may look professionally drawn; it may have specific features and details; it may have all the appearances of a genuine representation of actual land. Yet, it is based upon human imagination, not the way things really are. It does not matter how good your map is if indeed it is in error; likewise, it does not matter how "good" your attitude seems if indeed it is based upon anything less than God's truth.

One's personal truth does not accurately reflect the way things really are, only how he wants them to be. When he leaves this life, however, he will also leave behind all false "maps" of his own making. Many people believe that all of their private convictions, personally-drawn "maps," and artificially-made "truths" will carry over into the afterlife. There is nothing in Scripture or earthly existence that supports such an idea except in the human imagination. When we stand before God—and every person *will* stand before Him in due time—we will not be attended by the mental or emotional baggage that we lugged around with us in this earthly life. Instead, we will be confronted with

God's reality—a reality in which Jesus lived and taught—and we will be judged by what *is* true, not what we *imagined* was true.

We cannot think that it makes no difference whether or not we accept God's truth. There are serious and irrevocable consequences for *rejecting* His truth—whether individually or as a society.[80] On the other hand, there are also serious responsibilities incurred by *accepting* His truth. Every person alive on the planet right now will either *accept* or *reject* His truth; there is no third option. One who rejects God's truth jeopardizes his own soul—no matter how good he thinks his attitude to be. It does not matter what factual information about God he has accepted—i.e., God's existence, Jesus' incarnation, isolated truths of Scripture, etc. Rejecting His *truth* means refusing to obey Him, since this is the only correct and acceptable response to His truth. Thus, whoever does not obey God has rejected His truth, and whoever has rejected His truth manifests this in his disobedience. Jesus said, "If you continue in My word, then you are truly disciples of Mine; and you will know the truth, and the truth will make you free" (John 8:31-32). He never said, "As long as you have a *good attitude,* then you must be right and you will be free." Spiritual freedom from divine condemnation (Romans 8:1) is only obtained through *hearing* the Word of God and then *acting* upon it in a manner consistent with its instructions (cf. Matthew 7:24-27, Romans 10:17).

Christian Thinking
What do *you* think?

1.) Is it important to understand what "truth" *actually* is versus something that a person (including yourself) *thinks* it is? Why or why not?

2.) This statement was made above: "What is true to you may not be 'the' truth." Is God obligated to change His truth to accommodate your truth—or the alleged truth as determined by any given church or religion?

    a. If so, then what does this say about the nature of God's truth?

    b. If not, then what does this say about the nature of man-made truth?

3.) If you believe someone is truthful (as in honest, sincere, and well-intentioned), does this mean that his (or her) *authority* is to be valued equally with God's truth? Does one's personal claim to truthfulness mean that he (or she) cannot be challenged, questioned, or disbelieved? Please explain.

4.) How is God's *gospel truth* applicable and binding upon all people, regardless of who does or does not believe it? Is God "forcing" His truth upon us, or is there another way to look at this situation?

Section Three: Truth and Objectivity *(continued)*

Objective and Subjective Thinking

In order to make wise and beneficial decisions, we need clear, objective, and compelling reasons for action. A person cannot make intelligent decisions by way of an unintelligent or contrived method of discernment. "Discernment" means an accurate, perceptive, and discriminating way of separating what is *true* from what is *false* (or pretends to be true). It is the act of making a judicial estimation or decision about something, as weighed against a fixed and universal standard of authority—in this case, the Word of God.[81] This standard is transcendent in nature, since it is not based upon human feelings, emotions, or opinions. We can appeal to this standard even though it *transcends* our human realm. Because of its transcendent nature, this standard is out of reach, so to speak, of human tampering, corruption, or modification. Therefore, it does not define any person's situation based upon the opinions of others, consensus, or conventional wisdom. God's standard exposes each person as he really *is*, not as he wants to see himself or as others see him.

Discernment and objectivity are involved in a cognitive process known as "critical thinking." "Critical" (in this context) does not refer to nitpicking, finding fault (in order to look better by comparison), or meanness. Being a "critical thinker" does not mean you condemn people that are not like you or who do not think like you. On the contrary, it actually helps a person rise above such self-serving attitudes and perspectives.

> Critical thinking can be seen as having two components: 1) a set of information and belief generating and processing skills, and 2) the habit, based on intellectual commitment, of using those skills to guide behavior. It is thus to be contrasted with: 1) the mere acquisition and retention of information alone, because

it involves a particular way in which information is sought and treated; 2) the mere possession of a set of skills, because it involves the continual use of them; and 3) the mere use of those skills ("as an exercise") without acceptance of their results.[82]

Critical thinking refers to processing *intelligently* the evidence, reasoning, and various thoughts related to any given subject or situation. It is reflective, analytical, and probing; it tests traditional or conventional thinking to see whether or not it is sound or effective. It is not afraid to challenge the status quo or confident assertions. The goal of critical thinking is not to condemn traditions, shatter people's spirits, or win arguments. Rather, the goal is to appeal to an ideal standard—ultimately, God's Truth—in order to pursue the best possible course of action in any context.

Critical thinking is hardly limited to a religious context, however. It is something we are *expected* to use as intelligent human beings in any context. Consider what secular experts have discovered, for example, in the *absence* of critical thinking:

> All that we do, we do on the basis of some motivations or reasons. But we rarely examine our motivations to see if they make sense. We rarely scrutinize our reasons critically to see if they are rationally justified. As consumers we sometimes buy things impulsively and uncritically, without stopping to determine whether we really need what we are inclined to buy or whether we can afford it or whether it's good for our health or whether the price is competitive. As parents we often respond to our children impulsively and uncritically, without stopping to determine whether our actions are consistent with how we want to act as parents or whether we are contributing to their self-esteem or whether we are discouraging them from thinking or from taking responsibility for their own behavior.
> As citizens, too often we vote impulsively and uncritically, without taking the time to familiarize ourselves with the relevant

issues and positions, without thinking about the long-run implications of what is being proposed, without paying attention to how politicians manipulate us by flattery or vague and empty promises. As friends, too often we become the victims of our own infantile needs, "getting involved" with people who bring out the worst in us or who stimulate us to act in ways that we have been trying to change. As husbands or wives, too often we think only of our own desires and points of view, uncritically ignoring the needs and perspectives of our mates, assuming that what we want and what we think is clearly justified and true, and that when they disagree with us they are being unreasonable and unfair.[83]

Objectivity is a key ingredient in critical thinking. An objective-thinking person analyzes a problem, situation, biblical passage, etc., while being removed from its essential context. Thus, he does not allow himself to be *involved* in the situation itself nor does he try to *influence* its outcome. (This does not mean the conclusion has no bearing upon him; it means he does not concern himself *with* this until the matter is factually and accurately determined.) This "outside" perspective allows him to see the situation (far more) clearly and pragmatically. In contrast, a subjective-thinking person makes himself directly involved in whatever he analyzes, and thus personally directs its outcome toward a conclusion that meets his own pre-determined beliefs, value system, preference, or status. Because he is so involved, he remains unable to allow the thing being analyzed to reach its natural or necessary conclusion. The English philosopher John Locke defined subjective-thinking people as "prone to error." These people, he says, are:

- "Those who seldom reason at all, but think and act as those around them do—parents, neighbors, the clergy, or anyone else they admire and respect. Such people want to avoid the difficulty that accompanies thinking for themselves."
- "Those who are determined to let passion rather than reason govern their lives. Those people are influenced only by reasoning that supports their prejudices."

Christian Thinking

❑ "Those who sincerely follow reason, but lack sound, overall good sense, and so do not look at all sides of an issue. They tend to talk with one type of person, read one type of book, and so are exposed to only one viewpoint."[84]

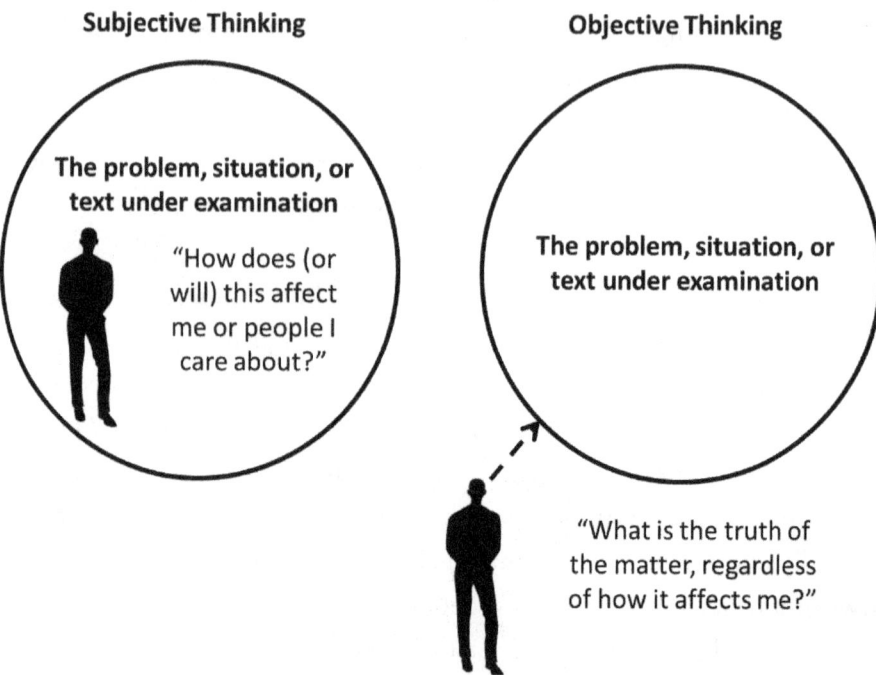

Absolute objectivity is humanly impossible, since none of us can *completely* divorce ourselves from our own biases, prejudices, and personal beliefs. Nonetheless, we can strive to be more objective by viewing any given subject by its facts (including its virtues or defects) rather than by how we feel about it. Objective thinking is not *mere* "open-mindedness," although having one's mind "open" to relevant possibilities is certainly a large part of it. It is better to say that objective thinking exercises discernment with a mind that will accept conclusions and solutions that a "closed" mind would have resisted or been blinded to altogether.

Objective thinking means at least the following:

- Seeking truth and reality for what they are, rather than what you want them to be.
- Facing the reality of who *you* are rather than what you project to others (or, what you have thought yourself to be), based upon a fixed and universal standard (truth).
- Not taking *personally* everything that you hear, see, or experience—i.e., it is not all about you, and how it affects you is not as important as whether or not it is true.
- You allow the truth to reach its logical and necessary conclusion, regardless of the consequences or how it affects you personally: if it is the right thing to do, then it must be done, period. If it is *not* the right thing to do, then no amount of justifying or rationalizing will *make* it right.

This (type of thinking) allows you to live responsibly according to a transcendent and universal standard.

Subjective thinking is not evil in itself. Everyone is "subjective" at some time; any person who offers his opinion ("This coffee tastes delicious!") or creative preference ("I think we should go to this other movie instead") exercises his subjective thought process. But we cannot make intelligent decisions concerning *the truth* with this method. Especially, a subjective method is not something in which you should place the future of your eternal soul. Subjective thinking typically manifests itself in the following ways:

- You will evaluate evidence, situations, and "truth" based upon how it affects you personally (or, how it affects someone or something you deeply care about).
- You will not accept the truth of who you really are, unless (you believe) it puts you in a favorable or acceptable light or is consistent with what you already believe *is* "true."

- ❏ You purposely allow your emotions, memories, or pre-formed conceptions (about anyone or anything) to bias your judgment in how you think and reach conclusions.
- ❏ You decide every situation, argument, or personal belief by how it affects you personally rather than whether or not it is *true* or the *right thing to do*.
- ❏ You cling tenaciously to conclusions decided by people you love and admire—parents, grandparents, mentors, preachers, celebrities, etc.—and are unwilling to consider that these people may be *wrong*, and (thus) you will not change your mind (out of respect for them rather than a love for the truth).

This type of thinking enables irresponsibility or self-deception, in that you will live only according to what *you believe* to be right or justifiable, not according to a transcendent and universal standard. Simply put, subjective thinking is a foolish way to live your earthly life and is an extremely dangerous way to prepare your soul for the life to come. In cases where decisions are insignificant (e.g., which kind of music you think is better than another), there is no harm done. But in cases where the mental process you use to determine what is right, how you evaluate others, or how you decide what is best for your soul, your conclusions will be founded upon an inherently-flawed system of thinking.

Objective thinking provides *freedom*: you are not trapped by or obligated to uphold any personal views, prejudices, or beliefs. "It was for freedom that Christ set us free…" (Galatians 5:1)—not to be bound or re-bound by someone else's thinking (1 Corinthians 7:23). Objective thinking has a realistic, practical, and beneficial focus—ideally, to *live in truth*—and thus is goal-oriented.

Subjective thinking leads to mental *paralysis* and *imprisonment*: you will be trapped by your own finite, self-made, and (often) immature thinking. You will not be open-minded or willing to entertain new ideas; instead, you will be narrow-minded and defensive, and will use irrational or even outright foolish logic to preserve your status quo beliefs. Subjective thinking has a personal agenda to uphold, usually one that only benefits the one with whom that agenda originated and those who also buy into it. Any so-called "subjective reality" is a contradictory idea.

Examples of Objective Thinking:	Examples of Subjective Thinking:
"Our Law does not judge a man unless it first hears from him and knows what he is doing, does it?" (Nicodemus, John 7:51)	"…The Jews had already agreed that if anyone confessed Him to be Christ, he was to be put out of the synagogue." (John 9:22; see also John 12:42-43)
"If this man [Jesus] were not from God, He could do nothing [miraculous]." (John 9:33, bracketed words added)	"The Jews answered and said to Him, 'Do we not say rightly that You are a Samaritan and have a demon?'" (John 8:48)
"If I do not do the works of My Father, do not believe Me; but if I do them, though you do not believe Me, believe the works…" (Jesus, John 10:37-38)	"But when the Pharisees heard this, they said, 'This man [Jesus] casts out demons only by Beelzebul the ruler of the demons'" (Matthew 12:24).
"If…I am a wrongdoer and have committed anything worthy of death, I do not refuse to die; but if none of those things is true of which these men accuse me, no one can hand me over to them." (Paul, Acts 25:11)	"Pilate said to them, 'Then what shall I do with Jesus who is called Christ?' They all said, 'Crucify Him!' And he said, 'Why, what evil has He done?' But they kept shouting all the more, saying, 'Crucify Him!'" (Matthew 27:22-23)

When it comes to mathematics, science, engineering, or financial data—things that require a strict adherence to laws, formulas, and measurements—we want objective information, not subjective feelings or opinions. A person does not want someone's *opinion* that the plane he is about to board can fly; he wants this premise to be substantiated with proven evidence. Likewise, you do not want to hear your bank's *subjective interpretation* concerning your savings account; you want to know factually and precisely how much money you have.

When it comes to things that are spiritual in nature, however, many people throw the need for factual, objective, and relevant information out the window. It is common for people to reduce biblical authority to a personal *evaluation* of what God said rather than seeking to be *obedient* to what is said ("This is how *I* see the words of Jesus"; "This is what the gospel means *to me*"). In the context of God's world, it is irrelevant what the gospel means to *you* or *me* or *anyone else*. It matters instead what the gospel means to God, and whatever or however the gospel is important to Him, so it must be important to those who wish to be saved by Him.

For example, consider one who is evaluating his spiritual well-being and his soul's future existence in the afterlife. God's Word serves as an absolute authority of the spiritual realm, the heavenly world, and the afterlife. Indeed, we have no factual and credible source for this kind of information otherwise. His revealed Word is timeless, changeless, universally-applied, and reaches a singular conclusion concerning one's spiritual state of being. It is balanced, impartial, and authoritative. Nonetheless, someone will respond:

- ❑ "I don't feel the need to respond to that Word."
- ❑ "I don't believe that God will condemn what I believe in *my heart* to be true."
- ❑ "I don't need your religion to tell me how to live; God is my judge, not you or your religion."
- ❑ "That's your 'take' on the Bible; I have a completely different 'take.'"
- ❑ "This does not fit in with my present worldview."
- ❑ "I just need God to validate my *feelings*; I don't need anyone to preach to me."

God has defined and proven His transcendent truth through: objective reasoning; physical, moral, and spiritual evidences; numerous eyewitness accounts of His activity among men; historical evidences; and the flesh-and-blood Person of Jesus Christ. Nonetheless, someone will respond:

- ❏ "I believe *my* sense of truth is equally acceptable to God."
- ❏ "I choose not to accept those proofs. To me, they are unconvincing."
- ❏ "I refuse to accept the implications of God's Truth; therefore, I reject it altogether."
- ❏ "I feel comfortable with what I have already come to believe."
- ❏ "I am uncomfortable making any change to my belief system that will be critical of other people's beliefs—I am in no position to judge others."[85]
- ❏ "I don't care about all of these details. I just want to know that everything's going to work out for me—that everything's going to be all right."

God offers redemption for the corrupted human soul in exchange for that person's obedient faith in Him. This is a profound and priceless offer that cannot be duplicated, superseded, or neglected without the severest of consequences. Nothing less than the eternal destination of a person's soul is at stake. Nonetheless, someone will respond:

- ❏ "I appreciate God's concern for me, But I'm not a bad person (and if I agree to what God says about me, it will mean that I *am* a bad person—which I am not)."
- ❏ "I do not need my soul to be redeemed. I just need redemption from my mistakes so that I can be relieved of my guilt and live happily from now on."
- ❏ "I am more interested in my connections with family and other people than in having to follow some organized religion's dogma."
- ❏ "It is more important for me to embrace my youth culture [or other generational experience] than to have specific religious beliefs."
- ❏ "I am happy where I am at right now; I'm in a good place in my life. Therefore, I do not feel the need for 'salvation' or 'redemption.'"

In each case expressed above, the person has been deluded into thinking that his (or her) response is equal in substance to that which is offered him. This is a fallacy, but he remains either carelessly oblivious to or woefully ignorant of it. Furthermore, he maintains his subjective position without any proof, relevant evidence, or sound reasoning. His position does not have to be *proved* to be true; it is true to *him*, and that is enough. This kind of rationale is the hallmark of a self-absorbed society that does not want to answer to an authority higher than itself and does not want to have any restrictions on what it wants to do.

It is amazing to see people reason so wisely and thoughtfully on non-spiritual subjects, and then toss all objectivity aside when it comes to spiritual matters. These people may invest their money wisely, get several quotes for their home remodels, and seek the best course of action for purchasing a car. Yet, when it comes to the most important decision of all—planning for their future spiritual existence—they put full confidence in their own opinion about their soul. Or, they entrust their soul to the opinion of someone no more qualified than themselves. The truth is: no soul is either saved or lost based solely upon an opinion. This is true no matter how long that opinion has been around, how passionately it is defended, or how many people have adopted it. Salvation rests upon the *truth* of one's standing with God, not his (or anyone else's) *opinion* of that standing.[86]

God Has No Opinion of You

God's own holy nature cannot be defined or sustained by ever-changing or benign opinions. As a self-existent and sovereign Divine Being, He is defined by absolute values that cannot change. He can never be more or less than what He is right now, which is what He will be throughout eternity. Since He is perfect, He operates on perfectly-known and completely objective facts. He never changes His mind (about what is true); He never lies (because this would violate His holy nature); He never changes the rules in the middle of the game, so to speak; and He never fails or disappoints in anything He does (Romans 10:11, 2 Timothy 2:13, Titus 1:2, Hebrews 6:17-18, et al).

Truth and Objectivity

Because God is completely objective and not subjective, there are some things that He would never say, such as:

- *"I think [insert: you, me, or anyone else's name] is a servant of Mine."* God does not "think" about anything; He does not sit down and process information, sorting out facts and seeking various alternatives. He already *knows* who belongs to Him and who does not; He already *knows* the full and accurate situation—no matter what that situation is. Thus, you either are or are not His servant (and the same goes for me); there is no third option or "gray area." God does not have to weigh the evidence or take time to analyze the data. Because He is God, He knows everything and He knows it exactly as it is, not as someone wants Him to know it.

- *"In My opinion, you are a sinner who stands in condemnation of Me."* God's position on sin is not an opinion; it is an unquestionable constant. Sin is, always has been, and always will be repulsive to God.[87] Whatever violates His holy nature is sinful, whether today, tomorrow, or 3,000 years ago. Since God never changes, so His position on sin never changes. Likewise, whether or not you are indeed a sinner—one who remains outside of God's fellowship and therefore in a state of condemnation—is not determined by anything less than factual, accurate, and credible information. Again, you cannot be saved *or* condemned by an opinion—and God has no opinion of you.

- *"I suggest that you obey Me."* Because God's holy and self-existent nature is the governing law and moral influence for all of His Creation, He cannot offer "suggestions" as to what to do. Instead, He tells us exactly what to do—and how and when to do it. God cannot "suggest" that you be obedient to Him, because it is your *moral responsibility* as one made "in His own image" (cf. Genesis 1:27) to be obedient to your Creator. For Him to "suggest" otherwise would reduce His moral nature to a mere interpretation of what is right rather than the *standard* of righteousness. He may put His instruction in the form of a rhetorical question ("What will it profit a man if he gains the whole world and forfeits his soul?"—Matthew 16:26) or an invitation ("Be saved from this perverse generation!"—Acts 2:40), but it is a straightforward and non-negotiable message all the same.

While we cannot assume a god-like objectivity in our finite, earth-bound existence, we *can* and are *expected* to accept God's objective evaluations as being superior to our own. We cannot say something like, "I know God says this-or-that, *but...*" because that is the language of subjective reasoning and modern liberalism. If we accept that God's knowledge and His scope of vision, so to speak, are far superior to our own, then it stands to reason that we should always accept His conclusions over ours, no matter how they impact our current situation or beliefs. This is what it means to "walk in the Light as He Himself is in the Light" (1 John 1:7) rather than to live in the darkness of (mere) human understanding.

TRUTH AND OBJECTIVITY

What do *you* think?

1.) Why is it *extremely Beneficial* to know God's truth (or, to be exposed by His "Light"—see John 3:18-21 and 1 John 1:5-7), even when it reveals our own "truth" to be irrelevant or in error?

2.) Are you able to know where *you* stand with God unless or until you know exactly where *God* stands, so to speak? Please explain.

3.) Consider any of Jesus' discussions with or teachings to the people of His day (as in John 5:31-47, for example). Did He reveal Himself to be a subjective thinker or an objective one? How do you know, one way or the other?

4.) Why do you suppose people become so insistent on facts when it comes to their bank accounts (for example) but careless or uninterested when it comes to responding to God's message for their souls?

5.) It is common to hear someone put their opinion about their soul (in "I think," "I feel," or "I believe" statements) on par with—or even superior to—what God's revealed gospel teaches. Why do people do this? Is God obligated to honor their private beliefs, regardless of what they are?

6.) Why does God have no opinion about you? (There are several answers.)

Section Three: Truth and Objectivity *(continued)*

Who Are You to Judge?

The above question is a good one to ask ourselves, and needs to be addressed. Unfortunately, this "question" is usually one's response to an argument he is unable to counter with objective reasoning. In this sense, the interjection, "Who are you to judge?" is more of an accusation than an actual query into the judgment process of intelligent human beings. It is meant to *end* dialogue rather than promote it.

Jesus said, "Do not judge so that you will not be judged. For in the way you judge, you will be judged; and by your standard of measure, it will be measured to you" (Matthew 7:1-2). This has often been construed to mean that Christians are forbidden to level any judgment against anyone or anything for any reason at all. Apparently there is some confusion going on about "who gets to judge whom"—and who is assumedly prevented from even engaging in the process. There is also an inconsistency in the logic of those who would invoke statements that are self-incriminating. (Any person that condemns others for "judging" is guilty of having made a judgment of their own. Their "argument" is actually self-refuting and therefore illogical.) As intelligent, rational people, we need to know what we are talking about when we challenge another person's position. This pertains to statements of religious beliefs as much as those regarding any other context.

Christians do not have the right or authority to condemn someone to hell, nor should we be engaged in that business. We are not to *personally* condemn people who stand already condemned by Christ any more than we are to justify those whom He has not justified. Yet, we are forced to make judgments and decisions concerning what is *true*, what is *real*, and what is *of God*. God has given us a "measure" by which to judge (i.e., His Word) as well as the ability to make judgments (through love and wisdom, as learned through His Word). We should not be afraid to "judge," then, when deferring to an authority higher than any human authority. In this case, it simply means that we have reached a decision that has already been made by and is consistent with God's own decision. According to its own inferior standard, the ungodly world has already judged the Lord Jesus to be an impostor and those who follow Him to be foolish; we must consider the source of such statements and the subjective wisdom that produced them. People who argue only with human wisdom also succumb to the error and limitations of that wisdom. Furthermore, they ultimately have nothing to substantiate their arguments other than their own insistence that such things are true. Thus, what they call "arguments" are, in fact, merely their opinions.

Christians must be honest—and courageous—enough to allow themselves to be subjected to the same formal criticism that we apply to those who are outside of Christ (see 2 Corinthians 13:1-5). This means, *you* must subject *yourself* to this same standard:

- What source of information do you use in order to make the most important decisions in your life? Are you consistent in using this source regardless of the outcome, or do you only use this source when it agrees with what you wanted to do in the first place?
- Can you defend your religious faith with evidence and sound reasoning, or do you simply have strong opinions about what you believe?
- Where do you stand concerning contemporary issues (e.g., capital punishment, abortion, homosexual marriages, and euthanasia)—and is your stance consistent with your spiritual belief system?
- When someone challenges your beliefs, how do you react or respond? Do you get emotionally upset, or do you reply with reasoned answers—and what is the authoritative basis for your reasoning?
- Are you a critical thinker who seeks objective and truthful answers, or are you merely critical of everyone who does not believe like you?

Christian Thinking

As the finest human being that has ever lived, Jesus was also the most objective thinker the world has ever known. As a Divine Being (the Son of God), He was not bound by the same limitations and finite knowledge that impede the rest of us. Just as God has no opinion about you, so Jesus had no opinions about what is true or not: He knew it absolutely. Thus, He spoke with crystal-clear and inerrant objectivity. When we accept His evidence and reasoning, we will reach conclusions that are superior to those of the secular world (see 1 Corinthians 1:18-25, John 12:44-50, and 1 John 4:4-6).

What Would You Say? (Special Exercise)

Imagine that you are the defense lawyer of one of the greatest trials in all of history: *Modern society v. Jesus Christ*. Jesus is the defendant *in absentia*, and the secular, godless world is the plaintiff. The charge: **Jesus, being an inadequate leader, is GUILTY of extreme misrepresentation.** As the prosecuting attorney lays out his case, you are required to examine the facts and provide an adequate response. The jury is composed of twelve men and women between 18 and 20 years of age who are ready to go into the world carrying whatever decision is rendered. The effectiveness of your case, then, will affect the rest of their lives, and possibly an entire generation. The prosecution then lays out its best evidence:

Point #1: Jesus had **no formal training** as a leader. He wanted people to follow Him, but offered no previous record of leadership. He has duped people into believing He is someone or something that He is not. He was an unskilled, unprofessional, and manipulative fraud. (**Your response?**)

Point #2: Jesus had **no education** with which to lead. He spoke of great things with feigned eloquence, but offered no record of academic achievement. His words of instruction were actually deceptive and seditious; He was an uninformed man who was also an opportunist who preyed upon the naiveté and gullibility of His audience. (**Your response?**)

Point #3: Jesus had **no experience handling money, no actual job, and no domestic responsibilities.** He lived in a world where He did not have to contribute to society or feed Himself, unlike the rest of us who must contend with jobs, bills, and the pressures of *real* life. His teachings are utopian; they would only work in a perfect rendition of His own self-made world. They have no practical value and defy any literal application. (**Your response?**)

Point #4: Jesus was **never married or had any children,** yet wants men and women, most of who *are* married and with children, to follow in His footsteps. He speaks confidently about situations with which He has no actual experience. This is a hollow example to others, and destroys all credibility of His so-called "wisdom," as He has exempted Himself from the rest of mankind but then wants to lead us. (**Your response?**)

Point #5: Jesus is just another **radical visionary,** an **egomaniac** who craves everyone's attention but has nothing substantive to offer. His teachings encourage rebellion against secular authority; He justifies this through His claim to have a divine nature. His followers are brainwashed into following Him, sometimes paying for this with their very lives—much like followers of Jim Jones or David Koresh have done in modern times. He is not an ideal role model, but leads the people into moral and mental confusion. (**Your response?**)

Point #6: Jesus is **offensive.** Much of what He says is not designed to unite people, but to destroy whatever functional cohesion we (as a modern, progressive society) have tried so hard to achieve. He is not a leader, but a rebel; His teachings are hard to understand, impossible to implement, and are fracturing the world's global interests everywhere. Instead of being honored, He ought to be exposed as a heretic and publicly condemned. (**Your response?**)

The prosecution rests upon saying, "We, the court, find this man a pathetic excuse for a leader for ours or any other society. He has no experience, no education, no grasp of reality, and no functional relationships. He is a radical extremist and is offensive to society; He is a troublemaker, not a peacemaker. We find this man GUILTY of severe misrepresentation and ask that from this day forward His teachings be BANNED from all society." (**Your response?**)

Perceptions and Reality

Perceptions are not always inaccurate, but they fall into the realm of opinions rather than being interchangeable with facts. The "rules" of perception manifest a subjective outlook that is riddled with bias, self-promotion, and conflicts of interest, as well as one that adopts the views of those who lack credibility but are very influential nonetheless. The "rules" include:[88]

- ❑ Two or more people often perceive the same things in different ways—sometimes *radically* different ways. (If you have ever seen an angry parent argue with the umpire at a Little League game, you know what this means.)
- ❑ Our self-concept (i.e., our collection of personal convictions through which we see the world) has a powerful effect on how we make, substantiate, and refute claims with which we are confronted.
- ❑ Our perceptions can be altered or influenced by others, either negatively or positively. We tend to allow those closest to us (whom we trust the most) to have the greatest influence on us, even though their claims may remain questionable or unsubstantiated. (This happens in religion *a lot*: a family member will hang his eternal

Truth and Objectivity

future on the decision of a beloved relative; a church member will regard his minister's advice as the gospel truth; or a person's spiritual convictions may have an almost hypnotic effect on his or her best friend.)

- ❑ Different people see us differently, regardless of the perception we have of ourselves, or the image of ourselves that we wish to project upon them (i.e., how we want them to see us).
- ❑ We tend to judge ourselves (and people we love) more favorably and generously than we do others. (Think of it: when *you* commit a traffic violation, it is an "honest mistake" or you "didn't mean to do that"; when someone *else* does the exact same thing, you may call him a "careless driver," "an idiot," or someone whose license needs to be revoked.)
- ❑ We tend to be influenced by what is most obvious, attractive, or immediately gratifying, not necessarily by what is best. (The world of modern advertising capitalizes on this.)
- ❑ We tend to cling to first impressions, even if they are wrong. (It is much harder to undo *first* impressions than it is to take the time to seek *accurate* ones.)
- ❑ We tend to blame innocent victims for their misfortunes rather than evaluate objectively what happened to them. ("I know that pedestrian got hit crossing the street, but that's a bad intersection and he should have paid more attention"; "It is tragic that she was raped, but girls are wearing such seductive clothing today—well, it's no wonder"; "It serves him right for getting cancer, since he never really paid much attention to his health.")

Perceptions and opinions *by themselves* are unreliable for guiding us through life. An opinion is a statement of personal understanding or conviction. It is "a view, judgment, or appraisal formed in the mind about a particular matter" or a "belief stronger than impression and less strong than positive knowledge."[89] This does not mean that all opinions are necessarily incorrect, but that they are not to be accepted on par with proven facts. This also does not mean that perceptions or opinions are wholly lacking in truth, but that these cannot be interchangeable *with* the truth. Factors that affect the worthiness or credibility of one opinion over another include:

- ❑ The credentials of the one offering it. Certainly a financial expert's opinion is far more convincing regarding your estate planning than that of an auto mechanic. However, if your car's engine won't start, you would be wise to listen to the opinion of a professional auto mechanic over that of a financial planner.
- ❑ The sincerity and objectivity of the one offering it. The opinions of those who have a vested interest in a certain subject will likely influence you to support whatever conclusions that have a direct effect on their status, financial standing, future employment, etc. For example, if you wish to deal with a medical issue, a surgeon will likely advise surgery; a medical doctor will advise prescription medication and treatment; and a chiropractor will likely advise spinal manipulation and/or related therapies. All three are intelligent and well-educated people, yet their personal perceptions of "what to do" will be influenced by their individual professions.
- ❑ Their access to relevant knowledge. Just because someone is well-educated (with college degrees) does not mean he knows everything about *everything*. If you wish to have some welding done, you likely will not consult a Harvard graduate with an MBA; you will seek the professional advice of a trade-school-educated welder. However, if you wish to start a new business, a consultation with an MBA degree holder would be the wiser choice.

Since God's gospel—the message of redemption of human souls through the saving work of Jesus Christ—is the revealed work of God Himself, it is objective (the truth) and not subjective. It does not rest upon mere the perceptions, secular education, or credentials of men. The message of redemptions through Jesus Christ—what we call "the gospel"—did not originate and was not promoted as an *opinion* of God, since God has no opinion about anything. Instead, it has been revealed by God's Holy Spirit (Ephesians 3:4-7), promoted by God's own Son (Mark 1:15, Ephesians 3:11-12), and confirmed by miracles for which only a Divine Being could be responsible (John 5:36, Hebrews 2:3b-4). Thus, the gospel of Christ is not merely the Christian's *perception* of what is true, it *is* the truth—regardless of who does or does not believe it.

What do *you* think?

1.) People discern (or, make judgments) all the time between what is absolutely *true* and what is absolutely *false*. Without this discerning process, no one could make an intelligent decision about *anything*. Christians must use this same process when determining what is *of God* (true) and what is *not* (false) (see 1 John 4:1). For example, we could not practice "righteousness" unless God had absolutely defined it for us in His revealed Word (Romans 1:17).

   a. What are some other examples of things Christians are required to discern (or judge) that are critical to salvation and our identity as God's people? (There are several answers.)

   b. What are some examples of things that we *cannot* discern with certainty, or that we have no business judging at all? (Consider Romans 14:1-10, 1 Corinthians 5:9-13, and James 4:11-12, for example.)

2.) Are all perceptions false or misleading just because they *are* perceptions? Regardless, what are the limitations of all human perceptions?

3.) Given the value and duration of your soul's future existence in the afterlife, which would be the wisest course of action: to rely upon your perceptions or opinions about what is best for you, or to put your full confidence in what God says is true? Please defend your answer with Scripture.

Section Four: Godly Love

What Is "Godly" Love?

"Love" (*agape*), as it is used in the New Testament, is the charitable goodwill of one person as shown to another.[90] It is an act of benevolence (however expressed) that serves the best interest of the one receiving it. Love is sacrificial in nature, since the one who demonstrates love always does so at his own expense, thus incurring some measure of personal loss. Godly love is based upon God's own divine nature: "…God is love" (1 John 4:8). Since God's nature never changes, therefore His love never changes; since God's nature is unique, constant, and unconditional, therefore His love shares these same attributes.

God's love is best defined in 1 Corinthians 13:4-7:

- **Patient**—willing to endure time and difficulty in anticipation of a good outcome.
- **Kind**—love does no harm to anyone (cf. Romans 13:10).
- **Not jealous**—does not seek to save face; is not insecure, threatened, or fearful of loss.
- **Does not brag**—is not motivated by pride, but always acts in humility.
- **Is not arrogant**—is not smug, over-confident, or pretentious.
- **Does not act unbecomingly**—does not conduct itself in an undignified manner.
- **Does not seek its own**—is not self-serving, self-protective, or vindictive.
- **Is not provoked**—is not coerced or instigated by evil, but seeks only what is good and honorable.
- **Does not take into account a wrong suffered**—does not keep a list of offenses, hold grudges, or stew in bitterness over past crimes.
- **Does not rejoice in unrighteousness**—never condones or gives approval to wicked behavior, but only approves of godly behavior.

Godly Love

- **Rejoices with the truth**—never rejoices with lies, half-truths, or deceptions.
- **Bears all things**—nothing is "too much" for love to deal with.
- **Believes all things**—love is always positive, optimistic, and joyful.
- **Hopes all things**—love is based upon the promises of God, which are infallible.
- **Endures all things**—love will prevail into eternity, even though the world and all those who conform to it will be destroyed.
- **Love never fails**—because God never fails, and "God is love."

Godly love does not wait for someone else to act first, but takes the initiative (Matthew 7:12). It does not only act in hope of reciprocation (Matthew 5:46-48, Luke 14:12-14), but acts anyway. It is unconditional: it is not offered *if* certain conditions exist or *when* someone performs appropriately, but only because it is the right thing to do. Christians are expected to *think upon* and *internalize* the characteristics of God's love.

> The core, central, primary characteristic of God...is love. Not the silly, finite, flimsy, emotional, wax-fruit imposter we sometimes call love, but a boundless, eternal, bottomless, never-ending reality of goodness on which the cosmos is built! A love that lasts, that creates, that is constant.[91]

Love requires demonstration in order for it actually to exist (or, to be *godly* love). God has shown His love for us through the giving of His Son (1 John 4:9-10). We are to show our love for God by keeping His commandments (John 14:15, 1 John 5:3) *and* loving the brethren (1 John 2:9-10, 4:20-21). Our love for God, then, is manifested in *obedience* as well as *servitude*. Love without servitude is like faith without works, grace without forgiveness, or mercy without compassion. In other words, godly love simply cannot exist or function as a mere concept; it must be *acted out* in a manner consistent with Christ's own conduct (1 John 2:6).

Godly love is a *binding force*: it is the "glue" that holds all other Christian virtues together. It is the foundation of all of God's laws (Romans 13:8-10, Galatians 5:14) *as well as* the pinnacle of one's faith in Him (2 Peter 1:7, 1 John 4:17-18)—in effect, the base and crown of everything believers pursue in Christ. Love is "the perfect bond of unity" among believers (Colossians 3:14): when we *love like God loves*, this will inspire, condition, and define every other appropriate action or behavior within Christ's church. Our unity with our brothers and sisters in Christ is founded upon our common love for God and whatever or whomever He loves.

God So Loved the World

"For God so loved the world, that He gave His only begotten Son, that whoever believes in Him shall not perish, but have eternal life" (John 3:16). This is one of the most well-known and oft-quoted passages in the Bible. It is also one that is often misunderstood or taken out of context. Many people use this passage to claim that God will automatically *save* them simply because He *loves* them. This is simply not true. In fact, all will "perish" who do not rightly *respond* to His love—so says the passage.

Others will claim that the only thing necessary for salvation is to "believe" in Jesus and nothing more. In this latter case, "believe" is thought to be a mere acknowledgement of Jesus and a measure of gratitude. Thus, if you just "ask Jesus into your heart," you demonstrate your *belief* in Him and are thus *saved* by Him—all because He *loves* you so much. (Such is the gospel of our modern world and cheap, plastic religion.) This also is simply not true. God is not interested in token acknowledgement, but the unconditional surrender of one's heart.

John 3:16 sums up God's plan of redemption but does not itemize it. In other words, it provides a succinct and accurate overview of *what* God did as well as *why* He did it; at the same time, there is far more to the story than what is stated here. God's love is the most powerful *motivation* in the entire universe, yet it cannot save anyone *by itself*. No one is saved by God only because He loves them. First, there is absolutely zero proof of this in the Bible. Second, the Bible teaches that while God's love is unconditional, salvation is most certainly conditional. (If there is *anything* that you must do to make your salvation possible, then it is *conditioned* upon you doing it.) Third, we should not confuse what *motivates* God to act with what is necessary to *fulfill* that motivation. God's love is what led Him and His Son to act in our best interest, but it was still necessary that Jesus went to the cross *and* that we give Him our allegiance. God's love inspires us to believe—"We love because He first loved us" (1 John 4:19)—but it is not a replacement for our belief. "Believe" does not mean merely "agree to" or "give acknowledgement of" something. In the context of the New Testament, it necessarily implies obedience (see John 3:36). To ask Jesus into your heart may sound appropriate at first, but it fails to do what Jesus truly asked of *us* (see Matthew 16:24, for example). Thus, it fails to obey His gospel. No one can rightly respond to God's love through willful disobedience or rebellion.

The brief statement of John 3:16 nonetheless does provide profound insight into both God and His love:

- ❑ **Author.** "God"—our Creator, our Father, "the Almighty" (Revelation 1:8)—is the *source* of all love. We love because of Him; any godly love that we demonstrate toward one another is simply a reflection of and emulation of His love for us. Our world is filled with hatred, greed, vice, and despair, but these things are inconsistent with God's holy nature, and "…you did not learn Christ in this way…" (Ephesians 4:20). Spiritual and moral confusion result from satanic influences, not godly love.
- ❑ **Depth.** God "so loved" us—not with a passive, obligatory, or cursory love, but a love that is deep, caring, and unstoppable. There is nothing that God withheld in making our fellowship with Him possible and fully rewarding. It is "His great love with which

Christian Thinking

He loved us" that provided for our salvation even while we were "dead" in our sins (Ephesians 2:1-5). On the other hand, it is also His great love which allowed us to exercise our own *free will* either to accept or reject that salvation. His love is a *saving* love, not a *coercive* love.

- ❏ **Object.** "God so loved the *world*"—not the physical universe, but *all of humankind* (as in John 4:42, 1 John 2:2, and 4:14). God's love is directed at people, not things. God did not make the earth, fish, birds, or land animals "in His image," but only mankind (Genesis 1:26-27). Thus, we are the object and desire of His love, and receive the full attention of His love. Jesus did not die to save the physical earth, but only human souls. The *fact* that God's Son died for us—and now lives to intercede for us—is proof positive of just how much He loves us (Romans 5:6, Hebrews 7:25).

- ❏ **Gift.** "His only begotten Son" is God's gift to us because of His great love for us. No one asked God for this; no one even thought to ask for it. Yet, even as God created us "in His image," He knew that we would sin against Him and that it would require the sacrifice of His Son to restore the fellowship that our sin had destroyed. "Gift" necessarily implies something that we did not deserve, cannot earn, are unable to duplicate, and without which (in this context) *we cannot survive*. We all "fall short" of God's holiness, but we can all be "justified as a gift by His grace through the redemption which is in Christ Jesus" (cf. Romans 3:23-24). God's *love* is not the gift in this case; God's Son is the Gift. In love, He offers the gift; also in love, He lets us decide whether or not to receive this priceless gift.

- ❏ **Reason (or purpose).** "That whoever believes in Him...eternal life"—God's love is not without purpose. There is always a (stated or implied) "so that" or "in order to" that follows it. In other words, God does not love for *no reason*; His love is objective in nature and practical in application. It does not merely exist; it performs. The only appropriate *response* to God's love is also through objective performance on *our* part, which is our obedience ("If you love Me, you will keep My commandments"—John

14:15). God's love *by itself* does not save us from "perishing"; it can only provide the *means* for that salvation. What does save us is God's grace that is only *prompted* by human faith. Grace is what God does for us that we cannot do for ourselves; faith is what we do for God to prove that we believe and trust Him (Ephesians 2:8-10, Hebrews 10:38-39). We are not saved by grace *alone* any more than we are saved by faith *alone*. Many people will "perish" even though God loves them, because they rejected His "way of escape" from divine condemnation. Such people resisted God's grace because they refused to put their faith in the One who could have saved them. Christians are those who *believe* in this grace and demonstrate that belief in works of faith. (*Anything* that is done by God's request—believing, repenting, confessing, being baptized, praying, forgiving, walking in a manner worthy of the gospel, etc.— is a *work of faith*.) "Faith is not a part of the Christian life; *it's the whole thing*."[92]

Jesus was once asked, "Teacher, what is the great commandment in the Law?" To which the Master replied (quoting from Deuteronomy 6:5), "You shall love the LORD your God with all your heart, and with all your soul, and with all your mind.' This is the great and foremost commandment." (Matthew 22:37-38). This is how important *love* is for the believer: he cannot fulfill any other commandment of God successfully apart from his love for God. John Piper asks rhetorically, "What does it mean to love God 'with all your mind'? I take it to mean that we direct our thinking in a certain way; namely, *our thinking should be wholly engaged to do all it can to awaken and express the heartfelt fullness of treasuring God above all things.*"[93]

Love requires *understanding*, and understanding requires *thinking*—in this case, thinking about what God has revealed in His Word. Yet, thinking is not a replacement for love, and we cannot merely "think" that we love God with all of our heart, soul, and mind. Rather, we earnestly focus our thinking mind upon the *act* of loving God— discovering what this means, how to do this, what impact it must have upon our everyday lives, etc. Then, we bring that thoughtful contemplation *about* loving God into reality by actually carrying out those actions. But we cannot claim to "act in love" if we do not understand what it *means* to love in the manner in which God expects of us. Piper continues: "God is not honored by groundless love. In fact, there is no such thing. If we do not know anything about God, there is nothing in our mind to awaken love. If love does not come from knowing God, there is no point in calling it love *for God*."[94] Another writer adds succinctly: "Deficient love is always central to our problems."[95]

Jesus says (bluntly) that if your love for Him does not surpass your love for others, you *cannot* be His disciple—not, "You *may* not be My disciple," but "You are *unable* to be My disciple" (see Luke 14:26). Greg Sidders writes: "His warning is not, 'Love me supremely or I will abandon you.' His warning is, 'Love me supremely or you will abandon me.'" This, because it is just a matter of time before something or someone will come along to steal your heart and draw you away. You need to decide ahead of time who *owns* your heart.[96] Sidders continues: "Loving him [Christ] supremely is the secret to a life that is incomparably better than the life we leave behind (Luke 18:29-30). But loving him requires 'hating' some others along the way."[97] This "hating others" refers to the *willful decision* to give full allegiance to Christ *ahead of* and *more importantly* than any other allegiance (the essential meaning of Luke 14:26).[98]

What do *you* think?

1.) How is *godly* love distinctly different than: self-serving love (1 Corinthians 13:1-3)? Love of the world (1 John 2:15)? Love given only to those who love equally in return (Matthew 5:43-47)?

2.) Since love for God requires obedience to His commandments, what shall we say about a person who claims to love God but refuses to obey Him? On the other hand, is commandment-keeping equal to or a replacement for godly love?

3.) Peter says that we are to have a "sincere love of the brethren" and "fervently love one another from the heart" (1 Peter 1:22). What do these statements mean, exactly?

   a. How are these instructions actually carried out in real life?

   b. What do these have to do with our having been "born again" (1:23)?

4.) Do Christians have to be educated and trained in *how* to love with a godly love?

   a. Or, is this something that just comes natural to us once we have been Christians for a while?

   b. Or, is this an expectation only for Christians who *want* to love like this, but not all Christians?

5.) What does Jesus mean when He says that we need to "hate" those closest to us in order to be His disciple (Luke 14:26)?

   a. How can we be told to *love* our spouses (Ephesians 5:22ff), our children (Titus 2:4), and fellow believers (Hebrews 13:1), and at the same time "hate" all these people in our decision to serve Christ?

   b. Are we really supposed to hate our friends but love our enemies?

Section Four: Godly Love *(continued)*

How Can a Loving God Allow ... ?

People tend to impose upon God their own conception of Him. A "loving God," some believe, is a God who will not inflict pain or punishment upon anyone, and especially will not send a person to hell. A "loving God" cannot allow evil to exist in the world, since this causes pain and suffering.[99] A "loving God" cannot allow human suffering, because (they believe) it is His responsibility to *prevent* all such suffering. Yet, since hell, evil, and suffering do indeed exist, this forces people to draw certain conclusions about God that are based upon artificial premises:

- ❏ "God is not truly a *loving* God." He is a capricious, temperamental, even malevolent God. Since *love* (allegedly) forbids condemnation, punishment, or the destruction of one's soul, a God that inflicts these things is not exercising it. God's love *for* the world ought to remove everything evil *in* the world, since the presence of evil is not consistent with the presence of a loving God.[100] This does not mean that God is incapable of showing love; it means that He also shows other (unloving) attributes as well.
  - This view is entirely dependent upon a subjective interpretation of "love" in the first place—one that is inconsistent with the biblical portrayal of God's love. We should remember that the only source of *factual* information about God is in Scripture, and Scripture never defines God or His love in this way.
  - It is always amazing to see mortal, finite, and sinful people telling an eternal, infinite, and holy God what He "must" do, how He must do it, and how He must *love*. It is not our place to judge God, but He is *our* Judge instead. Since God is far superior to us in every respect, it is entirely appropriate that He tell *us* what a "loving God" should do rather than being handcuffed to our short-sighted expectations.

- ❏ "God is a loving God, but is limited in what He can do." This view reduces God to a benevolent but hapless Being who wants to help us but is not much more capable than ourselves. He shows us love when He can, but He is also unable to shield us from the overwhelming tide of evil that is in the world. He smiles, encourages, and wants to see us succeed, but He is powerless to *deliver* us.
  - This view is purely subjective. It compromises God's power and authority in order to provide a workable explanation for the presence of evil and suffering without completely abandoning one's "faith" in Him.[101]
  - This view also completely contradicts God's own holy nature and ability to perform as portrayed throughout the entire Bible. Again, the only *factual* information we have concerning God is in the Bible; anything beyond this is speculation; anything in contradiction to this is a delusion.
- ❏ "God does not really exist." Since there is "no good reason" why a loving God would allow human suffering, therefore He simply cannot be real.[102] He is a figment of our imagination, the product of millennia of myths, legends, and superstitious beliefs. The presence of evil, war, pain, suffering, and death is wholly inconsistent with a kind and benevolent Creator who seeks the best interest of His Creation.
  - This is the atheist's finest argument (as he would see it). Yet, among other things, it fails to explain either "good" or "evil" in the world. Atheists believe evil is real but God is not, yet this is an impossible position to defend. "If there is a moral law demanding that we ought to always be just, this leads us right back to a Moral Lawgiver."[103]
  - Atheists spend a great deal of time *ridiculing* and *trashing* God, but they have no consistent or workable alternative of a world *without* Him. They are fond of critiquing and mocking Christianity, and yet never really prove *anything* of their own. One's contempt for God (because He does not operate

according to his personal expectations) is hardly a "proof" for His non-existence.

- The presence of evil, war, pain, death, and suffering is *not* inconsistent with a kind and benevolent Creator. The idea that if God is forever perfect, His world should also be forever perfect, is false from the beginning. The Bible clearly puts the blame at *man's* feet, not God's, for the moral (and physical) corruption of the world that God created.

People want a paradise on earth, but they still want to do whatever they want to do without consequence. This is an inconsistent, unrealistic, and immature view of human life. As many people see it, God either refuses to provide this (untenable) situation or He interferes with it with His laws, morality, and accountability.[104] Or, people will take a different route: since God will not remove everything bad in the world, therefore He must be responsible for it. Since God created the world, and the world has evil in it, therefore God created evil. But this view assumes very much and yet proves nothing. It seeks to put the burden for *our (mankind's) irresponsibility* upon the God who entrusted us to be responsible. This is like blaming a car manufacturer for an accident caused entirely by the car owner's reckless driving. It appears to be momentarily gratifying, perhaps, but it will not hold up in court, so to speak. Likewise, all of man's accusations against God—and our subjective interpretations of God's love—will not hold up in our presentation before His Tribunal.

People want a paradise on earth, but they forget that when God *created* Man, He put him *in* a paradise. It was Man's sin—not God's lack of love or power—that forfeited that beautiful life. Even so, God continued to provide for peoples' inadequacy through His grace and mercy—extensions of His love for us—throughout history. The gospel of Christ is the ultimate expression of that grace and mercy: even though we have all chosen to sin against Him, He nonetheless has provided a means of redemption from the condemnation that we have incurred because of *our* sins. "Therefore there is now no condemnation for those who are in Christ Jesus. For the law of the Spirit of life in Christ Jesus has set you free from the law of sin and of death" (Romans 8:1-2).

The Evidence of God's Love

Christ's self-sacrifice is the proof of His love for us. "But God demonstrates His own love toward us, in that while we were yet sinners, Christ died for us. Much more then, having now been justified by His blood, we shall be saved from the wrath of God through Him" (Romans 5:8-9). It is through His means of blood-bought redemption that we are saved from His wrath—the divine condemnation that we bring upon ourselves for having willfully sinned against our Creator, the source of our existence and well-being (see John 3:36, Romans 1:18, and Ephesians 5:6). "For God has not destined us for wrath, but for obtaining salvation through our Lord Jesus Christ..." (1 Thessalonians 5:9; see 1 Timothy 2:3-4). John Piper makes a good observation here: "We may conclude that the ultimate difference between God's wisdom and man's wisdom is how they relate to the glory of God's grace in Christ crucified. *God's wisdom* makes the glory of God's grace our supreme treasure. But *man's wisdom* delights in seeing himself as resourceful, self-sufficient, self-determining, and not utterly dependent upon God's free grace."[105]

The problem with the world—its evil, war, injustice, pain, suffering, etc.—is *not* that God is "unloving" or that He has maliciously withheld His love. Rather, it is that people have not responded rightly *to* that love. More specifically, we have largely failed to reflect that love in our dealings with one another. We have *all* sinned and fallen short of His holiness (Romans 3:23); we could *all* accept the terms and conditions of His gospel; we could *all* be saved by the blood of His Son (1 John 2:1-2). Yet, many of us resist the solution to our spiritual demise that He offers *in love*, then turn around and accuse Him of *not loving us*. This is short-sighted, self-serving, and irresponsible on our part.

Godly Love

"God so loved the world" (cf. John 3:16) that He did not sit idly by and watch us destroy ourselves without offering to rescue us. "God so loved the world" that He acted and continues to act in our best interest, even if we do not always understand what it is that He is doing for us. "God so loved the world" that He did not send a committee, form a bureaucracy, or establish a political party in order to address our problem. Instead, He sent the cherished "Son of His love" (cf. Colossians 1:13) as an offering for *our* sins. "By this the love of God was manifested in us, that God has sent His only begotten Son into the world so that we might live through Him. In this is love, not that we loved God, but that He loved us and sent His Son to be the propitiation for our sins" (1 John 4:9-10). No matter how badly we mess up, no matter how often we sin, and regardless of whether others forgive us, *God's love* has provided a means by which we can have fellowship with Him—now and forever. He not only *takes* us back, but—because He loves us!—He *wants* us back. Thus, "*Future hope is more valuable than present relief.* Until we realize this, we are not on the path to finding God."[106]

God's love does not treat us coldly and clinically, as though we were the nameless subjects of some scientific experiment. He treats us with undeserved dignity and respect. Even though we have sinned against Him, He shows us patience and kindness. He does not rub our faces in our own mistakes and make us feel guiltier than we already feel. In His love—and because of His love—He provides a workable recourse for our sin. In other words, He provides an effective means by which we are able to deal with our sins against Him without us being debased or destroyed in the process. His intent for us is either reconciliation or restoration: both actions serve our very best interest. He desires those who are outside of Christ to be reconciled to Him (2 Corinthians 5:18-21). He desires those who are already Christians but have sinned against Him to be restored (Galatians 6:1). In either case, God shows patience, mercy, and grace as we come to our senses and take advantage of His offer of fellowship.

Just because He provides a loving *recourse* from our sins, however, does not for a moment soften God's *position* on sin. All sin is an offense against God's holiness, His authority, and His will; all sin is therefore condemned by Him. We who "died to sin" are no longer to live in it (Romans 6:2)—thus, we cannot think that God's love will excuse our sins at any time. Christ came "to destroy the works of the devil" (1 John 3:8), not perpetuate them, soften their effect, or allow us opportunity to indulge in them (and offer a mere "Sorry about that" afterward). Likewise, just because He saves us from the ruin of our sin does not mean that He removes all of the pain and consequences our sins may have incurred. It is completely unnecessary—and unrealistic—to think that God must remove all of our pain before we can be inwardly at peace with Him. Pain is not the problem; rather, it is our seeking to *alleviate* or *remove* pain at any cost, and especially at the expense of genuine faith in God.[107]

The fact that God loves us does not mean He cannot be angry toward us for our offenses against Him. "For God so loved the world..." (John 3:16), but God does not love what we (sinners) have done *in* the world or what we have done *to* the pristine world He created. We should not assume that His love *prevents* or *nullifies* His "wrath" against all unrighteousness (Romans 1:18). God is angry with you when you sin because sin destroys your relationship with Him and He *does not want to lose you*. He is angry when you continue to sin and refuse to repent, because He knows how much harm sin does to you and the ultimate price that you will pay for your sins if you resist Him (Romans 6:23). He has every *right* to be angry over such things, just as a parent has a right to be angry when his child willfully puts himself in harm's way after being specifically warned against this. "...[God] desires all men to be saved and to come to the knowledge of the truth" (1 Timothy 2:4) because *this is in your best interest* and *this keeps you out of harm's way*. If God did not love you, then He would not care what happened to you. If He did not love you, He would not have provided you with a "way of escape" from your spiritual demise (1 Corinthians 10:13). If He did not love you, He would give you cold, hard *justice*, not mercy, grace, and forgiveness. If He did not love you, you would have no hope in the life to come. It is only *because* He loves you that He has made redemption possible.

What do *you* think?

1.) Why do you suppose that mortal and imperfect sinners feel justified in telling an eternal, all-powerful, and all-knowing God how He must love people and otherwise do His job? What is the motive behind such critiques?

2.) Why is it so easy to blame God for all of the world's problems? What kinds of errors in reasoning do we commit when we do this?

3.) If someone cites his personal suffering or the evil that is in the world as "proof" that God does not exist, how would you respond to him?

   a. What *factual* evidence—not opinions or suppositions—has anyone ever produced that *proves* conclusively that God does not exist?

   b. What *factual* evidence—not opinions or suppositions—has anyone ever produced that *proves* conclusively that God is "unloving"?

   c. If a husband and wife bring a child into the world knowing full well that he will be subjected to all sorts of sin, injustice, and suffering, does this mean that they "obviously" do not love their child? Or, is there another explanation(s)?

4.) Can God be very angry with us because of our sins and still love us unconditionally? Can He punish us? Can He destroy us?

   a. Is God's love for us *consistent* with His divine nature, or must His love for us be demonstrated *at the expense* of His divine nature? In other words, must He deny His other attributes (such as holiness, righteousness, justice, etc.) in order to "love" us?

   b. When God is compelled to punish or destroy people because of His righteous justice, is this because *He* is "unloving" or because the recipients of His actions did not love *Him*?

   c. Are we *forced* to love God only to avoid being destroyed by Him? Or, are we *expected* to love Him because He is our Creator and Life-giver? Or...what do you think?

Section Four: Godly Love *(continued)*

Loving One Another

How Christians deal with *all* people—the righteous and the wicked—must deliberately imitate the love God has shown to us. "We love, because He first loved us" (1 John 4:19)—the passage does *not* say, "We love *Him* because...," but simply, "*We love*, because..." Everything we do must be done in love (1 Corinthians 16:14); every expression of our love must be a reflection of the love Christ has both *shown* to us and *taught* us to have.

One of the foundational passages of the Christian belief system is in John 13:34-35: "A new commandment I give to you, that you love one another, even as I have loved you, that you also love one another. By this all men will know that you are My disciples, if you have love for one another." This commandment is not "new" because it has never been heard before (see Leviticus 19:18, Matthew 22:37-40), but because it never had the *full meaning* that Christ gave to it through the example of His own life. It is not "new" in *time*, but in *understanding* and *application*. In this sense, it is superior to whatever was commanded of men in the past.[108]

To "love" others in this manner means to act in those people's best interest even to our own hurt. All love—God's as well as yours and mine—requires some level of *sacrifice* by the one who offers it. In our case, this sacrifice may be small, such as a kind word, a smile, a meal, or a ride. At other times, it may be considerably greater, such as the donation of a vehicle, a place to live, the forgiveness of a large debt, or a kidney. Because of His *love* for us, Jesus laid down His *life* for us; if necessary, He expects us to do the same for a fellow Christian (compare John 15:12-13 and 1 John 3:16). Obviously, this is an extreme case—and relatively few Christians will ever need to go this far—but this is what *love* may require of us.

Christian Thinking

We are to love and "do good" to those who are in Christ, to be sure, but our love is not limited to fellow believers. We are to love our enemies, those who persecute us, those who hate us, and all men in general (Galatians 6:9-10). This is required of us for at least the following reasons:

- ❏ It reflects God's own benevolent nature toward all people, whether they are Christians or not (Matthew 5:43-47). Likewise, we are to show—proactively and without prompting—the highest and most noble form of human decency with no regard for one's moral condition. "God is love," and while people cannot see God Himself, they most certainly will be able to see His love in us (1 John 4:12).
- ❏ It is the most dignified and appropriate response from one person to another, especially among those who are enlightened by God. Instead of the repayment of evil for evil, we are to show love and generosity toward all men (Matthew 5:38-47, Romans 12:17-21).[109] This transcendent behavior will not only set us apart from our world of hatred and vengeance, it will also identify us with our heavenly Father—the inspiration for our otherworldly actions.
- ❏ It makes people more receptive to hearing the gospel of Christ. A stated purpose for God's own patience and kindness is to turn men's hearts to the One who has shown them such goodwill (Romans 2:4, 2 Peter 3:9). This must be our stated purpose as well. If we let our "light" shine to others in the form of love and good deeds, then this will turn men's attention to the God who inspired us to act this way (Matthew 5:16). Likewise, our conduct in teaching men about the Lord must exhibit mercy and gentleness so that they will perhaps "come to their senses" and give their hearts to Him (2 Timothy 2:24-26).

The selfish and wicked world must not merely be countered with Christian love and kindness; it will also be *profoundly affected* by this. We are not merely acting differently *than* the world; we are tacitly condemning the world's actions and also challenging those ensnared by it to consider a superior manner of living. Many conversion stories *begin* with someone having been deeply touched by the demonstration of a Christian's love.

If God deals with our own sin because of love *and* in a loving manner, then we ought to show this same decency and dignity toward others who sin. If they sin against God, then we are to demonstrate loving compassion in helping them to address that sin. After all, we are no better than them, since we also have sinned against Him. If they sin against us, then we are to forgive them of their offense when they take responsibility for their action and ask us for our forgiveness (Colossians 3:12-14). This is what God does for us *in love*; this must be what we do for others for this same reason.

Such talk can easily be taken out of context and misrepresented, however. Some think, for example, that love *by itself*—the showering of kindness and affection—is to be our only response to sinners. This is not true. God requires us to take responsibility for our sins against Him, and we must hold people responsible for their own sins. We love unconditionally, but the *manifestation* of this love is to tell people the truth about their sinful condition *and* lead them to the One who can resolve their spiritual predicament. "Above all, keep fervent in your love for one another, because love covers a multitude of sins" (1 Peter 4:8; see also James 5:20). Some have taken this to mean, "Simply *loving* people is how we deal with their sins," but this also is not true. God loves *all* people, but they will still "perish"—even though He loves them!—if they will not take responsibility for their own souls (John 3:16).

"Love covers a multitude of sins" *does* mean, however, that it does not matter how *many* or how *grievous* those sins may be: if we rightly exercise godly love, then both the sinner and those who love him will deal with that person's sins in an appropriate manner. "Love covers… sins" does not mean that love *hides* sin, as if to pretend that it does not exist. God never pretends anything, and neither should we; God never conceals sin, but exposes it with the light of His Word (John 3:18-21, Ephesians 5:7-13). God either charges a person *with* sin, or He forgives him *of* sin, depending upon whether or not that person does what is necessary to address that problem. When God "covers" our sin, He atones for it through the blood of His Son. (In Romans 4:7—a quotation from Psalm 32:1—for example, "covered" is used synonymously with "forgiven.")

God so loves the world that He proclaims His gospel to those who are in sin and thus provides hope to those who wish to escape their awful situation (John 3:16). God's love never ignores, enables, or tolerates sin; our love must never do these things, either. If we truly love someone, then we will lead them to the truth, since the truth will make them "free" (John 8:32). There is nothing better you can do for someone than to lead them to Christ; this serves a person's very best interest. It is godly love that inspires us to act upon this, and it is godly love that must govern how we carry this out. We are to be "speaking the truth in love" (Ephesians 4:15)—not just speaking truth, and not just acting in a loving way, but communicating God's truth in a Christ-like manner.

H. C. Mattern's formula for happiness is this: "Keep your heart free from hate, your mind from worry. Live simply, expect little, give much. Fill your life with love. Scatter sunshine. Forget self, think of others. Do as you would be done by. Try this for a week and you will be surprised."[110] While this "formula" cannot overcome sin or replace one's fellowship with God, it does capture the essence of the genuine Christian's attitude.

What do *you* think?

1.) When John says, "We love, because He first loved us," does he mean that *every human manifestation* of "love" originates from God?

> a. If so, then how do we explain (for example) the "love" shared between two people in an immoral relationship that God does not condone?
>
> b. If not, then what is the context in which John makes his statement—and how do you know this?

2.) Is godly love the *very best* manner in which to deal with any person at any time—no exceptions? Or, are there times when godly love just will not work and something else must be done instead (and if so, please give some examples)?

3.) What are some reasons why we are to show *love* to sinners— and to those "in Christ" who sin?

> a. Is forgiveness of a person's sins against *us* a demonstration of godly love, an act of moral obligation, or both?
>
> b. If someone who sins against us refuses to repent or take responsibility for this, are we justified in withholding godly love from him? Do we just forgive him anyway?

4.) If someone's love for another person can "die" (as in the case of an estranged spouse or a friendship that has deteriorated), then can our love for *people in general* also "die"? If so, how does this affect our Christian responsibility to "love one another"— including our enemies? If not, why not?

5.) How can we reconcile having Christian "love" for someone with whom we refuse to share the gospel of Christ?

Section Five: Disciples of the Master

What a Disciple Is (and Is Not)

One of the great barriers to having an appropriate (and rewarding) Christian perspective is the misunderstanding of what it means to be Christ's *disciple* in the first place. Many people today assume things about their identification with Christ that are simply not supported by facts. In his book, *Not a Fan*, Kyle Idleman says:

> It may seem that there are many followers of Jesus, but if they were honestly to define the relationship they have with Him I am not sure it would be accurate to describe them as followers. It seems to me that there is a more suitable word to describe them. They are not *followers* of Jesus. They are *fans* of Jesus. Here is the most basic description of fan in the dictionary: "An enthusiastic admirer." … And I think Jesus has a lot of fans these days. Fans who cheer for Him when things are going well, but who walk away when it's a difficult season. Fans who sit safely in the stands cheering, but they know nothing of the sacrifice and pain of the field. Fans of Jesus who know all about Him, but they don't *know* Him. … They want to be close enough to Jesus to get all the benefits, but not so close that it requires anything of them.[111]

Fans and disciples are two very different things. "Disciple" means a student, learner, pupil, or follower (of a master).[112] Disciple*ship* refers to a standardized practice of being a disciple; it necessarily involves the beliefs and lifestyle of one who actually *is* a disciple. While the word "Christian" has been heavily abused, misapplied, and often hijacked for purposes other than what was ever intended within the early church, "disciple" remains a fixed and constant designation. "Christian" has lost so much of its original meaning in modern religion. If a person says, "I am a Christian," we need clarification: What *kind* of Christian is he? Traditional or contemporary? Denominational or non-denominational? Catholic or Protestant? Calvinist or non-Calvinist? Neo-orthodoxy or fundamentalist? Institutional or non-institutional? Instrumental or *a capella*? One cup or multiple cups? The list goes on and on, to the point of absurdity.

But one who is a *disciple* of Christ must, by definition, be a student of the Master, period. This means: Christ is His Lord and Teacher; he is Christ's student and follower; whatever the Master says, he listens; whatever the Master teaches, he obeys; etc. Many contemporary Christians (and those who *think* they are Christians) automatically consider themselves to be "disciples" of Christ simply because they have adopted His *name*. But discipleship describes a lifestyle of one who has voluntarily and consistently put himself under the tutelage of His Master for the purpose of becoming more and more *like* Him. McGuiggan aptly writes:

> Granting that disciples had to submit their hearts to the Master on his terms, it is useful to say that they came in all shapes and sizes. There are weak ones and strong ones, very gifted ones and less gifted ones. Some of them have an awful struggle with the pull of the flesh, while others grapple with dispositional weaknesses (pride, arrogance, and the like). Whatever their place on the ladder of moral excellence they are all dedicated to growth out of sinfulness into the likeness of the Master. They **all** have that in common. He who has no intention of growing into the likeness of his Master is not a disciple! Disciples, all of them, share a common struggle and a common purpose: To increasingly leave aside sin and increasingly (which is the same thing stated positively) to become like their Master.[113]

The one who says, "Lord, this is how I *feel* about what You said" is living by his emotions rather than practicing discipleship. What Jesus *commands* must be more important than what a person *feels* about His commands. If Christ is truly *your* Lord and Savior, then you will obey His commandments rather than try to interpret, re-define, or psycho-analyze them.

The New Testament Pattern

Consider an illustration: For centuries, smoke from candles and torches blackened Michelangelo's paintings on the ceiling of the Sistine Chapel in Rome. The artwork and magnificent detail of that great artist were obscured, thus preventing people from seeing his masterpieces as they originally had been created. In recent years, however, elaborate restoration efforts have removed this soot and have allowed Michelangelo's art to be seen in all of its glory once again.

Similarly, centuries of misinterpretation, misunderstanding, conflicts of interest, and sheer lethargy have obscured the true meaning of discipleship to Christ. We do not need a "restoration movement," however, to learn the original intentions of the Master; we simply need to read the primary source document (the New Testament) in its context and accept the conclusions that it draws as our own. When we do this—paying special attention to Christ's own instructions on this subject—the true meaning of discipleship will emerge intact. What we quickly discover is that His definition of discipleship is at serious odds with what many contemporary Christians call "Christianity." Like the veil that covered the Jews' hearts in the time of Paul (2 Corinthians 3:14-16), there may be a veil over our own hearts today that obscures the true meaning of what Jesus calls us to be.

Modern Christianity is often a mere *version* of New Testament Christianity, not always an accurate description. Because of this, many Christians have conditioned themselves (or allowed themselves to *be* conditioned) to read New Testament passages differently than what was originally intended. For example, when Jesus said, "If anyone wishes to come after Me, he must deny himself, and take up his cross and follow Me" (Matthew 16:24), this does not necessarily mean to us what it meant to Him. To Christ, this meant: discipleship is an all-or-nothing commitment that demands your primary attention, all your effort, and the loss of everything else in this life. In the mind of the contemporary Christian, however, this may translate to:

- ❏ Wear a crucifix as jewelry around your neck, or hang a cross on your rear-view mirror.
- ❏ Watch a Hollywood movie or Discovery Channel documentary on the crucifixion of Christ and get a dramatic and stylized picture in your head of what He must have endured.
- ❏ Listen to a series of lessons on "discipleship," but afterward resume your life as before, untouched and unchanged by what you heard.
- ❏ Deny yourself the luxury of sleeping in on Sunday morning because you have to go to church ("Christianity is *so hard*—I hope Jesus appreciates all that I do for Him!").
- ❏ Take up your crutches—i.e., offer your reasons and excuses as to why you *personally* cannot do everything Jesus asked of His disciples. In other words, minimize your responsibility, justify your lack of participation, or wait to be told what to do.
- ❏ Hobble after Jesus *on* your crutches—i.e., be willing to do *some* of what He asked, but exempt and excuse yourself from whatever seems uncomfortable, unreasonable, or simply too difficult.

When Paul wrote, "Put on the full armor of God" (Ephesians 6:10-17), this does not necessarily mean to the modern Christian what it meant to him. To Paul, this meant: prepare to engage in the spiritual war that is all around us; prepare to engage the enemies of the church; and fully trust in the providential protection of God ("Be strong in the Lord and in the strength of His might"). To the contemporary Christian, however, this may mean:

- ❏ Have the preacher give a nice series of lessons on the "full armor of God."
- ❏ Hire a prominent and eloquent speaker from the Bible Belt to offer this series.

- ❏ Have an involved discussion about each piece of "armor" in an adult Bible class.
- ❏ Sing a bunch of hymns about being soldiers of Christ, sounding the battle cry, or "The Fight Is On."
- ❏ Download a music video of a song that some famous "Christian rock" singer has performed and play it for your congregation to inspire everyone.

When Paul wrote, "Suffer hardship with me, as a good soldier of Jesus Christ" (2 Timothy 2:3), this does not necessarily mean to the modern Christian what it meant to him. To Paul, this meant: be willing to endure any hardship or loss for the sake of Christ; serve Him to your own hurt; and put aside those things that would compromise this service. Today, however, this may mean:

- ❏ Endure the arduous task of having to go to church and listen to sermons.
- ❏ Suffer the pain and hardship of having to make a financial contribution to the Lord's work.
- ❏ Suffer the pain and hardship of having to attend special classes or anything else that exceeds the "normal expectations" of the Sunday and Wednesday assemblies.
- ❏ Spend an hour—an *entire hour!*—of Bible study in someone's home that is not as nice and comfortable as your own home.
- ❏ Tolerate the human imperfections (including the off-key singing and annoying idiosyncrasies) of fellow believers.
- ❏ Sit through an entire church service painfully deprived of the comfort and convenience of your cell phone, e-mail, and latest video game obsession.

Given our modern "take" on Christianity, we may fail to make any practical application or any serious implementation of what Christ or Paul originally meant. Proportionately, few of us have actually "come after" Christ in the manner in which He instructed us. Few of us may be prepared to suffer what Christians in the early centuries of the church had to suffer. We say the words, we sing the songs, and we preach the sermons, but this does not mean we understand or appreciate the concept.

Instead of re-interpreting Christ's or Paul's words to accommodate what we have come to *believe* as "Christianity," we are to view the world, the gospel, the church, and our own selves from a heavenly point-of-view, not as we choose to see them. For example, when Paul (by inspiration of the Holy Spirit) said that the church is Christ's body, we cannot view the church as a mere institution, religion, building, or (an) owner of real estate and bank accounts. These things may be what *we* have come to believe about "church," but they have nothing to do with what *Christ* meant. Instead, His church is a spiritual and living organism that pulses with His blood and breathes with God's Spirit. When Christ said, "...Those who worship Him [God] must worship in spirit and truth" (John 4:24), we are not permitted to reduce this "worship" to a Sunday service, a special series of lessons, any single event, or any traditional ritual (such as a singing or prayer meeting). Christ was talking to individual believers, not a corporate church. He was telling us what actually must be done, not our *take* on what we *think* must be done. Thus, He meant (at least):

- ❑ Be filled with the Holy Spirit.[114]
- ❑ Be immersed in Christ's teachings.
- ❑ Partake of holy communion with the Father.
- ❑ Live as true believers.

When Christ said, "Come to Me... [T]ake My yoke upon you and learn from Me..." (Matthew 11:28-29), we cannot reduce this to, "Call yourself a Christian," "Come to church services," "Read your Bible," or "Partake of the Lord's Supper." Such conclusions have little to do with what Christ actually meant in the context of His own ministry and teaching. What He meant was (at least):

- ❏ Surrender everything in your heart to Him.
- ❏ Put yourself at the feet of the Master.
- ❏ Defend His cause with everything you have—even your own life, if necessary.
- ❏ Lay all of your fears, doubts, cares, and worries at His feet.[115]

When Paul said, "Have this attitude in yourselves which was also in Christ Jesus" (Philippians 2:5), he did *not* mean: "Every church is to use the exact same worship service format," "Make baptism, non-instrumental music, and marriage-and-divorce issues the core of your preaching," "There cannot be any kitchens in the church building," or "Only fellowship with those who agree with you entirely." Such conclusions are apparently what many Christians have *interpreted* Paul to mean (by their actions), but this severely limits whatever Paul *did* mean. It is clear in the context of Philippians (and the rest of Paul's epistles) that he meant at least:

- ❏ Treat one another with the same decency, respect, and forbearance as Christ Himself would do for you if He was here in person.
- ❏ Allow Christ's love to condition your heart and express itself in genuine acts of mercy and kindness, rather than succumbing to the short-sighted and self-serving gestures of the world.
- ❏ Allow for *no other* attitude to prevail, but allow only *His* attitude to rule your heart, fill your soul, and dictate your behavior.
- ❏ Be obedient to His instructions, as you best understand them, but also realize that there is always room for personal improvement (Philippians 3:12-16, Colossians 2:6-7, 1 Thessalonians 4:1, et al).
- ❏ God's objective is that "Christ is proclaimed" (Philippians 1:15-18), not that your private understanding of Christ's gospel is proclaimed.

"Radical" Discipleship

Denominationalism is a system of church organization that—like any "-ism"—is foreign to the New Testament.[116] Yet, just because you may be in a "non-denominational" (or the increasingly popular "*un*-denominational") church does not mean you are automatically free from denominational *thinking*. If you are not living like the Lord or His apostles instructed you to live, then you are re-defining "discipleship" to accommodate your own beliefs and perspectives. How is this any different—or any *better*—than those who attempt to validate an unbiblical system of church organization? Jesus has not softened, minimized, or modified His expectations for discipleship for any of us, no matter what we think of ourselves. Sadly, what passes for "Christianity" today has often become a religion of accommodation rather than that of genuine discipleship. If anyone has gotten soft, it is *us*, not Christ. Jesus Himself describes the character and disposition of those who are genuine disciples:

- Disciples sit at the feet (so to speak) of their Master in order to *learn* from Him and be *like* Him in every respect (Matthew 10:24-25). They regard Jesus alone as "Teacher" and "Lord"; they implement His teaching examples in their own lives (John 13:13-16). Jesus said, "A pupil is not above his teacher; but everyone, after he has been fully trained, will be like his teacher" (Luke 6:40). Thus, while others will be busy with mundane and unprofitable tasks, His disciples choose to sit at His feet and learn from Him (as in Luke 10:38-42). In simple language, this means to immerse oneself in Christ's teaching and internalize His holy character in order to conform to Him.
- Disciples are the "light of the world" and "salt of the earth" (Matthew 5:13-16). This refers to the moral illumination and preservation they provide for the society in which they live. Disciples do not just practice "religion," but share—through their words *and* conduct—a life-giving and life-saving message. In order to be a "light" to someone else, however, disciples themselves must first be illumined by God (Philippians 2:15). Likewise, in order to provide "salt" for the world, disciples must internalize a character that is morally superior to that of the world's own self-serving character.

Christian Thinking

- Disciples take care of their own in honor of their Master (Matthew 25:34-40). The "one another" principle permeates the entire gospel of Christ, and His disciples take it seriously. By tending to the needs of fellow believers, they express deep respect for the Master Himself. For this reason, they will inherit that which God has prepared for them "from the foundation of the world."
- Disciples are "slaves" (servants) of the Master, His kingdom, and righteousness (Luke 12:37-38). They do not try to avoid work but are always vigilant for opportunities to serve Him and His people. They are willing to leave behind everything and everyone else in order to accomplish this (Mark 10:29-30). They are also prepared for and eagerly await His return (Hebrews 9:28, 1 John 3:2-3).
- Disciples are willing to endure persecution and other hardships for the sake of righteousness (Matthew 5:10-12). They are willing to identify with their Master in the most difficult and sacrificial manner (Romans 8:16-17). They possess strong convictions and exercise moral excellence in their service to the Lord (1 Peter 3:17, 2 Peter 1:5).[117]

Modern representations of discipleship often pale in comparison to what Christ actually describes in the gospels. Many Christians (or those who *think* of themselves as Christians) have subscribed to a dumbed-down and mild *version* of discipleship that corresponds to the pre-occupied, entertainment-driven, and often lazy expectations of a spiritually-lukewarm religious world. Many Christians are comfortable with practicing *religion*, but do not understand the *calling* to which they have been called.[118] Many people are looking for a church-owned community center to which they can bring their families and have some high-energy "pastor" validate their private beliefs. Relatively few have come with a full surrender of their hearts or looking to have their lives literally transformed by the renewing of their minds (cf. Romans 12:2). And some Christians are more concerned about their piety and clean hands than they are about holiness and the dirty work of discipleship.

Yet, Christ did not call us to be churchgoers, church members, mere participants in a church service, or mere entries in a church directory. He called us through His gospel to be His dedicated, exclusive, and very active followers. We are to represent accurately who He is and what He teaches, not re-package His persona or His message in a context that suits our personal objectives. He also called us to be *vocal* about the gospel message and our Master's love for people—not just vocal when in the company of friends and fellow believers, but even in the company of unbelievers and personal enemies.

This perspective *does* sound radical, revolutionary, and even militant. The truth is: discipleship *is* radical, since it is in direct conflict with the worldly life and its expectations (Galatians 5:16-17). It *is* revolutionary in that it does not seek to preserve the world's mentality in a different packaging but to overthrow it altogether (2 Corinthians 10:3-5). And it *is* militant in a certain sense, since we are not in a state of peaceful coexistence with the unbelieving world but at war with it (Ephesians 6:10-13). Christ is our Captain and Leader; He leads us into this battle between the Light of the world and the satanic darkness which presently engulfs the world (1 John 5:19).

However, this is not a call to *physical* warfare and spilling of blood in an attempt to advance the cause of our Master. We are not to strap bombs to our chests for Jesus; we are not to behead people for Jesus; we are not to hijack planes and carry out suicide missions for Jesus. These are things that people do who do not *know* Jesus, and therefore do not know the Father—which is exactly what Jesus said about religious zealots throughout the ages: "They will make you outcasts from the synagogue, but an hour is coming for everyone who kills you to think that he is offering service to God. These things they will do because they have not known the Father or Me" (John 16:2-3).

Instead, we are called to convince men of God's truth, not declare war on them to force *our* "truth" down their throats. We are called to love those who are our enemies, not execute them. Thus, we are engaged in *spiritual* warfare, but it is really Christ who fights for us. Jesus Himself said: "My kingdom is not of this world. If My kingdom were of this world, then My servants would be fighting [to protect Me]...; but as it is, My kingdom is not of this realm" (John 18:36, bracketed words are mine). We are never called to kill unbelievers, but to reason with them (if they will listen to reason) by the gospel of Christ. We are not to shed blood and then call it "divine vengeance"; in fact, we are not even to be "quarrelsome," but are to do our best to persuade people to be saved from their own spiritual ruin (2 Timothy 2:24-26).

But this representing, reasoning, and persuading takes time, energy, education, and *work*. It is not something we do in a Sunday morning church service; it is something to which we *commit* in identifying with Christ. Christians cannot be expected to put on the "full armor of God" in order to sing songs, hear sermons, and play church. The only reason for donning armor is to engage in battle—not by our own strength, but certainly by our own decision and resolve. If necessary, the blood that is spilled in that battle ought to be ours, not our enemy's. We must be willing to die for what we believe in, not kill those who will not believe our message. Before we can make such a commitment, however, we must first be willing to *live* for what we believe.

What do *you* think?

1.) Sometimes Christians seem to manifest a split personality. On the one hand, we may talk like aggressive soldiers ("The fight is on!"; "Soldiers of Christ arise!"; "Faith is the victory!"; "Sound the battle cry!"). On the other hand, we may *act* like passive civilians, oblivious to the war all around us and our enlistment in the holy army that fights it ("I'm pretty busy right now; God will understand").

   a. Why do Christians fail to recognize the true nature of discipleship and the level of commitment that this requires?
   b. What do you suppose it is going to take for us to get out of "passive" mode and engage the enemy, so to speak, with our "full armor of God"?
   c. Which personality do *you* manifest?

2.) In an earthly battle, some soldiers are on the front lines in actual combat while others remain behind offering tactical or provisional support. Yet, Paul tells *every* Christian to put on the full armor of God. Why is this?

   a. Can we personally choose to remain behind the battle lines, so to speak, and let others fight our (moral or spiritual) battles?

   b. Does the aggressive nature of discipleship to Christ sound disagreeable to you? If so, how would *you* characterize it instead—and can you support this characterization with Scripture?

3.) Can you conform to a more accurate understanding of discipleship without making any changes to your present lifestyle and habits?

4.) In describing our discipleship to Christ, John wrote: "We know love by this, that He laid down His life for us; and we ought to lay down our lives for the brethren" (1 John 3:16).

   a. Is John saying that we may *literally* have to lay down our lives for our fellow believers, if necessary? Or, is this just figurative language? (Did Jesus just figuratively lay down *His* life for *you*?)

   b. When we made a commitment to serve Christ, did we also make a commitment to make sacrifices for those who belong to Him?

Section Five: Disciples of the Master *(continued)*

A Christian's Vocation

Instead of identifying with our present view of religion, we would do well to see the Christian walk as a *vocation*. "Vocation" in this context does not mean what you or I do for a living (as a job, career, or profession). In contemporary usage of this word, God has been omitted from the picture altogether. Yet, when God calls people to Himself, He is not asking us to switch jobs, change careers, or go back to school for a better skill set. Rather, "vocation" refers to one's *calling*—specifically, God's having called a person into His service. (This is what the word originally meant as it came into the English language in the 15th century.) It means, in essence, "I [God] need you to give yourself entirely to Me and submit your heart and your life to My oversight." Consider, for example, some very specific "callings" in Scripture:

- "Then I heard the voice of the Lord, saying, 'Whom shall I send, and who will go for Us?' Then I said, 'Here am I. Send me!'" (Isaiah 6:8). God did not say to Isaiah, "I need someone to start a religion," or "...get spiritual," or "...build a church," but *carry out My will as My servant.*
- "Now the word of the LORD came to me saying, 'Before I formed you in the womb I knew you, and before you were born I consecrated you; I have appointed you a prophet to the nations'" (Jeremiah 1:4-5). God did not tell Jeremiah, "I need you to go to church," or "...write some material for Me," or "...follow this spiritual 'movement' I have put together," but *follow Me and become My disciple.*
- "As Jesus went on from there, He saw a man called Matthew, sitting in the tax collector's booth; and He said to him, 'Follow Me!' And he got up and followed Him" (Matthew 9:9). Jesus did not tell Matthew, "I need you to go to church," or "...identify with this synagogue or that one," or "...follow this spiritual 'movement' I am putting together," but *follow Me and become My disciple.*

❑ "Jesus said to him [the rich young ruler], 'If you wish to be complete, go and sell your possessions and give to the poor, and you will have treasure in heaven; and come, follow Me'" (Matthew 19:21). Jesus did not tell this man, "You need to feel more spiritual," or "…join a church," or "…get more involved in organized religion," but *follow Me and leave behind everything and everyone that prevents you from following Me.*

Being a part of a local congregation is certainly important, and provides for a collective worship of God *and* individual opportunities to edify fellow believers in a variety of ways. Yet, God's calling of your heart—your vocation—is not to be interpreted as a mere summons to seek membership in a congregation. Sadly, this seems to be a primary goal of many Christians today ("I want a 'home church' I can identify with"; "I want a 'church family' that will keep my kids interested in the Christian lifestyle"; etc.). Christ did not call you through His gospel (cf. 2 Thessalonians 2:14) to provide you with a new social group for you and your family. Rather, Christ calls all of us out of the world and into His fellowship so that each of us can be transformed into a genuine follower of Him. Not surprisingly, Christians collectively are referred to as a "called" or "chosen" people (as in Romans 1:6 and 1 Peter 2:9).[119] God chose the spiritual body of Christ—His church—to be glorified (Romans 8:29-30); thus, all who are added *to* that church will be glorified *with* it.

Christians are not "called" to attend church services, classes, Bible studies, or potlucks.[120] While it is true that we engage in these activities, they are by no means the reason for which we were called. Paul identifies our true objective: "Therefore do not be ashamed of the testimony of our Lord or of me His prisoner, but join with me in suffering for the gospel according to the power of God, who has saved us and called us with a holy calling, not according to our works, but according to His own purpose and grace which was granted us in Christ Jesus from all eternity…" (2 Timothy 1:8-9). God did not call us because of what *we* did, but because of what His *Son* did. We are to honor the Son's work by responding rightly to our calling. This response includes:

- Proclaiming the "excellencies" of God (1 Peter 2:9).
- Walking in a manner worthy of our calling (Ephesians 4:1, Philippians 1:27).
- Preparing (purifying) ourselves for the Master's service (2 Corinthians 7:1, Hebrews 13:20-21).
- Growing in the knowledge and grace of the Lord (Colossians 2:6-7, 2 Peter 3:18).
- Manifesting the "fruit" or visible evidence of that growth (Colossians 1:9-10).
- Suffering for the sake of Christ and righteousness (Matthew 5:10-12, Romans 8:16-17, et al).

While many people today easily adopt the name "Christian," it is those who actually *follow* Christ that belong to Him (Matthew 16:24, John 10:27, Revelation 14:4b). Those who will not follow the Master are really not identified with Him at all. Thus, one's vocation—his having been called *by* God to enter into a sacred ministry *to* God—has little to do with his identification with a particular congregation but has everything to do with his heart's devotion to Christ as his Master.

The Lord Who Calls Us

This concept of absolute allegiance to the Lord—even to one's own hurt—is virtually a foreign concept to many churchgoers today. Much of the reason for this foreignness is the erroneous manner in which people "see" Christ in the first place. For example, depending upon one's cultural background, past religious experience, ingrained teaching, etc., a person may see Christ as:

- **The CEO of His church.** Jesus is merely a corporate executive who sits in His celestial boardroom and is surrounded by "yes men" (angels). He attends to the administrative business of the church, but is unconcerned with its individual people or day-to-day operations. He is disconnected, unavailable, and out-of-touch ("Jesus doesn't know what I'm going through"; "He cannot relate to my real-life world because He's stuck in His corporate world"; "He's too busy").

- (Christ *is* the head of His church, but He is deeply concerned with His "bride." He *does* know what you are going through because He has faced far more than you will ever face, "yet without sin" [see Hebrews 4:14-16]. He *can* relate to your world because He knows all things—and He knows *your* world even better and more accurately than you do.)

❑ **The Great Problem-solver.** If you have problems, concerns, or crises, just bring them to Jesus and He will solve them. He is the One you go to when all of your own efforts and solutions have failed. Yet, He does not ask much in return—just a token nod, a thank-you, or a little something in the collection plate now and then. After that, you can resume your life where you left off—until, of course, the next crisis arises, in which case you can go running back to Him.

- (Christ *can* remove whatever trouble or crisis you are facing, but that may not be His purpose for you. It is more important that you learn to trust Him and put your faith in Him than it is for Him to deliver you from every "scrape" in which you find yourself. Instead of a token nod of thanks, He expects—and deserves—a lifetime of respect, obedience, and gratitude.)

❑ **A Magic Genie.** When you read Scripture, something mysterious happens—your mind is *magically* or *miraculously* opened up and enlightened. It is like unlocking a secret code and bringing its message to life. When you say prayers (especially repeatedly), it is like rubbing a lamp getting your wishes answered. Saying "in Jesus' name" serves as a special code-phrase, magic formula, or secret chant—mysteriously, things begin to happen (and if they do not, then you did not use the right formula or sequence).

- (Christ *will* give "wisdom" to whoever asks for it, but this will always be in the context of His will [see James 1:5-8].

Reading Scripture is enlightening, but not miraculously so; it is educational, but not in some magical way. The Word of God does impart spiritual understanding, but not apart from your own effort, diligent study, and prayerful entreaties.)

- ❏ **A Great Enigma.** Jesus is not Someone to whom you "draw near"; rather, He is a puzzle or riddle to solve—and He has all kinds of secret and hidden knowledge to give to those who *do* solve Him. When you read Scripture, it is like deciphering a long-held secret—you are unlocking transcendent messages that few others will ever see. Your objective is not to imitate His character, but to become wise and illuminated. Jesus is your route to personal enlightenment.
  - (Jesus is a *Divine Person* and a *Personal Savior*, not an abstract puzzle to be solved. There are certainly things about Him that are mysterious and intriguing—such are the very attributes of "sacred"—yet you are not to dwell upon what cannot be known about Him but what He has revealed to you through Scripture.[121] Your objective *is* to imitate His character and to "walk" like He did [see 1 John 2:3-6].)
- ❏ **A Good but Helpless Friend.** You are not trying to be disrespectful to Jesus, but (frankly) He can only do so much. His hands are tied, His power is limited, and His mindset is stuck in the ancient past. He will listen to all that you tell Him and will console you as best as He can, but there is really little that He can do. In the end, He is more like a cheerleader on the sidelines watching you getting pummeled and beaten by your opponents, but not able to join you in the struggle.
  - (Jesus has authority over *all things*, and has been given control of the *entire universe* [Matthew 28:18, Colossians 1:15-17, Hebrews 1:1-2, et al]. He is not stuck in the past, your circumstances, or even your perception of Him. He can do far *more* than you think He can [Ephesians 3:20-21], not less. He is not just cheering you on, but is there to help you bear your cross, walk you through the fire, and do whatever else is necessary to bring you home to Him.)

Christian Thinking

- ❑ **The Ultimate Life Coach.** Jesus is like a therapeutic guru who tries to bring you in touch with your "inner self." He offers suggestions (not commandments); He gives compliments (not criticism); He makes no demands other than what you want to do. He accepts every form of praise, worship, and acknowledgement, regardless of whether or not it conforms to His instructions (because He does not want to suppress your creativity or make you feel unfulfilled). In the end, He will say to you, "Well done!" no matter how well you did or didn't do.
  - (Jesus never asked you to get in touch with your "inner self"; rather, He expects you to sanctify *Him* as Lord in your heart [1 Peter 3:15]. He does make demands of you and He does expect you to keep His commands, but these are all designed to improve your character, not crush your spirit. He will not accept just any worship that *you* come up with, but requires you to follow the pattern that *He* provided in the gospel message [the New Testament]. He will only say "Well done" to those who are good, faithful, and genuine servants [cf. Matthew 25:21].)
- ❑ **The Consummate Critic.** Jesus stands in heaven with His arms folded and His eyes gloweringly narrowed at you. He is unrealistic and unfair; He burdens you with unattainable expectations. He earned perfect scores in *everything*, while you are always a failing student—and He reminds you of this constantly. He finds fault with everything you do; He is not happy even when you give Him your best. After years of hard work and good behavior, all He can say is, "Excel still more." Frankly, He seems ungrateful, unappreciative, and unrealistic.
  - (The Lord is not unaware of your hard work; the letters to the seven churches [Revelation 2 – 3] reveal this. Holding you to a higher standard than that with which you are comfortable is not being unfair or ungrateful. Instead, it challenges you to do more than you thought was possible—largely because He is helping you all along the way. Jesus *was* perfect—this was necessary if He is to save your soul—but He gives you mercy

and grace for your imperfections. He *does* tell you to "excel still more" [cf. 1 Thessalonians 4:1]—not because He is unappreciative of your hard work so far, but because He needs you to remain committed to that which you started [1 Corinthians 15:58, Philippians 2:13, Hebrews 10:35-39, et al].)

All such portrayals or characterizations (above, in bold type) are untrue, unbiblical, and unwarranted. Yet, this does not stop people from clinging to them as though they were genuine. Such views are based upon personal opinions, not biblical facts. "The great irony," writes Jared Wilson, "is that, despite being the most discussed and confessed figure in all of history, no historical figure has been more marginalized and commoditized than Jesus. For many today he is a generic brand, a logo, a catchphrase, a pick-me-up...He's been romanticized by countless admirers, and sanitized by the Christian consumer culture."[122] Wrong conclusions about Christ lead to a failure to regard Him properly as both Lord and Savior. One's customized *portrayal* of Jesus does not change who He really is. Thus, it is extremely important that you learn instead His actual role as Master and your subordinate role as His disciple.

Christ's title and position as "Lord" in the New Testament is due to His supreme authority over all other authorities (Ephesians 1:20-21). (In most cases, "Master" is translated from the same Greek word [*kurios*] as that from which we get "Lord.") As far as God the Father is concerned, His Son (Christ) is worthy of and has been given "all authority in heaven and on earth" (Matthew 17:5, 28:18). This makes Him the King of kings and Lord of lords (cf. Revelation 17:14, 19:16). He is the "exact representation" of His Father (John 14:7-9, Hebrews 1:1-3a). He is the reason *for* and sustainer *of* all creation (Colossians 1:15-17). Such things are not and cannot be said of anyone else; Jesus is not "Lord" only because He is the head of His church, but because He exercises divine, sovereign, and invincible power and authority over *all of creation*.[123] This is not a ceremonial title; it commands respect and obedience. Ideally, *all* those who derive their existence and authority from Christ should regard Him as Lord; yet those who voluntarily submit to His authority most certainly must regard Him in this way.

What Christ's Lordship Requires of Us

Since Jesus *is* Lord, what does this fact require of those who are not yet Christians? What does this require of those who *are* Christians? What does *He* require of you *personally*? Respect and reverence, to be sure, but what does this mean to *Him*, not just to me or you? We cannot respect someone whom we will not obey; we cannot revere someone whom we do not respect. Thus, Jesus' identity—His power, authority, and position over all other powers, authorities, and positions *in existence*—demands our very best response. Nothing less than this is justifiable. No one is suggesting that this is easy to do, only that He is deserving of it and that He expects us (Christians) to strive for this very objective.

Sadly, many who identify themselves as Christians will call Jesus "Lord," but they act in a manner that does not *treat* Him as Lord. For example, they will:

- Focus on outward or external behaviors, but resist inward and internal transformation. Instead of a new *heart*, they simply try to maintain a Christian *image* or *ritual*.
- Question the Master's decisions and second-guess His conclusions. They imply that the Lord's commandments are open to interpretation or critique; His authority is presumed to be subject to their own approval. Thus, if they disagree with what He says, they feel justified in not obeying Him.
- Treat the Gospel as liberals and progressives do the United States Constitution—as an amendable document that can be re-interpreted and revised as social attitudes change. Since society is regarded as living, breathing, and fluid, these people regard the gospel in this same way.[124]

- ❏ Try to marry their personal *brand* of "Christianity" to what the Lord commanded. Instead of learning Christ's will and submitting to it, they customize their discipleship to agree with personal feelings, preferences, or schedules. They preach a gospel of accommodation rather than a radical departure from the world and its philosophies.
- ❏ Actually believe that their version of the gospel and their worship of God are just as valid, legitimate, and respectable as what the Master instructed in His Word. They are deceived by their own pride into thinking that they are able to know what is best for God *and* themselves—and that God will approve of whatever they come up with because, after all, He *loves* them so much.

In other words, such people call Jesus, "Lord, Lord," but they do not do what He says (cf. Luke 6:46). Their intentions may appear to be noble and good, but no one can be a disciple of the Lord based solely upon noble intentions. "Whatever may have been the degree of honor these people bestowed upon Jesus when they addressed him as 'Lord, Lord,' he stresses that they were dishonest," says Hendriksen; "for, while confessing him to be their Lord, they failed to render obedience to him."[125]

In John 6, we read that Jesus was being followed by a multitude of people, but many of these expected to be fed as before (6:26) or simply did not understand what discipleship to Him actually meant (6:15). Then Jesus began talking about eating His body and drinking His blood, and a number of people withdrew from Him (6:66)—not because they could not understand, but because Jesus did not fulfill their expectations of Messiah. Jesus said, "...the words that I have spoken to you are spirit and are life. But there are some of you who do not believe" (6:63-64a).

We see the same thing today: many claim to be "Christians," but only as long as they can define Christianity in the manner of their own liking or in support of their ethnic or social culture. Others practice what would by definition be called a hobby, not a spiritual vocation. Upon learning the true rigors of discipleship, many walk away and (proportionately) few remain. In such cases, Jesus' words still apply: "But there are some of you who do not believe." Discipleship does not cater to personal preferences; it will not conform to your present life; it does not seek popularity or the path of least resistance. It is difficult, expensive, time-consuming, and life-consuming. Yet, what better alternative do we have? As Peter said, "Lord, to whom shall we go? You have words of eternal life. We have believed and have come to know that You are the Holy One of God" (John 6:68-69).

Jesus said, "If anyone wishes to come after Me, he must deny himself, and take up his cross and follow Me" (Matthew 16:24). This means: choose to sanctify *Christ* as Lord in your heart (cf. 1 Peter 3:15) rather than yourself or anyone or anything else. Along with this, accept the sacrificial life of a true believer—the crown of life that you receive in heaven will be worth whatever losses you incur on the way (James 1:12).[126] And finally, honor Christ by serving and following Him—not just by doing what makes you *feel* special or involved, but by doing what is *necessary* to be involved. From this point forward, live for His sake, not your own (Galatians 2:20). "When Christ speaks of 'self-denial' He speaks of choosing Him as Lord and the dethroning of ourselves. *We are not permitted to play god* [sic]. We must renounce our own will in favor of His."[127]

These are difficult statements to hear, and are even more difficult to put into practice. But discipleship is not for those who choose to be weak, the timid, the unprepared, or the Sunday-morning churchgoer. Discipleship is a vocation, not a church service. Jesus never said, "If anyone wishes to use My name for his own religion, then second-guess everything I have told you, take up your crutches and hobble after Me." Some may call that a religion of sorts, but it is not discipleship to Christ. Responding to the call of heaven will take everything you own, affect every relationship you have, and put to test everything you profess to believe and claim to be. But *in the end*, you will meet the Master and He will present you to the Father—"...if indeed you continue in the faith firmly established and steadfast, and not moved away from the hope of the gospel that you have heard..." (Colossians 1:21-23).

Christian Thinking

What do *you* think?

1.) Are *all* Christians "called" (as a vocation) to serve Christ, or is this limited to preachers, elders, and missionaries?

2.) How will an inaccurate understanding of who Jesus really is affect our "discipleship" to Him?

   a. How do such inaccuracies get started in the first place?

   b. What is the only way in which we can *accurately* know who Jesus is?

3.) Why do people call Jesus "Lord" but do not do what He says? (There are several possible answers.)

4.) Many people want to be a "Christian" by their own definition, on their own terms, and on their own schedule. Why does *Christ* want us to be a Christian? Are there justifiable reasons other than His for becoming one?

5.) Jesus said, "If anyone wishes to come after Me, he must deny himself, and take up his cross and follow Me" (Matthew 16:24). Are these actions still necessary today in order to "come after" Him? Or, was that limited to believers in the first century (and now it is considerably different)?

   a. If it *is* considerably different for us today, then how do we know this, and in what ways is it different (and how do we know *that*)?

   b. If Jesus' requirements for discipleship today are *not* different than they were for believers in the first century, then how are we expected to respond to the passage cited?

Section Five: Disciples of the Master *(continued)*

Christ the Teacher

Jesus said, "But do not be called Rabbi; for One is your Teacher, and you are all brothers. ... Do not be called leaders; for One is your Leader, that is, Christ" (Matthew 23:8-10). Christ alone has the authority, responsibility, and ability to serve as the exclusive Teacher for all those who disciple themselves after Him. He is called "Teacher" more than any other single designation. All teaching that is about Him, salvation, and fellowship with the Father must originate with Him, either from His own words or the teachings of His hand-picked apostles. He is the "Light of the world" (John 8:12) because no one can be illuminated spiritually apart from Him; no amount of human wisdom or experience can provide what He alone is able to give to the human soul. No one comes to the Father except through Him (John 14:6), and those who will not listen to Him will not inherit the kingdom of heaven (Matthew 7:21).[128]

Jesus was uniquely and authoritatively able to disclose what is impossible for men to know otherwise (John 1:18). Having full knowledge of what is in the human heart (John 2:24-25), He could speak directly to this without bias or error. He also knew people in general—that is, the social dynamics of people, how they think, and how they learn. This made Him not only a good teacher, but a highly effective one. Daniel King observes:

> Jesus possessed a sympathetic insight into the nature, structure, and functioning of human personality and of social groups. This made it possible for him to meet the learning needs of such. In other words, he discerned their deficiencies and knew what kind of help they needed in order to enable him to "fill the gaps" of both knowledge and understanding. Also, he possessed unparalleled skill in mediating the subject matter

of his curriculum in such a way that the learning needs of the pupils would be met with the greatest economy, efficiency, and permanency.[129]

But Jesus never allowed His teaching to be separated from His own personal identity as "the Christ, the Son of the living God" (Matthew 16:16). Whatever He taught, and whenever He taught it, was always couched in the context of His role as the world's Redeemer. Alfred Edersheim, in his seminal work, *Jesus the Messiah*, says this:

> Christ came to found a Kingdom, not a School; to institute a fellowship, not to propound a system. To the first disciples all doctrinal teaching sprang out of fellowship with Him. They saw Him, and therefore believed; they believed, and therefore learned the truths connected with Him, and springing out of Him. So to speak, the seed of truth which fell on their hearts was carried... from the flower of His Person and Life.[130]

Given this, Jesus never descended into sophistry or esoteric philosophizing, as many other men have done who have allowed their great learning to obscure any practical value to their words. His teaching was not designed to impress people; it was designed first to *enlighten* them with heavenly insight ("This is what you should know"), and then put that knowledge into a practical *lifestyle* ("This is what you must do"). In this sense

> ...the teaching of Jesus was characterized by the utmost simplicity. His instruction was free from over-adornment and ornateness, complex construction, and obscure thoughts. He did not attempt to secure a reputation for learning through a mystical, intangible, and unintelligible message. As to his words and phrases, they were familiar to all, though filled with new contents and broader applications. He made the simple folk and the poor his major concern; those attracted out of other classes could understand and appreciate his message, too, but

if he had operated in the reverse, the uneducated and poor would have been altogether left out. To accomplish his aim of teaching, he made his life a simple one: his personal wants were few, no display or splendor. ... His ambitions were also simple: his desire was not to be quoted as a man of letters, a philosopher, or an earthly king. He was a Savior. His sole ambition was to be a Savior and communicate to others the benefits of his office for them.[131]

As the Teacher of His disciples, there are things Christ does *not* teach us as well as things He *does* teach. For example, He does *not* teach:

- What we eventually can learn on our own. He did not bring us any technological innovations; He did not introduce us to higher math; He did not invent a new language; and He did not conduct scientific experiments. These are things that men would learn or discover over time, but have nothing directly to do with the redemption of their souls.
- How to take advantage of people and exploit their gullibility. Many televangelists, religious hucksters, and self-proclaimed gurus today have become rich and famous by capitalizing on the fear, emotions, and/or ignorance of good people who thought these men were something when they in fact were nothing.
- How to get ahead in life at the expense of others. This is a common and pervasive problem in the world: in order for *a few* to succeed, *many* must pay the price for this "success." Thus, a majority of the world's population at any given time suffers for the benefit of a relatively small percentage of people.
- How to become rich, powerful, and arrogant. Christ did not teach us how to exercise control over people in the manner of men or how to dominate and exploit the weak. In fact, He taught just the opposite (Matthew 20:25-28). "He taught the highest moral and spiritual truths: God is father, man is brother, the will is free, the soul is immortal, [the lives of] women and children are of equal worth and are to be honored along with men, the life of sacrificial

love is supreme, etc. Yet he presented these profound truths simply, clearly, and skillfully."[132]

- That we need seminaries, formal ordination, and church approval to carry out the most important business on earth: teaching people how to become disciples of the Lord and (thus) children of God. The church was never empowered with the authority to decide *for* God or *instead* of Him who would or would not be qualified to act as His representative or spokesman.

- How to use politics, bureaucracy, or formalism to manage (or oversee) His people. He did not teach us how to build a religion, but how to build a *life with God*. The Pharisees were experts in politics and formalism, and Christ openly condemned their brand of "righteousness" (cf. Matthew 5:20).

- How to distinguish ourselves or fellow believers as more "enlightened" or closer to God through academic achievements, seminary studies, or titles that men give to one another (e.g., Rabbi, Reverend, Father, Bishop, Pastor, etc.). While our levels of learning will vary from disciple to disciple, we all remain equal in our standing before Christ. Jesus said, "You are all brothers" (see Matthew 23:8-10), and we have no reason to confer honorary titles upon those who are all of equal standing.[133]

- How to circumvent "the system," find loopholes, and look for escape clauses from personal responsibility. He did not teach us how to *avoid* work or moral responsibility (as people commonly do); He taught us to be good stewards, industrious, and active in His kingdom.

- How to turn the "path to heaven" into the path of least resistance. In other words, He did not teach us that God will be happy with whatever "path" we take, as long as we feel sincere or right in taking it. Instead, He taught that there is one "way" that leads to God, and no one is capable of coming to Him otherwise (Matthew 7:13-14, John 14:6).

- How to love only when it is convenient, comfortable, materially-rewarding, and/or self-gratifying. He taught us to love one another in the manner that *He* loves—unconditionally, no matter what, and even to one's own hurt (John 13:34-35).

- How to walk in darkness and call it "enlightenment"; how to live without hope and call it "fulfilling"; or how to live in delusion and call it "truth." Ungodly and unconverted people live and reason with such contradictions, but genuine disciples "did not learn Christ in this way" (Ephesians 4:20)—He did not teach us these things. These are from the world, not from heaven (see James 3:13-18).

In a positive sense, Christ *does* teach His disciples how to live the most rewarding, fulfilling, and morally-responsible life possible. He does not provide a variety of options from which to pick and choose, but gives us one incredible, powerful, and life-changing message that *can* and *will* improve the life (and spiritual future) of every single person who embraces it. He does not set us on our own course to pilot and navigate ourselves as we see fit, but He provides all the wisdom, strength, and resources we need to walk the path that leads to God. In light of this, Christ taught us:

- Who God really is—not just by way of explanation, but through His *personal representation* of Him. He is the "exact" character of God (Hebrews 1:3); He alone has revealed God to us (John 1:18); if we have seen Christ (through the record of Scripture), then we have "seen" the Father (John 14:7-9).
- What is important to God—and therefore what must be of supreme importance to each one of us. We are not left to wonder where God stands, or where we stand with God, because He (Christ) has told us these things exactly. "My Father is glorified by this, that you bear much fruit, and so prove to be My disciples" (John 15:8). We cannot bear "fruit" or prove ourselves to be Christ's disciples unless we are told by Him what we are to know and do.
- How to honor God and worship Him—not just in a church service, but with our *entire lives*. Very little of our discipleship to Christ *can* be demonstrated "at church" (so to speak), but

most of it will be manifested in our everyday walk—what some have called "life worship." God is not to be honored only during a few hours of the week, but every day, by every follower, and through every experience.

- How to establish and maintain a right relationship with God through entering into a covenant agreement with Him. This agreement—the terms and conditions of which are spelled out in the gospel—is filled with benefits, blessings, promises, and *hope for the future*, including our future beyond this life. It is also filled with instructions, commandments, principles, and warnings to govern our lives while we remain here upon the earth. Whatever we *need* to know, He has revealed; whatever is *necessary* for salvation, He has made available.

- How we can deal with the flaws, imperfections, and varying temperaments of others. Since all people—including you and me—are unique and important, we need a means by which we can all achieve *collective action* (brotherly fellowship) despite our human differences. This is accomplished through patience, toleration, mercy, and grace. We "forebear" in the case of differences of personality and opinions; we "forgive" in the case of actual sin against one another (cf. Colossians 3:12 15).[134]

- How to rise above the greed, corruption, and selfishness of this world and serve as "lights" and "salt" instead (cf. Matthew 5:13-16). In other words, He has taught us how to live *in* the world but not be *of* the world; He raises our view to heaven rather than letting it be fixated on things here below (see Colossians 3:1-3).

- How to treat people with dignity, compassion, and respect. Instead of stepping on people to get where we (feel that we) need to go, He has taught us how to *serve* them instead (John 13:13-17). If we do this, then Christ Himself will take us where we need to go.

- How to separate the religions, philosophies, and teachings of men from the infallible and eternal truths of God. He has

taught us how to rise above all moral confusion and the swamp of misinformation contained in all man-made religion and to *know* and *understand* the truth instead (2 Corinthians 1:13, Ephesians 3:4-5).
- ❏ How to be noble-minded, pure in heart, and free in conscience. Despite human efforts to achieve this in vain (through philosophy, psychology, or therapy), Christ has given us the best prescription for human thinking and human life that exists, period. He has shown us how to live *as* and *among* the best people on earth without letting it go to our heads in succumbing to elitism or intellectualism.
- ❏ How to imitate God Himself: His virtues, His character, and His love. Christians are to be "imitators of God, as beloved children" (Ephesians 5:1), but this would be impossible if not for the model example of Christ Himself *and* the divine grace that He provides to overcome our sins, failings, and limitations of understanding.[135]

Becoming Perfectly Human

Given these last points, it is important to understand that Jesus was not teaching His followers how to be *less* human, but to strive for a *more perfect* human life than we could ever attain without Him. It is evil to embrace the satanic world and gratify wicked lusts; it is our *divinely-inspired mission* to follow the Teacher into the role of an ideal human being. Christ Himself did not use His role as Teacher to separate Himself from people, but fully identified *with* human life in order to provide a model example of what this life could be if every person on earth patterned himself after Him. On this, Dr. Geikie eloquently comments:

> Nothing could better illustrate His perfect manhood, than His identifying Himself thus with the humble incidents of a private circle. He had grown up under the common ordinances of human existence, as a child, a son, a brother, a friend, and a neighbour [*sic*]. As a Jew, He had shared in the social, civil, and religious life of His nation. ...Neither His nationality, nor

education, nor mental characteristics, nor natural temperament, narrowed His sympathies. Though burdened with the high commission of the Messiah, He retained a vivid interest in all things human. With us, any supreme pre-occupation leaves only apathy for other things. But in Christ, no one faculty or emotion appeared in excess. His fullness of nature suited itself to every occasion. Strength and grace, wisdom and love, courage and purity, which are the one side of our being, were never displayed so harmoniously, and so perfectly, as in Him. … In the fullest sense He was a man, but not in the sense in which manly virtues are opposed to those of woman, for He showed no less the gentleness, purity, and tenderness of the one sex, than the strength and nobility of the other. He was the Son of Man, in the grand sense of being representative of humanity as a whole. Man and woman alike, have in Him their perfect ideal.[136]

Worldly thinking follows the carnal and self-serving human passions; Christian thinking follows the heavenly and selfless desire of Christ Himself. "You are from below," Jesus told His unbelieving countrymen, "I am from above; you are of this world, I am not of this world" (John 8:23). Therefore, the mind of Jesus does not follow the mind of the human world; instead, "…I speak these things as the Father has taught Me …" and "… which I have seen with My Father …" (John 8:28, 38).[137] The source of Jesus' knowledge and information is not of the world or human origin, but God Himself.

Jesus' thinking was not merely different than the world's thinking, but far superior to it. Human wisdom cannot transcend its own limitations, just as a stream cannot rise above its source. Apart from divine enlightenment, people cannot help but think *like* people. With such enlightenment, however, we are able to think above and beyond whatever we could have done otherwise. Just as the Father's "thoughts" and "ways" are higher than those of earthly men (Isaiah 55:8-9), so Jesus' thoughts and ways exceeded those taught by men.

And as He thought, so we (Christians) can think—*if indeed* we adopt His "mind" and follow His Spirit (Romans 8:12-14, Galatians 5:25). This does not mean we develop a higher intelligence than those who are not Christians. Rather, it means: our perspective has increased dramatically; we are brought into contact with knowledge and wisdom that exceeds human comprehension; we are taught to think, love, and live more fully than what the world teaches us to do; and we walk through life with an eternal purpose, an undeterred hope, and a brimming anticipation of an even better existence in the life to come.

The New Testament teaches that when we enter into glory in the afterlife we will be given a heavenly body that is spiritual in nature (1 Corinthians 15:40-49, 2 Corinthians 5:1-4). This new body will not be of "flesh and blood" (1 Corinthians 15:50-53), but will conform to a glory consistent with the One who has raised us from the dead (Philippians 3:20-21, 1 John 3:2). The New Testament never teaches that we will cease to be *human*, however. On the contrary, whatever we become in our glorified existence will be *perfectly* human—without mortality, sinful corruptions, and physical limitations that we must presently endure—and not *un*-human. In heaven, there will be Deity (the Father, Son, and Holy Spirit), angels (of many different forms), and *humans*—those who have experienced life on earth *and* have walked by faith in God (2 Corinthians 5:7). We cannot become divine beings; we will be 'like" angels in some respects (Matthew 22:30), but we will not become angels. Instead, we will "become more human than you ever succeeded in being on earth"[138]—not by our own doing, but by following the One who has taught us this. When we follow the Teacher, we become like Him; and when we become like Him, then we follow Him wherever He goes (John 10:27, Revelation 14:4), even beyond this earthly life and into eternal glory.

The Teacher, then, forces us to reconsider and recalibrate what we *define* "human" to be. If Jesus found favor with God the Father by living as a perfect human being, then it stands to reason that He

Christian Thinking

[Jesus] does not want us to shed our humanity, but to live to a far higher standard than we had chosen to live while we remained in our unconverted state. By rejecting the Teacher, we accept an inferior mode of thinking, which translates to an inferior lifestyle. By accepting the teachings and modeling ourselves after the behavior of the Teacher, however, we ascend beyond the examples of those who want us to follow *them* rather than the Son of God. "His method and approach was thus to be distinguished from that of the rabbis of Judaism, the philosophers of Greece, and the rhetoricians of Rome. He was a man of the people, and a teacher of the people."[139]

Again, becoming a Christian does not mean that our personal level of intelligence increases, or that we become morally superior to everyone else. It *does* mean, however, that we have made a decision to sit at the feet of the greatest Man in all of history—a Man whose teachings bring us into eternal fellowship with God Himself. "It is the Spirit who gives life," Jesus said. "The flesh profits nothing; the words that I have spoken to you are spirit and are life" (John 6:63). Not only did He say these words but He also proved them to be true through the miracles He performed, culminating in His resurrection from the dead (John 2:19-21, 10:18).

What do *you* think?

1.) Is knowing *about* Jesus—even in great detail—the same thing as *knowing* Jesus? Why or why not?

2.) Why is it important to know what Jesus did *not* teach us as well as what He *did* teach? How does this (distinguishing the one from the other) also help us to identify what is so profoundly different between His teachings and what men teach?

3.) Why is the world's knowledge—regardless of how profound it may seem to one another—profoundly inferior to Jesus' knowledge? What does Jesus' superior knowledge necessarily imply concerning our expected *obedience* to Him?

4.) Based upon Jesus' own teaching and personal example, who is *more* human in God's sight: the Christian who follows in His footsteps, or the one who conforms himself to the world? How did you arrive at your answer?

Section Six: Greatness through Servitude

Disciples Are Servants, Not Spectators

There is a saying among Marines: "Every Marine a rifleman." While Marines all have different functions while serving their country—scouts, snipers, administrators, tacticians, computer engineers, cooks, doctors, etc.—nonetheless *every* Marine is trained and expected to pick up his rifle and fight the enemy, when necessary. Similarly, every Christian is a servant. Even though we have different responsibilities and functions within Christ's church—deacons, elders, teachers, preachers, evangelists, mentors, encouragers, spouses, parents, etc.—nonetheless *every* Christian is to be trained and expected to function as a servant. This is what Jesus taught, and He led the way through His own profound example. Unfortunately, the concept of "servitude" has been greatly obscured in contemporary churches, having been replaced by (among other things) *spectatorship*.

Spectatorship directly interferes (and is incompatible) with discipleship. Voyeurism—secretly or anonymously spying on other people—has become an American pastime, as manifested through our fascination with so-called "reality" television shows of every kind. Social media (Facebook, MySpace, etc.) allows people to be involved in someone else's life as a "friend" and yet remain otherwise disconnected from that person. Thus, we can peer into the lives of other people and follow their petty thoughts, mundane activities, and even awkward moments or vulgar "likes" without any commitment or response required on our part. We have become a nation of bystanders and a society of passive and (often) disinterested observers. In a very real sense, we have stopped living our own lives and have chosen instead to live someone *else's* life—a decision that does not improve us in the least. We have made ourselves spectators rather than doers; we live to watch people rather than to be with God.

This cultural phenomenon has deeply affected the modern Christian perspective and our attitude toward personal involvement in the church. What often passes for Christianity today focuses largely on entertainment, sensory stimulation, and emotional gratification rather than expecting *all* members to roll up their sleeves and carry out what may be the dirty work of discipleship. Churchgoers have not only gotten soft and undisciplined because of this, but they have come to expect it as the norm. Now, *every* so-called "Christian" church is expected to offer a stimulating "worship package" to keep people enthralled with that group—otherwise, they will just go somewhere else. It is for this reason that we see many contemporary churches:

- Offer exciting video presentations.
- Offer cutting-edge yet simplistic messages filled with clever illustrations and emotional anecdotes.
- Headed by young, witty, and charismatic speakers (who tend to dress like they are going to a rock concert or football game rather than worshiping the God of heaven).
- Use celebrity speakers, singers, and musicians.
- Use self-promoting rock-and-roll bands thinly disguised as humble, soul-moving, and inspirational musicians—all with expensive, state-of-the-art sound systems and a team of roadies and sound engineers to run them.
- Provide an abundance of creature comforts, including coffee and refreshments, as part of the "worship" service.
- Offer separate church service for children, so parents do not have to be encumbered with the responsibility of having to tend to them, and so they can relax and soak up the spiritual ambiance their church has created for them.

People are willing to overlook the shameless hype, showmanship, and celebrity-ism these performances provide because they *just want to watch* without being overly involved. A nominal commitment is one thing; a full surrender is quite another. People do not necessarily attend these churches because they want to draw near to God—not in the manner in which He requires, at least—but because they just want to be infused and entertained by what someone *else* brings to the table. They are not really interested in conforming to Christ; they want to experience the spiritual "high" created by an artificially-stimulated "worship." They are not really interested in being servants; they are content with being mere spectators.

The word "spectator" is derived from a Latin word meaning "one who watches"; an "observer"; "one who looks on without interfering."[140] Some of the characteristics of being a spectator make it clear why it is so easy to become one:

- ❏ Spectators watch but do not perform. This takes no work, exercise, training, or special skills. You just sit in a chair or stand on your feet and watch.
- ❏ They have no vested interest in *what* they are watching—it just looked interesting, intriguing, or entertaining.
- ❏ They are often interested in what is new, exciting, and dramatic. They are not drawn to routine or mundane activities.
- ❏ They come and go whenever they want. Nothing compels them to stay, once their curiosity is satisfied. It is always up to the performers to keep them interested; if they cannot so perform, the spectator simply walks away.
- ❏ They have limits as to what they will endure. When they get uncomfortable, hungry, thirsty, or it's getting late, or something else "flashier" catches their attention, they leave. They feel entitled to do this without penalty, consequence, or apology. They have made little or no investment so far; therefore, they have no real obligation to stay.
- ❏ They may sympathize with those whom they are watching, but in the end, they completely disconnect themselves. They have entered the scene as strangers, and they leave the scene in the same way—nothing has really changed.

People who think they are Christians but actually act like spectators create a serious problem. Not only do they deceive themselves, they also misrepresent Christ and His church. Christians are defined in the New Testament as *disciples* of the Master and are therefore busy imitating Him (1 John 2:6), not just watching real disciples work. People may regard their presence in a church service or their membership in a congregation as equal to their commitment to the Lord, but these things are not necessarily related. Jesus said, "Whoever wishes to become great among you shall be your servant, and whoever wishes to be first among you shall be your slave" (Matthew 20:26-27). Jesus is not against greatness, but it must be pursued on His terms. Many Christians—real and imagined—are not pursuing greatness because they are content to *watch* rather than *serve*. So then, imagine an entire congregation filled with *spectators* but only a handful of genuine and active *disciples*:

- ❑ These spectating members watch but they do not *do* much of anything. Sitting in a church service requires little or nothing of them—no commitment, no homework, no special training, and no hands-on involvement. They are happy to be counted among the "faithful," even though they have thus far resisted what it takes to *be* faithful.
- ❑ They have no vested *interest* in watching real disciples work—it looks interesting, and they are glad the work's getting done (by someone else), but they do not feel the need to be so committed. When something needs to get done, they look around for someone to respond, but they do not think to volunteer.
- ❑ They are constantly wanting and anticipating something more flashy, stimulating, and dramatic. It is the minister's job to provide "powerful" lessons filled with "moving" illustrations; it is the spectating church member's job to soak it all up and be "stimulated" and "energized." Frankly, they find a skilled and practical exposition of the scriptures to be uninspiring because it lacks entertainment.

- ❏ They come and go whenever they want. They see no problem with coming late or leaving early, since it is only the *truly* committed that need to be on time and stay the course. Thus, when they want to come to the assembly, they come; when something more exciting is going on elsewhere, they go to that instead—or simply stay home and relax. They have no idea of (or appreciation for) all the work it takes to keep a congregation alive and healthy, but they expect that congregation to be there in full working order should they decide to show up.
- ❏ They have limits as to what they will endure. When they get uncomfortable, hungry, or thirsty, or when the service runs "too long," or they simply lose interest, they leave—without penalty, without consequence, and without concern for those who remain behind.
- ❏ They may sympathize with hard-working disciples, but in the end, they are able to disconnect from them and resume their own private lives. They enter as virtual strangers and they leave the same way—nothing has really changed. They are not *interested* in "change."

We must ask: Is this what Christ called us to engage in? When Jesus said, "Come, follow Me," is this what He had in mind? Did He die on the cross, resurrect from the dead, and ascend into heaven just to establish a church largely filled with bystanders, onlookers, and spectators? Did He establish a church that thrives on pushing the envelope on entertainment but failing to address the very real spiritual needs of both Christians and the lost? Nonetheless, many Christians—real and imagined—have convinced themselves that it is *perfectly acceptable* to be a spectator. They reason, in so many words: "I don't have to be 'actively' involved as long as I offer monetary support and cheer from the sidelines." Sadly, spectatorism has become the new "servant" role of 21st century Christianity—which pales in comparison to 1st century Christianity.

Slaves of Righteousness

While you and I cannot stop people from doing what they want to do, we can and must be responsible for doing what Christ called *us* to do. Jesus never said, "Whoever wishes to be great … must become a spectator," but "a servant." The word "servant" (in Matthew 20:26) is from *diakonos*, from which we get our English word "deacon." In this context, it does not refer to an appointed position within the church (as described in 1 Timothy 3:8-13) but is the expected role or function of *every member* of Christ's church. It defines a person who will "advance others' interests even at the sacrifice of their own"[141]—which sounds a lot like what Paul wrote in Philippians 2:3-5. A servant is a waiter (Acts 6:2-3), an attendant (John 2:5), a runner of essential errands (Romans 16:1-2), a minister of God's Word (as in Colossians 1:25), and, by implication, a representative of Christ (1 Corinthians 3:5). The responsibilities of each servant will vary according to ability, appointment, and/or opportunity, but the essential *expectation* remains the same: we are to serve, not spectate.

Even more direct than "servant" is the word *slave*—the most appropriate translation of the Greek word from which "servant" or "bond-servant" is derived. A slave is not a privileged consumer, looking to spend his time, money, and interests wherever he pleases. Rather, he is the *possession* of the one to whom he is enslaved (which is Paul's meaning of the word, both positively and negatively, in Romans 6:16-23). A slave has no civil rights, no personal property or possessions, no position or authority with which to negotiate or seek arbitration, no time off for a vacation, and no personal identity apart from his master. "A servant works for someone; a slave is owned by someone."[142]

While this sounds like a dismal career choice, it exactly describes the noble vocation of all genuine Christians: "You have been *bought with a price*"—namely, the blood of Christ—and therefore "you are not your own"—you do not *belong* to yourself and thus have no *right* to dictate the terms and conditions of your servitude to your Master (1 Corinthians 6:19-20, emphases added). This is strong language, which is why so-called modern Christianity shies away from it. Its constrictive, non-democratic, non-permissive demands are diametrically opposed to the soft, comfort-seeking, hobby-minded, non-committal attitude easily found in so many American churches.

Discipleship is a radical lifestyle, not a passive one. It is purposely disruptive and keeps us in a perpetual state of forward motion. It does not allow for standing still (as spectators do) or fading back into the crowd and slipping away (when things get, you know, a little too "uncomfortable"). We expect to have spectators at sporting events, craft bazaars, public demonstrations, and churches that simply want to make everyone feel unchallenged, unthreatened, and comfortable. We should *not* expect to have spectators claiming to be disciples of the Lord, because discipleship has nothing to do with sitting back and observing without actively participating. It has everything to do with serving the Master.

What do *you* think?

1.) Can believers legitimately practice discipleship without servitude? If so, can you produce relevant, biblical proof to substantiate this? If not, then what does this necessarily imply of *all* disciples?

2.) Why do you suppose some Christians have adopted the *role* of a spectator but want the *status* of a disciple? How has their view of "disciple" become something different to them than what Jesus or Paul actually described?

3.) Most people today have a very negative view toward "slavery," and yet Christians are called to be "slaves of righteousness" (Romans 6:18).

a. Are *all* people slaves to something (spiritually or otherwise)?

b. Do we always get to choose which form of slavery we will participate in (spiritually or otherwise)?

c. Why do people *choose* to be enslaved to Christ? What are the benefits to this decision? What are the consequences?

4.) How is discipleship, as Jesus defined and practiced it, "radical" in comparison to what we often see in churches today?

a. Does "radical" mean "unreasonable," "irresponsible," or "obnoxious"?

b. Was Jesus considered a "radical" in His own day? If so, what made Him so? If not, then why were the Jewish leaders so upset by Him and His teaching?

c. When we practice a contemporary and passive "discipleship," what will be the world's typical attitude toward us? If we practice discipleship like what Jesus defined, how will the world's attitude toward us change (see John 15:18-19)?

5.) Can we use the same words that the Bible uses (like "disciple," "fellowship," "service," "righteousness," "faithful," etc.) yet change the *meanings* of these words to accommodate our present *practice* of these things? Is this acceptable to God, or does this describe a "different gospel" than what was revealed to us (cf. Galatians 1:8-12)?

Section Six: Greatness through Servitude *(continued)*

The Nature of Our Servitude

As we have discussed previously, many Christians (including preachers) have watered down the biblical definition of "discipleship" to accommodate an increasingly comfort-seeking and self-absorbed social perspective. While most Christians may describe themselves as "students of the Bible," their studies are not necessarily leading them to *changed hearts* and *changed lives*, but only an increase of religious information. Thus, these people think that being well-versed in the Bible is equivalent to being a disciple of the Master. This is simply not true. Many atheists know the Bible—some of them better than a number of Christians—and yet they remain atheists. Satan is quite familiar with Scripture, yet he remains a wicked adversary of God's people.

Jesus' words, "Come to Me" (cf. Matthew 11:28-30), does not mean "Come to church," but *draw near to God*. "Take My yoke" does not mean "Use My name in your worship service," but *live in subjection to Me*. "Learn of Me" does not mean "Read the gospels," but *disciple yourself after Me*. Discipleship cannot be reduced to a comfortable, self-styled, and *easy* lifestyle. It is not something you approach conceptually and say, "Hmm, that is an interesting thought!" It is something you must choose for yourself and take personal ownership of.

In the same way, servitude to Christ is not self-defined. Imagine you are literally enslaved to an earthly master, and you say to him, "I will tell you what I will do for you—and you will like it!" That scenario will not go well for you. Likewise, it will not go well for those who use this same approach with Christ. Servitude is not an idea that you contemplate but do not act upon ("As I bask in fellowship with the Lord, I've been thinking about actually *serving* Him someday").

Rather, it is something you choose above every other choice because it is the very best choice of all. Instead of offering incidental acts of *service*, you must choose to be a *servant*. In Acts 6:1-6, for example, seven men were chosen to serve tables, but they had *already* proven themselves to be servants of the Lord. (Sometimes we get this backward: we appoint men to positions of responsibility hoping to motivate them to serve, when in fact they must prove themselves as servants *first*; see 1 Timothy 3:10.) Similarly, the Macedonian Christians gladly supported Paul financially, but only because they "first gave themselves to the Lord" (2 Corinthians 8:1-5). In other words, they did not commit themselves because they gave, but they gave because they were already committed.

"Service" to Christ has to be defined somehow, and it is Scripture that ultimately defines it. There are certain characteristics *of* service that make it "service to God" rather than simply something that you decided to do, even if the two actions are the same.

The gospel of Christ defines service in at least the following ways:

- It must be done "for the sake of righteousness" (1 Peter 3:14).
- It must be done in the name of the Lord (Matthew 19:29, Mark 9:41, Colossians 3:17).
- It must imitate what Jesus Himself did or would have done (John 13:15, 1 John 2:6).
- It must be lawful, profitable, and edifying (1 Corinthians 10:23, 14:26b ["Let all things be done for edification"]).
- It must not be for self-ambition, self-promotion, or to showcase one's own talents (1 Corinthians 10:31-33).
- It must be done with an attitude of humility and "in love" (Ephesians 4:2).

This, admittedly, is a broad definition, but it remains a definition all the same. Not all actions that seem outwardly "good" will fit the above biblical criteria. For example, suppose I am changing my car's flat tire on the side of the road. I am doing this out of necessity, not in service to Christ; it is simply something that needs to get done, not something I have chosen to do as a disciple of the Lord. Now suppose I am changing a flat tire on someone else's car on the side of the road—a person I do not know but who is unable to do this himself (or herself). I could have driven past him and let him deal with problem on his own, but instead I remembered the parable of the good Samaritan (Luke 10:30-37), the so-called "golden rule" (Matthew 7:12), and my responsibility to "do good" to others (Galatians 6:9-10). In other words, I remember that I am to manifest the light of Christ to the world as one of His representatives. So I stop to help, change the tire, and accept nothing for my trouble—because I did it for *Christ* more than anyone else. That is service to God. "Go and do the same" (Luke 10:37).

We sometimes draw on the ministry of the priests under the Law of Moses in order to describe Christians.[143] This provides an excellent analogy to our *own* priestly service to God, because:

- ❑ Priests never worked sitting down (like kings or lords), but always standing up. There were no chairs to sit upon in the original tabernacle courtyard; they literally worked on their feet. In the same way, we are not to be busy finding somewhere to sit down, so to speak, but looking for things to do as servants of God.
- ❑ Priests actively served, ministered, and offered sacrifices. That was their job. Any priest that did not do these things contradicted the very definition of his office. This would be like a fireman who did not fight fires, an electrician who did not work with electricity, or a quarterback who did not actually play football. Likewise, a Christian who does not serve *as* a Christian defies the very definition of his calling—and thus his priesthood to God.
- ❑ Priests were devoted to their ministry; they were consecrated for this very purpose. God told them, "…I am your portion and your inheritance among the sons of Israel" rather than a land inheritance (Numbers 18:20). Nothing was allowed to get in the way of their

ministry to God; when they wore their priestly garments, they were not allowed to engage in anything *except* this ministry. Likewise, Christians have no ties to the earth, so to speak, since God is our "portion," and, inasmuch as we are always "clothed" with Christ (cf. Galatians 3:27), we are always to be engaged in service to Him. We have been sanctified and consecrated for this very purpose.

- ❏ The Old Testament priests were ordained by the law of God, not by other priests. Their priesthood was regarded as a holy calling and a sacred profession—one that was critical to the welfare and success of Israel. Likewise, Christians are called by God with a "holy calling" (2 Timothy 1:9, 1 Peter 1:15); we are not ordained by other Christians, families, churches, synods, seminaries, or even ourselves. Our work and influence is critical to the welfare of our congregations and even the preservation of the world.
- ❏ Priests were (ideally) the closest people to God on earth. They literally interceded between God and His people through prayers, sacrifices, and pronouncements of forgiveness (Leviticus 4:20, 26, 31, 5:10, 13, et al). In like manner, Christ's physical church as a "holy priesthood" (cf. 1 Peter 2:9) is a group of people that most closely identifies with God of all the people on earth.

The point here is this: priests are not spectators, but workers. They are not observers, but active participants. They did not stay interested only when the job was interesting, or show up to the tabernacle only when they felt like it, but had a lifelong commitment to fulfill as ministers to God and His people. A Christian might respond, "Well, I never considered myself to be a 'priest' anyway"—but this misses the point entirely. *All* Christians are priests by definition and are to serve as priests in response to our heavenly calling. In fact, if you are *not* a priest of God, then you cannot be a Christian, and are certainly not a disciple of Christ. Jim McGuiggan writes:

> Service in the name of Christ isn't optional. We either serve or we reject the spirit of the Christ. It isn't that we're called to flawless service; that's beyond us (and the sooner we

acknowledge that the better!). But we are called to choose service in Christ's name. Service isn't an *extra*. It isn't something that "super disciples" get into. It's the fundamental call laid on all those who would claim to be followers of Christ.[144]

Our greatest example of servitude comes from the Lord Jesus Himself. Please read John 13:13-17, as it is a powerful passage and provides critical instruction. Jesus personally and pointedly admits His role as Lord and Teacher to those who follow Him. Given this, His acts of holiness, righteousness, and servitude provide model examples of what He expects of us—if not literally (as in the case of foot-washing), then at least in principle. "I gave you an example to do"—in other words, something to perform, not merely something to watch, talk about, discuss in a Bible class, debate in a lectureship, or include as bullet points in a PowerPoint presentation. It is disheartening to see how "wise" and "knowledgeable" some people portray themselves to be in a Bible class, but these same people may offer little or nothing in the way of actual performance. They talk about servitude, but they have not actually become servants. In contrast, it is encouraging to see other Christians who may not speak up in class so much but are very active in their servitude to others.

Even though we *imitate* Christ, we can never duplicate Him, replace Him, or supersede His role as our Teacher. He will always be our Teacher and therefore we must always serve as His disciples. We will never get to the point where we can say, "Okay, I've learned everything there is to know from You—I can take it from here." In fact, it should be just the opposite: the more we learn about Christ, the more we should realize just how *deeply* and *desperately* we need Him always to lead us.

"If you know these things, you are blessed if you do them" (John 13:17)—once again, this is not merely a thought-provoking idea, but a clarion call to action. No one becomes Christ's disciple by simply observing, spectating, or "knowing these things," but only by actually *implementing* His teaching in real life and thus *doing* what He commanded.

What do *you* think?

1.) What makes discipleship to Christ difficult? (There are several answers.)

2.) Are we allowed to define Christian servitude in whatever manner we choose?

   a. If what we are doing seems like "service" to us, then isn't this good enough for God—especially if it is something at which we are very proficient?

   b. If we are *comfortable* in how we are presently serving God, then isn't the fact that we are *serving* Him what really matters?

   c. Is personal comfort to be an objective of Christ's followers?

3.) Did you gain a better understanding of your servitude to Christ by examining the ministry of the Levitical priests? Why or why not?

4.) Jim McGuiggan was quoted as saying, "Service isn't an extra." Nonetheless, do Christians get it into their minds that service really *is* an above-and-beyond exertion of effort on their part?

   a. Where does this "extra" thinking come from?

   b. What is the fundamental flaw to this kind of thinking that needs to be identified, confronted, and corrected?

5.) Are we "blessed" if we *know* about the things believers are supposed to do, or if we actually *do* them—or both?

Section Six: Greatness through Servitude (*continued*)

Various Kinds of Service

A natural question at this point would be, "How *are* disciples supposed to serve?" There are some areas of service that are defined by Scripture (below); other areas are governed by biblical principles but cannot be imposed universally. This means that no Christian (or group of Christians) is allowed to define this latter area for the rest of the brotherhood of believers. A number of variables also affect the kind of service we perform in the name of Christ: your situation may not be the same as mine; your abilities may be different than mine; your opportunities to serve may be different than mine; and so on. Nonetheless, we would do well to learn what is expected of *all* of us:

- **Unconditional acts of love.** No matter what we do in service to God, it must be an act of love and inspired by love (Galatians 5:13-14). Love does not mean waiting for someone else to make the first move; Christians are to lead by example in this case. Loving service is proactive, not reactive; it seeks opportunity for expression rather than waiting for someone to compel us to show it. God loves *all kinds* of people—of every age, race, skin color, nationality, and ethnicity—and so we are to love these same people. This does not mean that we have to be personal *friends* with all people: to *love* someone is a command of God; to *like* someone is a personal (and thus optional) choice. It also does not mean that, in loving someone, we have to adopt their culture, learn their language, eat their ethnic food, or watch their TV shows (or vice versa). It *does* mean that we are to "do good" to them and act in their best interest (cf. Galatians 6:9-10).
- **Impartial kindness.** We cannot show kindness to someone only because we are trying to win that person's heart—for ourselves or the Lord. Rather, we are to show kindness and goodwill *regardless*

of what the recipient of these acts of service does in response to them. Jesus said that we are to love and pray for our enemies, even if they remain our enemies afterward (Matthew 5:43-47, Luke 6:31-36, and Romans 12:17-21).[145] We cannot only love people who are easy to love, so to speak; we cannot only accept those who are decent and successful. We must also love the unlovely and accept those who are struggling and fearful.[146]

- **Hospitality.** Christians are to be habitually "practicing hospitality" (Romans 12:13). "Hospitality" literally means "(being a) lover of strangers." In the New Testament context, "strangers" are fellow believers with whom we have not had previous acquaintance but share a common faith (3 John 5-8).[147] Showing hospitality in the Modern Age is becoming increasingly rare; our society is becoming increasingly impersonal and disconnected. Personal, face-to-face communication is being reduced to e-mails, social media, texting, video messaging, or form letters—or is disregarded altogether. Yet, discipleship cannot be conducted by e-mail; personal servitude cannot be replaced by digital communication; and hospitality cannot be carried out in a faceless, impersonal, and long-distance manner. Likewise, hospitality cannot become merely a matter of "good intentions" ("I *thought* about writing, calling, or having you over for dinner—I just haven't gotten around to it yet..."). It has to be something that you actually *do*: buying coffee, providing a meal, inviting someone into your home, offering to pay for something (that the other person cannot afford), running an errand (for the housebound), or visiting those in distress (cf. James 1:27). Hospitality forces us to see *ourselves* in the faces of those who are in need (Hebrews 13:3). John sums it up best: "But whoever has the world's goods, and sees his brother in need and closes his heart against him, how does the love of God abide in him? Little children, let us not love with word or with tongue, but in deed and truth" (1 John 3:17-18).
- **Personal sacrifice.** Discipleship to Christ requires personal sacrifice not only to Him but also to all people to whom He Himself would render service. Christians are to suffer loss—of time, money,

possessions, putting our interests first, reciprocation of action, etc.—because of our submissive commitment to the Master. This cannot be a mere acceptance of the *idea* of suffering loss (as in, "I *would* suffer loss, if indeed I was forced to do so"); it has to be a *lifestyle* of active sacrifice (as in, "I *am* suffering loss for my Lord in [an actual situation]"). Dr. Scott Stanley reminds us that "commitment requires action. You can't just sit back and reflect on it or wish you had it."[148] Just as Jesus laid down His life for us, so we must be ready to lay down our lives for our brethren (1 John 3:16-18).[149] Jesus had a servant's heart, and thus readily expressed His service—even to His own hurt—as He had opportunity (and He often *made* such opportunity). Part of our service *to* God is manifested in what we are willing to give up *for* God. In serving Him (and others), we may relinquish our "rights" (constitutional or otherwise), creature comforts, conveniences, privileges, or personal ambitions. We do this not because we are forced to, but because we choose to.

- ❑ **Forgiveness.** One specific form of personal sacrifice is that of forgiveness. How (or whether) we practice forgiveness directly affects our relationship with the Master. As the Lord has forgiven us, so we are to forgive others (Matthew 6:14-15, Colossians 3:12-13, et al).[150] Our forgiveness cannot accomplish what God's forgiveness is able to do—ours is limited to this life, His is not—but we are to demonstrate the same attitude *in* our forgiveness as what He demonstrates to us. This act of service does not make us weak (or weaklings), but actually makes us strong (and "great" in God's sight).

Our goal as servants of the Master is *not* to be flawless (because this is impossible) or only slightly better than the behavior of the world (because this profits nothing by itself). "Jesus doesn't expect followers to be perfect, but he does call them to be authentic."[151] This requires that we strive to "...cleanse ourselves from all defilement of flesh and spirit, perfecting holiness in the fear of God" (2 Corinthians 7:1).

Greatness through Servitude

When we focus on serving God and our fellow man, we stop fixating on self-gratification, personal ambitions, or petty problems. Learning the Bible, supporting our congregation, and adding to our faith are things disciples of the Lord *do*, but these are not final objectives in themselves. We learn, support, and "add" *in order to* love, serve, and represent God to others. No one has actually seen God, but *everyone* ought to see God in us, just as the twelve disciples could "see" the Father in Jesus (cf. John 14:7-10, 1 John 4:11-12).

All the book reading, sermon listening, Bible studying, and churchgoing in the world will not replace your *personal desire for* and your *personal effort toward* making this happen. This does not mean for a moment that you will be saved by your own desire and effort; it means that *without* your desire and effort you cannot be saved. God provides the opportunity, power, and instructions for your salvation, but He does not expect you to do nothing in response. God provides divine grace, you provide human faith. Your faith must be seen, not just experienced emotionally; you must pursue excellence, not just hear about it in a sermon; you must *strive* to enter into salvation, not just wait for it to happen (see Luke 13:22-30 and 1 Peter 1:6-9). One writer summarizes the situation well:

> ...Grace and faith are not opposites. Grace and *earning* are opposites. *Working for* your salvation is a heresy. *Working out* your salvation is basic Bible [cf. Philippians 2:12]. Grace and effort are allies. There are eight New Testament Scriptures that tell us that because God has already given us all things, we therefore must *make every effort* to do what leads to peace and mutual edification; *make every effort* to enter through the narrow door; *make every effort* to keep unity; *make every effort* to be holy; *make every effort* to be found spotless, blameless, and at peace with Him. Hebrews 4:11 is especially piquant [i.e., strong]: *Make every effort* to enter rest. Work to rest.[152]

Christian Thinking

Plainly said, Christians must be drawing near to God *through* service to Him rather than running away to *avoid* this. Those who remain elusive, fade into the background, or always expect someone else to do "the work" do not support their Master's calling, but they actually defy Him. Such people usually spend far more energy ducking their responsibility and coming up with excuses than in actually fulfilling their heavenly calling. On the other hand, those who live as servants of God—not in empty words, but in visible deeds—will be abundantly rewarded, as the record *of* those deeds will follow them into eternity (Revelation 14:13).

Jesus "went about doing good" (Acts 10:38). He did not just stumble into "doing good" by accident; He did not just sit back and watch others "do good"; and He did not just preach about "doing good" but refused to get His hands dirty. Instead, He went about showing *how* to do good and serve others. In order to teach us about discipleship, He had to prove Himself to be the greatest Disciple (to His Father) of all. When we serve as Christ served, people can see Him in us: we are a reflection of the Master. A refusal to serve as He served is a refusal of Christ Himself, since this violates our allegiance to Him. We cannot view these—active service in His name and allegiance to who He is—as two separate issues. We have been created anew "in Christ" for the very purpose of performing "good works" in His name (cf. Ephesians 2:10).

At this point, we should distinguish between being *productive* in our servitude to Christ and just being *busy*. It is common to hear people say, "I have been *so busy* lately," or, "I've been *too busy* to [insert: some Christian responsibility]." People use "busy" as an equivalent to or replacement for "doing something productive." Likewise, Christians may use "busy" as an equivalent to or replacement for *obedience* and *godly servitude*. In other words, because their plate is full, they assume that they must be serving God well or else consider themselves exempt from such service. Yet, just because a Christian is "busy" does not mean he is accomplishing anything of value. Wicked men are also very "busy," but they are busy engaging in worldly activities and their self-serving agendas. Satan himself is very busy, but nothing he does can be considered profitable or beneficial.

We cannot serve a "living God" with *dead works*—i.e., those inspired only of human imagination and good intentions that are of no value to God or the one who performs them. We have not been cleansed by the blood of Christ to fill our schedules with "stuff" that we deem important; rather, we have been cleansed to serve God with things that *He* deems important (Hebrews 9:13-14). Even when we *do* serve Him well, we should not expect to be praised for noteworthy behavior; we are merely doing what we should have done all along (Luke 17:10). Our service must not be offered out of mere obligation, but with "...joy in the Holy Spirit. For he who *in this way* serves Christ is acceptable to God and approved by men" (Romans 14:16-18, emphasis added).

What do *you* think?

1.) Please read Romans 12:9-21. What kind of service does God expect from you? Are there any of these things that you *cannot* do? Please explain.

2.) Despite the general descriptions of service offered in this section, is it my responsibility (as this section's author) or a preacher's responsibility (as one giving a lesson on "servitude") or the elders' responsibility (as overseers of their congregation) to provide detailed *jobs* for every Christian to carry out?

   a. Should Christians wait to be told what to do before they act?

   b. On the other hand, are there expectations, guidelines, and moral obligations that need to be honored in whatever *any* Christian does?

c. Suppose an earnest Christian who is young in the faith asks his elders (for example), "I don't know what I should be doing to fulfill my service to God." Would it be fitting for those elders to provide him with some specific answers? Or, should they say, "It's not our responsibility to tell you what to do—just read the Bible and discover that for yourself"?

3.) Please read Matthew 25:31-46. What criteria does Jesus use to identify men and women as either "sheep" or "goats"? What is conspicuously missing from these criteria (that many Christians might have expected to find)? (There are several answers.)

4.) What kind of service to God can Christians offer as a (an):

a. Husband or wife?
b. Father or mother?
c. Single person?
d. Teenager?
e. Employee?
f. Employer?
g. Citizen of his own country?

5.) Please read Mark 10:45. What do Jesus' words mean to you? What do His words have to do with a Christian attitude? A Christian's service to God?

Section Seven: Living with Gratitude

The Giving of Thanks

"Gratitude" in the New Testament is often translated from *eucharistia*, which means "blessing," "(giving of) thanks," "thankfulness," or "worthy of thanks."[153] Gratitude is a regular, rhythmic, and healthy aspect of the Christian lifestyle. Ingratitude—the lack of thankfulness, which is often accompanied by pride, bitterness, or resentment—is characteristic of the unconverted and those who have fallen away from the truth (2 Timothy 3:2). While ingratitude is a sign of unbelief in God, gratitude expresses a genuine belief in Him as the benevolent Giver of all good gifts to those who love Him. He is not only deserving of our gratitude, He also expects it and is pleased by it. This is a subject never far from the New Testament writers' minds (bracketed words are mine):

- "But thanks be to God, who always leads us in triumph in Christ, and manifests through us the sweet aroma of the knowledge of Him in every place." (2 Corinthians 2:14)
- "For this reason I too ... do not cease giving thanks for you, while making mention of you in my prayers..." (Ephesians 1:15-16)
- "[T]here must be no filthiness and silly talk, or coarse jesting, which are not fitting, but rather giving of thanks." (Ephesians 5:4)
- "[We should be] always giving thanks for all things in the name of our Lord Jesus Christ to God, even the Father..." (Ephesians 5:20)
- "Be anxious for nothing, but in everything by prayer and supplication with thanksgiving let your requests be made known to God." (Philippians 4:6)
- "We give thanks to God, the Father of our Lord Jesus Christ, praying always for you..." (Colossians 1:3)
- "[We pray that you will be] giving thanks to the Father, who has qualified us to share in the inheritance of the saints in Light." (Colossians 1:12)

- "Therefore as you have received Christ Jesus the Lord, so walk in Him, having been firmly rooted and now being built up in Him and established in your faith, just as you were instructed, and overflowing with gratitude." (Colossians 2:6-7)
- "Let the peace of Christ rule in your hearts, to which indeed you were called in one body; and be thankful. Let the word of Christ richly dwell within you... singing with thankfulness in your hearts to God. Whatever you do in word or deed, do all in the name of the Lord Jesus, giving thanks through Him to God the Father." (Colossians 3:15-17)
- "Devote yourselves to prayer, keeping alert in it with an attitude of thanksgiving..." (Colossians 4:2)
- "Rejoice always; pray without ceasing; in everything give thanks; for this is God's will for you in Christ Jesus." (1 Thessalonians 5:16-18)
- "For everything created by God is good, and nothing is to be rejected if it is received with gratitude..." (1 Timothy 4:4)
- "Therefore, since we receive a kingdom which cannot be shaken, let us show gratitude, by which we may offer to God an acceptable service with reverence and awe..." (Hebrews 12:28)
- "Through Him then, let us continually offer up a sacrifice of praise to God, that is, the fruit of lips that give thanks to His name." (Hebrews 13:15)
- "[And angels around the throne said,] 'Amen, blessing and glory and wisdom and thanksgiving and honor and power and might, be to our God forever and ever. Amen.'" (Revelation 7:12)

More than just a conspicuous theme, these passages manifest a *moral expectation* of those who have been redeemed by the blood of Christ. To "give thanks" or "be thankful" is more than just words; it is a heart-felt endeavor to communicate one's deep sense of indebtedness to God for the salvation He has freely offered. This does not mean we are paying off this debt *with* gratitude (or any form of penance). Rather, we acknowledge the enormity and difficulty of the price that Christ paid to remove it, and we appreciate what He has done on our behalf (see Romans 5:6-9). "Thanks be to God" (as in 2 Corinthians 9:15) is an expression that Paul uses several times in his epistles, and always in adoration of the One who has done something excellent and beneficial for His people.

Gratitude also necessarily implies a *satisfaction* with what God has done. Your agreement to God's decision(s) concerning you is expressed through your giving of thanks to Him. (The one who is ungrateful implies a disagreement with God's decisions—he is not satisfied with them and wants a different decision instead.) Being at peace with God's leadership and providential care naturally leads to one's gratitude toward Him. Whatever Paul says about "contentment" (as in Philippians 4:11-13) also has to do with gratitude: Paul is *grateful* to God because he finds his *contentment* in Him. Likewise, the believer is grateful to God when he does not seek gratification for his soul in anyone (or anything) other than God. This means he does not resent, begrudge, or question God's decisions for him regarding: what he has received; what he has been denied; what he has had to endure; or how God has determined to use him in His kingdom. Randy Alcorn writes: "Cultivating thankfulness today will allow us to cling to God's goodness and mercy in our darkest hours. Those hours lie ahead of us—but beyond them stretch unending millennia of inexpressible joy that we will appreciate more deeply because of these fleeting days of darkness."[154]

Gratitude as an Act of Worship

Giving of thanks to God is an act of worship. This means that our gratitude is not merely saying "Thank you" to God, but involves the performance of homage that can be rendered only to a Divine Being and no one (or nothing) else. We say "Thank you" to someone for a good deed or act of kindness, but we do not give *worship* to that person. In fact, we are expressly forbidden to do so (see Acts 10:25-26, Revelation 19:10 and 22:8-9). We might stand up and applaud men in appreciation for their gifts, talents, and performances, but we must prostrate ourselves—in spirit, if not literally—before God because He is our Creator and Source of every earthly and spiritual blessing. Thus, the gratitude we express to God must be special, unique, and superior to all other forms of gratitude shown to anyone else.[155] The *expression* of one's gratitude to Christ is demonstrated by at least three things:

- **Prayer.** Not all prayer can be categorized as "thankfulness," but certainly thankfulness is a necessary *ingredient* in all prayers to God, and some prayers are *devoted* to praise and gratitude (Philippians 4:6, Colossians 4:2, 1 Thessalonians 5:18). The things for which we are thankful can range from our "daily bread" to Christ's atoning sacrifice. A thank-*less* prayer is offensive to God: it does not demonstrate faith in His ability to control and provide, but smacks of self-will, disrespect, and evil motives (James 4:3).
- **Songs.** Many of the Psalms are hymns of praise and gratitude to God for His mercy ("lovingkindness"), providence, blessings, and love. Likewise, the instructions to the churches regarding singing includes "thankfulness" (Ephesians 5:19-20, Colossians 3:16-17, Hebrews 13:15). Our hymns must reflect gratitude and humility; our participation in singing these songs must be sincere and heartfelt. In other words, we cannot just sing *about* gratitude for Christ, but we must use songs to *express* that gratitude.
- **Sacrifices.** Our own sacrifices must never be put on par with Christ's, nor are ours even to be compared with His. However, Christians are to make sacrifices—of time, energy, convenience, comfort, "rights" (i.e., Christian liberties), etc.—for the sake of Christ. Such losses, deprivations, and gifts to others culminate in "a living and holy sacrifice" of one's entire life in service to God (cf. Romans 12:1). Whatever we relinquish in this life as an act of worship to God necessarily implies our gratitude for who He is and what He promises in compensation (Mark 10:29-30).

While certainly prayers, songs, and sacrifices are necessary expressions *of* gratitude to God, they are not enough by themselves. What must accompany them is an attitude that acknowledges the proper "place" of the one who offers them. "Place" has no reference here to geographical proximity, or even to one's season of life, but refers instead to a humble recognition of one's personal and moral inferiority as compared to a perfect and all-powerful Being. Prayers and such, if offered out of mere formality or with an attitude of smug self-righteousness, fail to *thank* God in the manner He so rightly deserves. Instead, they come across as mere gestures of politeness or manners of protocol—all "formal" and "official," but lacking any real depth or sincere meaning. Thus, gratitude is measured not only by visible or audible expressions, but also:

- ❏ **Love.** We have already had much to say on the subject of love. Suffice it to say here that no thanks to God is genuine apart from *love* for Him. Love is the "perfect bond of unity" between the believer and his God as well as fellow believers. If we are bound to God with love, then we will be at peace with Him and thankful for His having called us into the body of Christ (Colossians 3:14-15). "Gratitude," Hendriksen says, "is that which completes the circle whereby blessings that drop down into our hearts and lives return to the Giver in the form of unending, loving, and spontaneous adoration."[156]
- ❏ **Reverence.** Gratitude without reverence is hollow and pointless. While intended as an expression of thanks, the one doing the thanking remains untouched and unmoved by the One who is being praised ("You [God] are near to their lips but far from their mind"—Jeremiah 12:2b). Irreverence and ingratitude go hand-in-hand: if one is present, then so is the other. "Reverence" does not refer only to quietness or propriety, although these can be specific manifestations of reverence. More broadly, reverence describes one's deep and solemn respect for God that will not be compromised by self-interest, petty distractions, or inappropriate "talk" (Ephesians 5:4). Such reverence requires a genuine humility of heart. It also requires actual *demonstration*: all depictions of reverence toward God in Scripture ultimately are expressed through specific and visible actions.[157]

- **Obedience.** Gratitude without obedience is just empty words; it is lip service, nothing more. True gratitude will be expressed through obedience to what the Lord commands to be done. "The one who says, 'I have come to know Him,' and does not keep His commandments, is a liar, and the truth is not in him..." (1 John 2:4). The one who refuses to obey Christ cannot at the same time offer gratitude for who He is and what He has done. On the other hand, obedience that is offered *out* of gratitude is exactly what He desires. "If you love Me, you will keep My commandments" (John 14:15)—likewise, we prove our gratitude for Him through our obedience to His commandments.
- **Forgiveness (of others' sins against us).** Jesus said, "For if you forgive others for their transgressions, your heavenly Father will also forgive you. But if you do not forgive others, then your Father will not forgive your transgressions" (Matthew 6:14-15). This implies a rhetorical question: "How can you be grateful for God's forgiveness of *your* sins if you are unwilling to forgive the sins of others against *you*?" Thus, a lack of forgiveness of others indicates a lack of gratitude, whereas a willingness to forgive is consistent with (but not the entirety of) one's gratitude for God's kindness.

To summarize: gratitude is not merely a feeling, emotion, or spiritual sentiment. It is a *specific Christian attitude* that governs or conditions the heart of the believer. Gratitude (or thankfulness) must be specifically expressed in prayers, songs, and sacrifices to God. It also must be demonstrated in the form of love for Him, reverence for Him, obedience to Him, and forgiveness toward others. In other words, gratitude must never be reduced merely to a *heartfelt experience*, but must be *practically* and *visibly* manifested in the believer's life. The opposite is also true: prayers, songs, sacrifices, love, reverence, obedience, and forgiveness mean nothing without being offered with sincere *gratitude* to God.

What do *you* think?

1.) Does God have a right to expect Christians to be thankful? Why or why not?

2.) Why should gratitude to God be considered a moral expectation of *all* people? What makes this a "moral" action rather than a ritual or ceremonial one?

3.) Please read Luke 17:11-19. All ten lepers were healed of the same disease, yet only one returned to Jesus to give Him thanks. What does this account illustrate regarding our own situation before the Lord?

4.) Why is ingratitude directly linked to discontentment with God (or His decisions)? Can a person genuinely "give thanks" to God while at the same time look elsewhere for his spiritual completion? Please explain.

5.) Imagine a Christian who goes to church, offers prayers of thanks to God, sings songs of deep appreciation for God's blessings, and partakes of the Lord's Supper. Yet, this same person remains guilty of sins for which he has not repented and carries bitterness in his heart toward his wife. Will this man's gratitude be found acceptable to God *anyway*?

6.) It is popular among "contemporary" or "progressive" churches to spend a great deal of effort on youth ministries, music ministries, and "praise teams" in which gratitude to God is claimed to be a major focus. But what is often missing from these groups—and how critical is this omission? Will God accept their praises *anyway*?

Section Seven: Living with Gratitude *(continued)*

Acknowledging the Giver of Gifts

Gratitude is objective in nature. This means there must be a *reason* for it to exist, and that something—a person, governing authority, or God Himself—must be *responsible* for having produced this in a person's heart. When someone says, "I am so thankful *for* [insert: something]," what he necessarily implies is, "I am so thankful *to* [insert: the object of his gratitude] for having provided it or made it possible." Given this, gratitude in a godless and uncreated world makes no sense. Consider the following statements that people will use—people who do not believe in God, do not believe in God's providence, or attribute their "good circumstances" to luck, fate, chance, destiny, happy coincidence, serendipity, nameless gods, the harmony of the universe, "blind forces of nature," etc.:

- ❏ "I am so thankful to be born at this time in history." Thankful to *whom* or *what*? Such a statement lacks any specific point of reference and demands no further responsibility from the one who says it.
- ❏ "I have been so blessed to be able to have children." Blessed by *whom* or *what*? And who decided that this was a "blessing" rather than simply a natural and biological expectation of two people who had sex together?
- ❏ "I have been very lucky to have been spared all sorts of diseases in my life." But what *is* "luck," and how can anyone ascribe thankfulness to it? Who is in *charge* of "luck"—who gives it power to make decisions or choose one thing over another, and who decides what it will (or will not) do?
- ❏ "Fortunately, we are all the product of beneficial mutations caused by blind forces of nature"—so says the evolutionist. But what can be "fortunate" in a godless, amoral, mechanical, and purely material system that is devoid of mercy, love, or *your well-being*?

How can a system that has no plan, purpose, objective, or ideal model of anything be described as "beneficial"? How can a person be *grateful* to nameless, impersonal, and "blind" forces that cannot be identified or even described?

❑ "I believe that everyone should be thankful for what they have, and not begrudge what they do not have." A nice sentiment, to be sure. But thankful to *whom* or *what*—and for *what reason*? If there is no God to bless us, then there is no one to "thank" for any blessings for which we or other people are not completely responsible. Furthermore, if we are only governed by "natural selection" and "survival of the fittest"—and there is no moral reckoning for who we are or what we do—then it is *useless* to be "thankful" to anyone for anything. In such a case, there can be no crime against "begrudging" since nothing really matters anyway.

The point is: in order to be grateful or thankful, there must be a *cause* for whatever it is that we recognize is a blessing, advantage, or improvement to us. (Words like "blessing," "advantage," and "improvement" have zero value and no point of reference in a world without meaning, purpose, or an ultimate objective.) If we recognize the "cause" to be God, then this demands more of us than a mere acknowledgement of His providence. If we claim that there is some other unnamed, undefined, or unproved "god" or power that is responsible for such blessings, then we just *made that up*, and any "gratitude" we express is offered in sheer ignorance (Acts 17:23, 1 Corinthians 8:4-6).

A refusal to recognize God as the *Giver* of all blessings, advantages, etc. is a precursor to futile speculations, a (morally) darkened heart, and utter foolishness (see Romans 1:18-27). Such people "[do] not honor Him as God or give thanks…"—i.e., their refusal to *express gratitude* to the Creator leads to idolatry, moral depravity, sexual deviancy, and spiritual confusion. Such people are not improving over time, but are descending into something entirely base in character. As people abandon God, so God abandons them by "giving them over to" the infantile and animalistic lusts of their hearts (as in 2 Thessalonians 2:10-12). "[James] Denney says that 'to lose God is to lose everything; to lose the connection with him involved in constantly glorifying and giving him thanks, is to sink into an abyss of darkness, intellectual and moral.'"[158]

In contrast, Christians believe that God is the Giver of life (John 6:63), the Source of all earthly blessings (Matthew 5:44-45, Acts 14:14-17, James 1:17, et al), and the Protectorate of those who belong to Him (2 Timothy 2:19). In this perspective, gratitude has a *cause* (God's benevolence); it has a *purpose* (leading us to repentance—Romans 2:4); and it has a final *objective* ("And we know that God causes all things to work together for good..."—Romans 8:28). "For everything created by God is good, and nothing is to be rejected if it is received with gratitude; for it is sanctified by means of the word of God and prayer" (1 Timothy 4:4-5). Instead of offering up "thanks" to a concept, some mystical yet undefined "force," or an unknown god, Christians rationally offer up their thanks to the "living and true God" (cf. 1 Thessalonians 1:9) from whom "every good thing given and every perfect gift" is derived (cf. James 1:17).

What this means is: it is not enough to simply utter the words, "I am so thankful for [insert: the object of our gratitude]." We also need to follow-through with what is expected of grateful people. For example, suppose a prayer offered in a worship service uses one of the following statements:

- ❏ "We're so grateful for this opportunity to assemble in Your name." One with genuine gratitude:
    - Prepares his (or her) heart for the assembly with prayer, contemplation, and penitence.
    - Completes whatever preparation is necessary to make the most of his time and participation in the assembly.
    - Puts more value on *this* opportunity than he does on *other* opportunities that may have been available to him.

- ❏ "We are so grateful for Christ's death." One with genuine gratitude:
  - Prepares his (or her) heart ahead of time with prayer and meditation (see Philippians 4:8) concerning the effect of Christ's death upon his own life.
  - Honestly examines himself as instructed (1 Corinthians 11:28).
  - Makes Christ the sole focus of this memorial (1 Corinthians 11:24-25), rather than going through the motions of partaking simply because it is that time in the service when communion is offered.
  - Treats this memorial with reverence and awe (cf. Hebrews 12:28) and is not busy doing mundane things (e.g., writing notes, checking your e-mail, looking up something on your phone, or playing with a child).
  - Lives according to his professed gratitude for Christ's death by: seeking first His kingdom and His righteousness (cf. Matthew 6:33); sanctifying Him as Lord in his heart (cf. 1 Peter 3:15); holding fast to what is good and abstaining from every form of evil (cf. 1 Thessalonians 5:21-22); and actually doing what Christ says (Luke 6:46).
- ❏ "I'm so grateful for all of Your blessings." One with genuine gratitude:
  - Actually puts God's blessings to work rather than burying them (Luke 19:20) or hoarding them (Luke 12:16-18).
  - Thanks God for *all* blessings he has received—not just the ones that seem favorable, but even trials and deprivations.
  - Translates this into reverence for God, obedience to Christ, and forgiveness of those who have sinned against him.

Gratitude is a *lifestyle*, not an incidental act of piety or a verbal statement of "thanks." Those who are truly grateful to God for who He is and what He has done *live accordingly*. Their lives are molded by their deep appreciation for fellowship with their Creator rather than remembering (amidst the clutter of everyday mundane activities) to offer up a word of thanks every now and then.

Christian Thinking
What do *you* think?

1.) Suppose a Christian prayed to God for something, but the Lord denied his request. Should he be thankful to God for what he did *not* receive? Or should Christians only be thankful for what they *do* receive?

2.) When someone who is not a Christian tells you (for example), "I am so blessed to have such a wonderful life," how might you respond to this? (There is more than one answer.)

3.) Should Christians be teaching others—believers and unbelievers alike—*how* to be grateful people? If not, then who will? If so, then how is this to be done?

4.) How important is it that our expressions of gratitude are accompanied with demonstrations of obedience?

   a. Is gratitude without obedience acceptable to God?

   b. Is obedience without gratitude acceptable to God?

5.) What are the benefits to living a life of genuine thankfulness to God? (There are several answers.)

Section Seven: Living with Gratitude *(continued)*

God Is Good, No Matter What

"What are you thankful for?" In response to this question, most people (including Christians) will itemize things, people, or conditions that they deem *favorable* to their existence: "my good health"; "my wife (or husband)"; "my children"; "my democratic freedom"; "my congregation"; etc. It is unlikely that you will hear statements like the following:

- ❑ "I am thankful to have lost my job."
- ❑ "I have been blessed by God with the loss of one of my arms."
- ❑ "I am grateful that God has withheld from me good health."
- ❑ "I thank God all the time for the heartaches that I have had to face as a parent."
- ❑ "I am most thankful for the many insults I have received at work today for standing up for my faith in God."
- ❑ "It has been a tremendous blessing for me to have *suffered* for doing what is right."

People typically do not express *gratitude* for things that cause them discomfort, disappointment, ridicule, grief, loss, or suffering. If we receive these things because of our own poor decisions or sinful conduct, then there is no cause for thanks to *anyone*. In such cases, we are simply getting what we deserve (Luke 23:39-40, 1 Peter 2:20a, 4:15). No one should ever be thankful for being *punished* for their wicked behavior. But if we receive these things in the course of our *faithful service to God*, then we are able to understand them from an entirely different perspective.

People are often mistaken about what is "good," "right," "profitable," etc. Christians and non-believers alike often view their personal situations from a "This is what *I* think is in my best interest"-

perspective, which assumes they know what is best for them apart from divine omniscience or oversight. For Christians, this spills over into: our prayers; our views on discipleship, suffering, and endurance; and our belief in God's ability to perform. We tend to praise God for His "faithfulness" to us when He answers our prayers the way we *wanted* Him to answer them. But when this does not happen, we may question His decision or fall silent altogether.

Yet, God is faithful to us *even when we must suffer for His name.* (God was faithful to His Son in this same way—even as He went to the cross.) We must be careful not to place conditions on *our* faithfulness to *Him* based upon our private interpretations of His answers to our prayers, or our expectations of what we think "discipleship" should (or should not) require of us. Christians cannot be grateful to God only when it appears that everything is going our way, problems are absent, and "life is good." We must learn to be grateful to God no matter *what* our present situation looks like, as long as we are doing everything in our power to be faithful to God on *His* terms and not our own.

Our spiritual completion is not defined by or dependent upon the presence or absence of favorable circumstances.[159] We are made complete "in Christ" (Colossians 1:28), not in a trouble-free life. We have no right to question God's heavenly providence for us because of trials we endure while protected *by* that providence. And we have no right as heaven-bound people to be happy only in ideal and blissful earthly circumstances. Dr. Crabb concurs: "We must call God good even when we suffer—because He is! And, when things are going well, we must call Him good for reasons that go beyond our immediate blessings. Otherwise... *we will be more troubled by our discomfort than by our unholiness.*"[160] Christians who are more concerned about what is going on *around* them than what is going on *inside* of them have lost their focus and have forgotten about their purification (2 Peter 1:9).

The New Testament is not quiet about keeping a balanced perspective between being "blessed" and struggling to overcome the difficulties of discipleship (all bracketed words are mine):[161]

- "Blessed are those who have been persecuted for the sake of righteousness, for theirs is the kingdom of heaven. Blessed are you when people insult you and persecute you, and falsely say all kinds of evil against you because of Me. Rejoice and be glad, for your reward in heaven is great..." (Matthew 5:10-12)
- "Then Jesus said to His disciples, 'If anyone wishes to come after Me, he must deny himself, and take up his cross and follow Me.'" (Matthew 16:24)
- "They [the Council] took his [Gamaliel's] advice; and after calling the apostles in, they flogged them and ordered them not to speak in the name of Jesus, and then released them. So they went on their way from the presence of the Council, rejoicing that they had been considered worthy to suffer shame for His name." (Acts 5:40-41)
- "The Spirit Himself testifies with our spirit that we are children of God, and if children, heirs also, heirs of God and fellow heirs with Christ, if indeed we suffer with Him so that we may also be glorified with Him." (Romans 8:16-17)
- "Join with me in suffering for the gospel according to the power of God..." "For this reason I also suffer these things, but I am not ashamed; for I know whom I have believed and I am convinced that He is able to guard what I have entrusted to Him until that day." (2 Timothy 1:8, 12)
- "Suffer hardship with me, as a good soldier of Christ Jesus." (2 Timothy 2:3)
- "For this finds favor, if for the sake of conscience toward God a person bears up under sorrows when suffering unjustly." (1 Peter 2:19)
- "But even if you should suffer for the sake of righteousness, you are blessed. And do not fear their intimidation, and do not be troubled..." (1 Peter 3:14)
- "Beloved, do not be surprised at the fiery ordeal among you, which comes upon you for your testing, as though some strange

> thing were happening to you; but to the degree that you share the sufferings of Christ, keep on rejoicing, so that also at the revelation of His glory you may rejoice with exultation. ... [I]f anyone suffers as a Christian, he is not to be ashamed, but is to glorify God in this name." (1 Peter 4:12-16)

From God's perspective—which must also become the Christian's perspective—suffering is a means to an end. This is best expressed in James 1:2-4: *through* suffering, our faith learns to endure, and this endurance brings about a fitting conclusion, by which we are made "perfect and complete, lacking in nothing."[162] Jesus proved His own worthiness and obedience to the Father through the fact that He was willing to suffer for what is right. As a result of that decision, "He became to all those who obey Him the source of eternal salvation" (Hebrews 5:8-9).

Suffering for what is *right* is not to be viewed as punishment from God, but a further expression of our *gratitude* to Him. In choosing to suffer for what is right, we partake of Jesus' own sufferings for what was right—that which was done on our own behalf (1 Peter 2:20-24). As He chose to suffer, so we choose to suffer; as He sought our best interest in His suffering, so we praise what He did for us by imitating His actions—even to our own hurt. "Suffering, then, is the badge of true discipleship. ...The opposite of discipleship is to be ashamed of Christ and His cross and all the offence [sic] which the cross brings in its train."[163]

To clarify: suffering *by itself* does not make anyone righteous. Rather, those who are *made* righteous by God's grace must also be willing to suffer for what *is* right. The very act of suffering *by itself* is not a virtue, and people can suffer for things that are in error or have nothing to do with honoring Christ. Even some who claim to be suffering for the Lord may be purposely drawing attention to their own piety or doing things that the Lord never required of them. We need to be careful, then, not to confuse the mere *concept* of suffering with the biblical

Living with Gratitude

reality of submission to Christ. These are not necessarily the same thing.

To further clarify: we need to separate the things we have to endure because we live in a dynamic and unpredictable world from those things that we *choose* to endure because of our faith. For example, if you suffer the loss of your house because of a tornado that just ripped through your town, that is not "suffering for the Lord," but is a *common* suffering due to a *shared* experience. You may have suffered the exact same loss as did your atheist neighbor or a practicing witch that lives down your street. You did not *choose* to suffer this loss; it just happened to you because you live on a physical planet that sometimes produces tornadoes. Such natural events, taken alone, are neither good nor evil, right nor wrong, blessings nor curses. You are the victim of meteorology and geophysics, not persecution; the tornado did not single you out for what you believe, but simply *happened*, regardless of how (or whether) it affected you personally.

Having said this, it *is* true that how you *deal* with such events—natural calamities, extreme meteorological events, terrorist attacks, train wrecks, plane crashes, etc.—will reveal what kind of person you are. Ideally, your response to such trauma ought to be markedly different than that of unbelievers. Keeping with our hypothetical scenario (above), your atheist neighbor will not pray to God; he will rely solely upon his own resources, government intervention, or the kindness of his neighbors for help. Your Wiccan neighbor down the street also will not turn to God, but will call upon pagan "forces" and "Mother Earth" for answers and assistance. But you—if you truly rely upon God's providence in your life—will turn to God for divine help. You will not blame God for what happened, since you have no reason (or proof) to accuse Him of any wrongdoing. God has made no promise to protect you from everything bad that could happen to you, so you dare not assume otherwise. You will not ask for an explanation ("Why me?") because this is not necessary; faith in God does not require such answers. You will not expect God to replace everything you lost, because this also is not necessary; it may be that God closed that chapter in your life for His own purpose—and in your best interest. You will, however, trust that He *will indeed* take care of you—however, whenever, and through whatever means He determines is best. "The future will fully vindicate God's righteous integrity and the wisdom of his plan."[164]

What do *you* think?

1.) Please review the list at the beginning of this section regarding expressions of gratitude for things that do not appear to be positive. What *blessings* may be discovered in that list, if seen from the perspective of a faithful believer in God?

2.) Please read 2 Corinthians 12:9-10. If "power is perfected in weakness," then should we give thanks to God for difficulties that force us to rely upon His power? Is that what Paul did? Please explain.

3.) Should we be grateful for that which *makes* us suffer for the Lord's sake, or should we be grateful for the opportunity to *experience* suffering in this way? Is this distinction even necessary?

4.) Will those who suffer in this life—especially through no fault of theirs—be automatically escorted into heaven?

   a. If so, then what does obedience to God have to do with salvation in those cases (and who decides who *belongs* in those cases)?

   b. If not, what does this say about the *relationship* between suffering and obedience to God?

5.) Please read Matthew 5:10-12. What *qualifies* our suffering in God's eyes?

   a. What if someone suffers for something he believes in, seems good to him, or sounds noble and virtuous, but does *not* meet these qualifications?

   b. Does God look favorably on those who endure *any* suffering, regardless of their circumstances or the intent of their heart?

Section Seven: Living with Gratitude *(continued)*

Gratitude and Prayer

Gratitude must have a profound effect on a Christian's prayer life. The level of gratitude we have in our hearts affects *how* we pray, what we pray *for*, and even *whether* we pray to God. Our prayers of thanks to God must never be limited to His having fulfilled our wishes and expectations; likewise, we cannot withhold gratitude in every case that He does not perform as we had hoped. Atheists mock Christians—rightly so, at times—when we make a lot of noise for all the *good* things that God does but are rather quiet about the *bad* things that He allows to happen (or does not remove). They call this "counting the hits but not the misses." Sadly, this is often true.

It is not uncommon for an announcement concerning a fellow Christian's deliverance from his (or her) ordeal or his physical recovery to be worded as follows: "Brother Frank was released from the hospital today far ahead of his doctor's expectations! So then, God has answered our prayers." This begs the question: if Frank had *died*, then would this mean that God had *not* answered the many prayers offered on his behalf? Or, if Frank had remained in his sickness, then would this mean that God *failed* to answer such prayers? If He does not answer "yes" to our prayers, do we consider that a so-called "unanswered prayer"? Are we only to praise God for the "yes" answers to our prayers, or should we praise Him for *all* answers?

Hopefully, the responses to these rhetorical questions will be self-evident. If our belief in God can only be affirmed when He conforms to our pre-determined expectations, we open ourselves up to all sorts of reproach and ridicule. In such cases, we are no different than unbelievers who want a "yes" God but not one who is actually allowed to make His own decisions. This is not what we learned from the Bible. The early church did not fall silent in their prayers or give up on God because the apostles were jailed, Stephen was killed, Christians were imprisoned, and Paul suffered more than humanly imaginable. In fact, because of such difficulties, the early Christians learned to depend more and more upon the providence of God and less and less upon the fragility and instability of this world.

Whether God delivers you from your ordeals, heals you of your sicknesses, or even spares your life from death, must be *His* decision. Once He has purchased you with the blood of His Son, you belong to Him (1 Corinthians 6:19-20)—in good times and bad, in sickness and in health, and whether in your freedom or your imprisonment. This means that you are to have voluntarily and cheerfully—yes, even *gratefully*—subjected yourself to His will. It may be God's will for *you* to be healthy and physically intact in order to fulfill some spiritual objective that He has for you. His will for *me* (or someone else) may be just the opposite: He may need me to bear up under sickness, sorrow, or trial in order to fulfill some other spiritual objective. In either case, there is cause for *praise* and *gratitude*—whether we are free from difficulties or find ourselves under the weight of them.[165] It is not necessary that God explain or even reveal what His spiritual objective is for each of us; it is necessary that we believe He *has* such an objective and is completely capable of *fulfilling* it. Not only this, but you must believe He will *reward* those who, through their own faithful endurance, do not forfeit their confidence in Him simply because of what they must face in the meantime (Hebrews 10:35-39, 11:6).

Your belief in God's ability to perform—really, your decision to *let Him be God*—cannot be based upon your pre-scripted plan for your life. In order to draw near to God, you must trust His decisions for you, whether or not they are popular. Once you lay your petition before Him, you give Him the right to decide how that petition will be best answered. You must not place conditions upon your faith in Him, your trust in His judgment, or your confidence in how He answers your prayers. A Christian who prays to God but does not believe in the *power* of prayer or in the *One* to whom he prays is "double-minded" and "unstable in all his ways." As a result, he should not expect to receive *anything* from the Lord, since he manifests not faith in Him, but disbelief (cf. James 1:5-8). You cannot afford to be that person—and you have no *right* to be that person, if indeed God's divine grace has rescued from your own spiritual ruin!

Instead of doubting God, or falling silent when He allegedly "didn't answer" our prayers, we would do well to give thanks to Him for all the good that He has brought into our lives through Christ's redemption of our souls. "And we know that God causes all things to work together for good to those who love God, to those who are called according to His purpose" (Romans 8:28). Paul does *not* say, "God causes all prayers to be answered exactly how we asked them—or He doesn't answer them at all." We must be careful not to customize the gospel of Christ to accommodate our personal beliefs. Instead, we should allow the gospel to *determine* what we believe, and trust that God knows exactly what needs to be done—and the optimum time in which to do it.

What do *you* think?

1.) Take some time to list the blessings you have received from God—physical, personal, spiritual, etc. (You will need a separate page if you address this question in the way in which it is intended.)

   a. Are there only good and positive things on your list or (seemingly) "bad" and negative things as well?

   b. How have *all* of these things affected your view of God, His providence, and how He has used you for His purpose?

2.) It is not uncommon for Christians to say (in times of relative comfort), "Since the world reels from the effects of sin, negative consequences are inevitable." Yet, when some of these same people personally *experience* these negative consequences, they may doubt God's care for them or question His decision to allow them to suffer from these effects.

   a. Can we argue on one hand that pain, suffering, and loss are all a "natural" part of living in this world, yet at the same time assume that we (believers) should be immune to such pain, suffering, and loss?

   b. Have Christians *contributed* to the sinful world's problems in any way? Have you *personally* done this?

3.) Is God morally obligated to spare you from *anything* in this world? (Consider both 2 Corinthians 12:9-10 and 1 Corinthians 10:13 in your answer.)

Section Eight: Change Is a Gift

The Typical View toward "Change"

Generally-speaking, people do not like to change. The older we get, or the longer we have been conditioned by our routine life, the more resistant we become to anything that alters or disrupts the way to which we have become accustomed. Once we settle upon a course of action that seems easy, comfortable, and relatively free from conflict, we tend to remain there. This is human nature, which also parallels laws of nature. Isaac Newton's first Law of Motion, for example, states that an object remains at rest or continues to move at a constant velocity unless acted upon by an external force. Thus, nothing *different* happens until something *new* comes along to cause that difference. This "law" is just as true in human nature as it is in physics.

Christian thinking is not modeled after human nature, but is to be influenced by divine nature. The Christian life is not characterized by static thinking and comfortable routines, but by regular and necessary *change*. Any Scripture that talks about conversion (Matthew 18:1-3), transformation (Romans 12:1-2), growth (2 Peter 3:18), maturity (Hebrews 6:1), "reaching forward" (Philippians 3:13), or letting go (Luke 9:57-62), necessarily involves *change*. Yet, while this instruction is accurate and biblical, it is not always well received among the very ones who claim to embrace it—Christians themselves. "Most of us make it through life by coping, not changing," says Dr. Crabb. "We rearrange what we do, but somehow the core problems involving who we really are remain only partially addressed…"[166] In other words, we may make temporary, unimportant, or cosmetic changes now and then, but *how we see God, ourselves, and the world* and our habitual *patterns of thinking* remain virtually untouched. The Christian who decides to attend church services regularly (instead of his habit of "forsaking" the assembly—cf. Hebrews 10:25) has made a good decision, to be sure, but *by itself* it is superficial. It is his *heart* that needs to change, not just his attendance record; it is his *desire to serve Christ* that must motivate him, not guilt or peer pressure (as is so often the case). If he sanctified Christ as *Lord* in his heart (cf. 1 Peter 3:15), then the decision to assemble with God's people for all the right reasons would naturally follow. But his decision to assemble more often does not mean that anything else has changed.[167]

Much of our resistance of God's instruction *for* change is due to one or more simple facts that few Christians will openly admit:

- We have a negative view of "change" in the first place. ("I feel like God just doesn't want me to be happy" or "God keeps sabotaging my world so that I cannot do what brings me joy.")
- We do not (always) believe that we really *have* to change. ("Is this really necessary?")
- We do not (always) trust God to see us *through* the change. ("Will He really hold up His end of the agreement if I go through with this?")
- We are not always certain what actually *needs* to change.
- We are not always certain what we need to *become*. We may know what God says on paper (so to speak), but we may not know what this looks like in real life.
- **The conservative-minded person tends to regard change fearfully (as though fraught with potential dangers); the liberal-minded person tends to regard change unrealistically (either unconcerned with or oblivious to dangers).**
- Change requires learning, studying, and renewing the mind.
- Change is often hard because it requires time, energy, and sacrifice. Whatever time and energy is put toward making forward-moving changes must be diverted from things we *like* to do. This may create an underlying resentment toward the One who requests the change in the first place.
- Change is often inconvenient, disruptive, and uncomfortable. It often interferes with our plans, and especially those plans that follow the path of least resistance.

- ❏ Change is often viewed in terms of what is given *up* rather than what is *gained*.
- ❏ Change is often viewed as sorrowful rather than joyful.
- ❏ Change is often viewed as constrictive rather than liberating.
- ❏ We think we *did* "change" once—when we became Christians. Now we want just to settle into a quiet and comfortable routine (like going to church).

Those who do not *grow* also do not *change*—and vice versa. There are many Christians who have remained the same over periods of time: they have not learned anything new about the Bible; their prayers are predictable and mechanical; their level of service has remained unimproved over the years, despite all sorts of opportunities to do more. In contrast, there are other Christians who have grown immensely since their conversion, and they show no signs of slowing down: their study of the Bible has deepened; their prayers reflect an increasingly mature perspective; they have developed a lifestyle of service toward others. What is the difference between these two groups of people? It is not *what* they believe, since both read the same gospel. It is not *genetics*, since one's chemical makeup can neither increase nor prohibit his spiritual development. It is not *external circumstances*, since these things cannot prevent a person from drawing near to God.

Ultimately, the difference between these two groups of people comes down to *a desire to change* (or, the *lack* of this desire). Those in the first group refuse to let go of where they are—the reason does not matter, since the result is the same. They claim to want to draw near to God, but they are unwilling actually to move forward. Those in the second group have made change itself a regular and necessary part of their relationship with God. These people also claim to want to draw near to God, but they are doing something about it. They know that being "transformed by the renewing of your mind" (Romans 12:2) is necessary for this. They have chosen to immerse themselves in what God has revealed in His Word, coupled with a healthy prayer life that craves both help and intimacy with the Lord. They have not simply gone on to deeper and more difficult subjects in their studies, but whatever they have learned over time has become clearer and more meaningful than ever. C. S. Lewis writes: "As you advance to more real and more complicated levels, you do not leave behind you the things you found on simpler levels: you still have them, but combined in new ways—in ways you could not imagine if you knew only the simpler levels."[168]

Letting go of the things that hold us back—useless knowledge, erroneous ideas, empty traditions, long-held (but irrelevant) "positions," etc.—is critical to moving forward "in Christ." No one can truly live as a "new creature" in Christ (cf. 2 Corinthians 5:17) unless or until he forsakes the *old* creature that resisted God in the first place. Drawing *near* to God (cf. James 4:8) necessarily requires drawing *away* from those things that stand opposed to Him. Such "things" may be actual material things (such as money or possessions), personal beliefs, people (or relationships), or religious convictions (that contradict the Word of God).

Christ tells us to "…seek first His [God's] kingdom and His righteousness…" (Matthew 6:33), but this will not happen until we make everything else in our lives *second* to this noble pursuit. "Every effort to change must involve at its core a shift in direction away from dependence upon one's own resources for life to dependence upon God."[169] With the same power that you *chose* unprofitable beliefs or *chose* to include stumbling blocks in the first place, so you have the power to *un*-choose them. The one thing you *cannot* "un-choose," however, is your commitment to Christ: there is no turning back on this (without serious consequences; see 2 Peter 2:20-22). You can walk away from your commitment to God, but you cannot be "un-baptized."

Christian Thinking
What do *you* think?

1.) What is an appropriate and biblical response to each of the above bulleted statements (in bold type)?

2.) Are *spiritual growth* and the *need to change* always mutually dependent? Are all people who grow spiritually also *changed* in order to bring about that growth? Are all people who *change* also growing spiritually?

3.) Jesus said, "If anyone wishes to come after Me, he must deny himself, and take up his cross and follow Me" (Matthew 16:24). Is it possible to deny oneself by choosing to remain as he is? Can a person follow Christ by standing still?

Section Eight: Change Is a Gift *(continued)*

Gratitude versus Resistance

The following two things are impossible to reconcile: *gratitude to Christ* for His "ministry of reconciliation" (cf. 2 Corinthians 5:18-21) and *resistance to change* to accommodate His will. Gratitude for God's gift of salvation through Christ's sacrifice is incompatible with any resistance or reluctance to be "conformed to the image of His Son" (cf. Romans 8:29). Simply put: those who refuse to conform to Christ forfeit the promise of an eternal inheritance. Such promises are contingent upon faithful service, and faithful service is manifested through gradual but consistent conformity to Christ.

However, what if we saw change—the opportunity *for* it as well as its positive result—as a *gift* rather than a burden? Or, as an *invitation to glory* rather than something fearful to be avoided? This would turn the entire concept on its head. Through the continual conversion of our heart and transformation of our life, God provides a gift for improvement that we never could have had on our own (James 1:17). Left to ourselves, we are all doomed sinners with absolutely no recourse and no hope. But Christ provides a way *out* of that situation—not only through the process of becoming a Christian, but in drawing ever nearer to God thereafter. "In Him," "with Him," and "through Him" are regular expressions in the New Testament that indicate our full dependency upon Christ who—if we *let* Him—takes us from where we are presently to a far greater height (see Ephesians 3:14-21, for example).

In order for you to see change as a *gift*, however, certain conditions must be met:

- ❑ *You must believe that you are in need of this gift.* God is the dispenser of gifts, and especially of salvation and spiritual transformation. He wants you to open your mind and your heart to receive these gifts. Those who refuse God's gifts imply that they have already "arrived" or do not think His gifts will work. Either of these implications contradicts a claim of *gratitude* toward God.

- *You must believe that God can actually improve your situation.* If you doubt God's ability to perform, then you cannot possibly be grateful for His salvation, since salvation is absolutely dependent upon His performance for your benefit. It is impossible to *praise* Him and *doubt* Him all at once. This also defeats your prayer life: on the one hand, you pray for Him to intervene in your life; on the other hand, you do not believe that He will help you. If you believe that God cannot transform you in the here-and-now, then why should you believe that He will save your soul in the hereafter?

- *You must allow God to work His gift in you on His terms, for His purpose, and on His schedule.* Paul said, "For I am confident of this very thing, that He who began a good work in you will perfect it until the day of Christ Jesus" (Philippians 1:6)—but this is conditioned upon your submission to His will. Real gratitude will not only thank God for His gifts, but will also not stand in the way of God implementing them as He sees fit. And, not everything that happens to us looks like a "gift" up front. Let God decide what is best for you.

- *You must look past the difficulties and apprehension of "change" itself and focus instead upon the end result.* Christ did not fixate upon His crucifixion but upon the fruits of His obedience to God. The "joy" set before Him was not the cross itself but the great *victories* accomplished through it (Hebrews 12:1-3). When we submit to God's will—and *our spiritual transformation* is a major part of that will—then "…though our outer man is decaying, yet our inner man is being renewed day by day. For momentary, light affliction is producing for us an eternal weight of glory far beyond all comparison…" (2 Corinthians 4:16-17). As those who have been "bought with a price" (cf. 1 Corinthians 6:20), we must not keep our spiritual vision looking downward upon this life but upward where Christ is, seated at the right hand of God (Colossians 3:1-3).

❑ *You must be willing to get rid of anything that compromises or hinders God's gift of change.* Jesus warned us to gouge out or cut off (from our lives) whatever causes us to stumble (Matthew 5:29-30): *ingratitude*, *irreverence*, and *resistance of God's will* are stumbling blocks that must be entirely removed, not merely suppressed for a time. If your heart is filled with *any* attitude that prevents the reception and effectiveness of God's gifts, then you are not listening to Jesus but are standing in defiance of Him. Yet, if you allow Christ to determine what belongs in your heart as well as what must be removed from it, then you show great respect for His authority and prove to be His disciple.

For the true believer, change *is* a gift—a *priceless* one. God does not give us things to deceive us, trip us up, make us fail, or watch us suffer. He gives us gifts to make us better people, draw us closer to Him, and prepare us for our eternal life in heaven with Him (see 2 Corinthians 5:5-9). If He says (through His Word), "I need you to *get rid of your present attitude* and adopt *this new one* instead," then—as difficult as it may seem—we need to listen and comply. If we wish to have an attitude of thanksgiving, then we must follow what He prescribes for this.

Of course, not *all* change is automatically good, positive, or acceptable to God. Change merely for the sake of "change" means nothing by itself. A mere disruption or reordering of the status quo is not equivalent to making the kind of spiritual, moral, or lifestyle changes that God requires of us (or you). Just because a person does something *different* than what he did before does not mean that anything has actually improved.[170] For example, just because a person no longer shoplifts or steals from his neighbor does not mean that he now is walking "in the light." Or, just because a person stops swearing or lying does not mean that he proclaims the gospel of Christ. Thus, it is important to understand the proper *context* and *objective* for which all changes must be made. Any change that leads you away from God or is at the expense of your spiritual well-being must be rejected at once. Instead, you should accept only those changes that lead you closer to God and improve your spiritual well-being. God must be the One who decides these things for you and not you alone. Your responsibility is to listen, learn, and obey.

Many of the Jewish leaders of Jesus' day were not interested in improving their spiritual well-being. They believed that, because they were Jews, they were already close to God and therefore would be automatically ushered into the kingdom of Messiah (whenever He finally did reveal Himself). Yet, Jesus told them repeatedly that their conclusions about themselves were as wrong as their conclusions concerning Him. "You are those who justify yourselves in the sight of men," He told them, "but God knows your hearts; for that which is highly esteemed among men is detestable in the sight of God" (Luke 16:15). Their love of money (Luke 16:14), craving for human praise (Matthew 6:1-2), and contempt for the common people (Luke 18:9, John 7:43-49) blinded them to the reality of their situation. They refused to change their minds because they thought they had already arrived and knew more about God than could anyone else. They refused to change their ways because they would not do anything that threatened their status quo.

The Pharisees saw change as a detriment to their way of life; Jesus told them that *without* change, they would lose everything in the end (John 8:24). The Pharisees clung tenaciously to the only way of life that they had ever known; Jesus told them that that "way" was coming to an end and would be replaced by something far superior ("a more excellent ministry" and "a better covenant"—Hebrews 8:6). The Pharisees viewed anything that challenged their status quo as a threat; Jesus told them that their status quo was already condemned and therefore not worth preserving. The Pharisees let the things of this world cloud their judgment, corrupt their hearts, and interfere with their relationship with God. Jesus warned us that our righteousness must exceed the assumed "righteousness" of those men (Matthew 5:20). This means that we must not succumb to the same close-mindedness and errors of reasoning to which they succumbed.[171] Unfortunately, succumbing to their errors of reasoning is extremely easy to do, which means that we must continually strive to resist this.

Old Thinking, New Thinking

Years ago, I visited the United States Mint in Denver, Colorado, when the mint was in the process of stamping out dimes. Now suppose the supervisor of that facility told his crew, "We need to start stamping out quarters for the rest of the day," and everyone wrote down on their work orders, "Start stamping quarters." Hours later, the supervisor comes around and inspects what is happening, but sees that the workers are still stamping out dimes! "What is going on?" he demands. "I told you to stamp quarters, not dimes!" An employee steps up and says, "We heard what you said, and in our hearts, we *are* stamping quarters." And yet, no one changed the dies for the new coins, so it continued to stamp out what it had been producing previously. In other words, everyone *thought* about making a real change, but *nothing really changed*. The two things—what they *were* making and what they were *supposed* to make—were incompatible.

This is hardly a novel observation. In Luke 5:36-39, Jesus offered a parable about the incompatibility of *old* thinking with *new* thinking. It remains a powerful and relevant illustration for all Christians today.[172] New wine cannot go into old wineskins; new cloth cannot be sewed onto old cloth; and a "new creature" cannot be conformed to the old creature. You cannot hope to achieve an *improved* and *superior* life by basing everything you do on *faulty* and *inferior* thinking. You cannot learn anything *new* about Christ, the gospel, or salvation until the receptacle for those new things—your attitude toward Him—has surrendered to His will.

Christian Thinking

The Pharisees ran all the new thinking about Messiah, the kingdom of God, and their new life *in* that kingdom through their old mental machinery. Not surprisingly, their mind kept spitting out the same thing they had always concluded. They could not embrace what Jesus was saying because their attitude was not calibrated to *receive* that information in the way it was intended to be understood. Likewise, if you keep running new ideas, new ways of understanding the scriptures, or new ways of sharing the gospel through the same old thinking machinery that you have clung to for years (or decades), you should not be surprised when nothing *changes* in your spiritual life. You are trying to pour new wine into old wineskins, or put a new patch of cloth on an old garment. The two things are in fact incompatible.

"That's just the way that I am" or "That's just how I think" is the death-knell to any hope a person has of being *transformed* as a child of God. No person will ever hope to improve if he (or she) is already convinced that he *cannot* change or does not *need* to change. Paul taught, "Be transformed by the *renewing of your mind*" (Romans 12:2, emphasis added). This renewal is supposed to be an *ongoing* occurrence, not a one-time thing ("I changed years ago, so why should I change again?"). If your *mind* is not renewed, then whatever new information you feed through it will be of little or no benefit to you. You need to change the *way* you think, not just *what* you think about. Spiritual transformation does not come about merely by reading the Bible over and over. Such transformation occurs only when:

- ❑ You let God decide what kind of *mind* (or *heart*) you are to have in the first place. Your mind is to be conformed to the image of Christ, not your self-chosen image or the image of the world (Romans 8:29, 12:1-2). This means that you are not blindly stepping out into darkness in pursuit of an ideal that you cannot possibly know, but quite the opposite: you have your ideal in the person of Christ (1 John 2:6). This means you are not doing what is right in your own eyes (as Israel foolishly did; see Judges 21:25),

Change Is a Gift

but the revealed Word of God provides all the direction you need—"everything pertaining to life and godliness" (2 Peter 1:3).

- ❑ You seek God's approval rather than accepting anyone else's conclusions concerning you. One major reason why people resist change is because they already have a high estimation of themselves, either because of self-approval or the approval of others. Another major reason is that of self-loathing: people are so filled with guilt, shame, and discouragement that they do not think they can ever rise above these things. Yet, as we have seen (in Luke 16:15), God does not put any value on the approval of men—whether it is positive or negative. Those who approve of themselves by their own standard "are without understanding," since they lack truth and objectivity (2 Corinthians 10:12). Those who condemn themselves and shut off all opportunity for change also lack these same things. However, if God approves of you, then you are approved indeed—and it will not matter who else condemns you (Romans 8:33-34, 2 Corinthians 10:18).

- ❑ You surrender your inferior manner of *thinking* in light of superior *information*. Put another way: when the Word of God teaches you something that challenges what you presently believe, you yield to this new belief rather than try to reconcile it to your old, comfortable paradigm. You cannot stuff all the words of Christ, for example, into your own well-worn *image* of who He is and what His mission was all about. You cannot become a "new creature"—in any sense of the idea—without first putting to death the *old* life and laying aside the *old* manners of thinking (Romans 8:12-13, 2 Corinthians 5:17, Colossians 3:9-10).

- ❑ You look forward to and actively seek enlightenment from God. This enlightenment may come through His Word, wisdom gained from fellow believers, your own life experiences, or whatever way God chooses to give it to you. Regardless, the point here is that you are not only *open* to such spiritual illumination but are *eagerly seeking* it. This is not a passive search ("If I happen to learn anything from this Bible study, so be it"), but an active one ("I'm earnestly learning whatever I can so as to improve my walk with the Lord").

- ❏ You are actively putting into practice that which God has taught you. Having knowledge by itself does not make you wise; wisdom is gained through practice and experience. God is not seeking your Bible-quoting proficiency, for example, but your obedience to His will. "Potential" means nothing until it is actually *tapped*; otherwise, it will simply be the sad epitaph on the tombstone of one's life. (The servant who hid his one talent in the ground had all sorts of potential, but nothing to show for it; see Matthew 25:14-30.) Jesus was not interested in people merely *hearing* His words but also *acting* upon them (Matthew 7:24-27). It is good that you are gaining knowledge through studies like the one you are reading right now; but what will you do with all of this accumulated information?

- ❏ You persistently *ask God* for spiritual enlightenment. Through prayer, you ask God for help, seek His will as revealed in His Word, and knock on whatever doors are closed. (You must also give Him the right either to *leave* those doors locked or to open them up to you. Do not take a fireman's axe to any door that God refuses to open for you. Instead, find another door to knock upon.) God promises to "…[strengthen you] with power through His Spirit in the inner man…" and to do "…far more abundantly beyond all that we ask or think, according to the power that works within us…" (Ephesians 3:14-20). Do not regard these words lightly, but realize the tremendous help that is being offered to you—if you would just *ask* for it and believe it to be true. "If any of you lacks wisdom, let him ask of God, who gives to all generously and without reproach, and it will be given to him" (James 1:5). God will not miraculously make you wise, but because He is an all-wise and all-powerful Being, He can do things for you that you cannot do for yourself. If this were not true, then prayer is a pointless and hopeless ritual, nothing more. Unbelief is a sin, not a "phase" that Christians go through now and then. Your belief may need to be strengthened, but it must be *real* and *functional* if you wish to have fellowship with God. "Prayer," John Bunyan once wrote, "will make a man cease from sin, or sin will entice a man to cease from prayer."[173]

The point is: you must be more concerned with drawing near to God than trying to preserve your old way of thinking or living. It was your old way, after all, that led you into a life of sin; it is the continual "renewing of your mind" that will lead you to God. The opportunity for improvement is a gift from God, not a burden to shoulder and complain about. You are expected to show gratitude for God's gifts, not roll your eyes and say, "Will He never be satisfied?"

Christian Thinking
What do *you* think?

1.) Why should we consider change to be a *gift*—something that is given to us without having earned it—when in fact *we* are the ones making the decision to change?

2.) It is not uncommon to hear Christians say (in so many words), "I really want to change who I am," yet they seem perpetually to remain the same person, react in the same way, and do the same things.

   a. What is standing in the way of this person's transformation?

   b. Is personal desire alone sufficient to bring about necessary spiritual changes, especially when that desire appears very strong and sincere?

   c. Can necessary spiritual changes be made apart from personal desire?

3.) Why will "old thinking" never accommodate "newness of life"? Why will "newness of life" never accommodate "old thinking"?

4.) Since spiritual transformation involves "the renewing of your mind" (Romans 12:2), will your soul automatically be transformed if you just change your mind?

   a. If this is the case, what need is there for the blood of Christ? The guidance of the Holy Spirit? The instruction of God's Word?

   b. If this is *not* the case, then what exactly is *your* responsibility as a believer in the process of your spiritual transformation? What is *God's* responsibility in this?

Section Eight: Change Is a Gift *(continued)*

Repentance Is All about Change

The subject of repentance is an unpopular one. As with subjects like submission to God's will and the authority of Scripture, it forces people to take personal responsibility for their soul. Specifically, it grates against the modern perception of divine grace, which is allegedly supposed to cover *sin*, not transform the *sinner*. People will say (in so many words), "God will forgive me *when* I sin," rather than, "God's grace leads me into a life of righteousness, and thus *away* from sin." It is not that people think they are sinless, but that the responsibility for *dealing* with sin is God's, not their own. This translates to the following mentality: "Sin is God's problem, not mine. He is going to have to accept all my weaknesses and faults as part of the package; this is who I am and who I will always be. The burden is upon God to restore me when I stumble, because He loves me so."

As a result of this kind of thinking, what passes for modern "Christianity" often portrays God as being soft on sin—well, most sin, anyway—because He is so eager to embrace sinners. God's love is allegedly more powerful than His law; His love automatically nullifies His judgment against sinners. Thus, "Love wins!"—in the end, God will save *all* people because His love cannot allow a *single person* to be lost.[174] Because of this mentality, "sin" is minimalized to the point of irrelevance; sin no longer is viewed as *sinful*. It is no wonder, then, that modern theologians will tell you that it is *wrong* for you to judge others as being sinful—people whose choices, behaviors, and "orientations" are different than your own.[175] It is not *those* people who need to be reformed, but *you*—even though *they* are the ones who are in sin!

Given the premise of such an innovative gospel, it is clear why so many people—including many who call themselves Christians—are indifferent toward sin and stress love and forgiveness at the expense of obedience to God and personal responsibility. Yet, the New Testament opposes all such worldly and self-centered thinking. God requires people to turn *away* from sin, not just feel bad about it, attempt to minimize it, or pretend that it does not exist. It is not those who *identify* sin that are the problem, but those who actually *commit the act of sin* that need to change.

The opportunity for this change (repentance) is itself a gift of God: even though we have sinned, we have recourse, not immediate and irreversible condemnation. This opportunity is limited to this life, since there will be no chance (or purpose) for repentance in the life to come. By then, you will either have already repented of your sins and trusted in the grace of God, or you will have rejected these things and will thus suffer the consequences of your foolish decision—without reprieve or recourse. Randy Alcorn rightly notes: "God's grace is greater than my sin. But my ability to measure the greatness of His grace depends upon my willingness...to recognize the greatness of my sin."[176]

As we have maintained throughout this entire study, the gospel of Christ is not a gospel of accommodation but *conversion* and *transformation*. It does not cater to your or my feelings, but requires a transformation of the heart in order to conform to the Master (Christ). Jesus said of those who seek the kingdom of God, "Blessed are those who mourn, for they shall be comforted" (Matthew 5:4). Mourn over *what*? we should ask. In essence, we who are touched by God's love and Christ's sacrificial death are brought to our knees over all the harm, injury, and grief our sins have caused God. We look with horror—not a smug, "It's God's problem, not mine," but *personal humiliation*—at what we have done to the Giver of Life. It is true that sin *became* God's problem, in the sense that He could not have fellowship with us until it was taken care of. It is also true that He alone could take care of this problem through the blood of His Son. But having done this, our sin is now *our* problem, and it thus has to be dealt with by us in an appropriate and morally-responsible manner.[177] "Or do you think lightly of the riches of His kindness and tolerance and patience, not knowing that the kindness of God leads you to repentance?" Paul asks rhetorically (Romans 2:4). God is not merely a dispenser of kindness, tolerance, and patience (as though we deserve these things or He is obliged to give them unconditionally). Instead, He showers these upon us in order to get our attention, so that we will come to our senses and *repent*—while there is still time to do so.

The Components of Repentance

Repentance and conversion are closely related, but not interchangeable. Conversion involves a point of turning toward a new destination (having turned away from the old one). Repentance, however, involves turning to a previously-known destination which the one doing the repenting had once abandoned. When we are converted to Christ, this is a new experience for us—we never previously had salvation in Him. When we repent of our sins, however, we are returning to what we had left behind: truth, righteousness, and innocence. Both conversion and repentance are *objective* in nature, since there is a specific and definable thing to which we *are* turning, rather than just "turning." But repentance is *re*-turning—not just change leading in some other direction than before, but one that takes us back to where we once were.[178]

We are not born in sin; we are born innocent human beings. We are not born with the guilt of Adam, as Calvinism and the Doctrine of Original Sin teach; we are born without guilt and therefore without condemnation.[179] It is sin—not someone else's, but our *own*—that makes us guilty before God. At some point in our life, we cease to be innocent and become guilty; thus, we abandon what we know to be right and we choose to do wrong instead. The entire concept of "reconciliation" to God through Christ necessitates restoring (in a new *way*) something that had once existed: fellowship with God. It is impossible to be "reconciled" to Someone with whom we never had a relationship. Likewise, it is impossible to return (in repentance) to something we never left. Thus: we are converted to a new gospel; we repent of sin and thus return to practice the righteousness we had once forsaken; and we are reconciled to God with whom we once had a relationship, but had abandoned it for something else.[180] Conversion is about living in Christ; repentance is about living in righteousness; and reconciliation is about living in fellowship with God. *All* of these are required for salvation; *none* of these are possible apart from the blood of Christ.

In order for one to repent, at least three things are required:

- ❑ A person must know where he (or she) is presently—and that it is the *wrong* place to be. He acknowledges that he is indeed in sin, stands condemned by God, and cannot rescue himself from his perilous predicament. A person who refuses to acknowledge that he is a sinner not only insinuates that God is a liar (see 1 John 1:8, 10), but he will not change for the better. No one can return to where he *was* (as an innocent person) who refuses to confess that he is *guilty* of having abandoned what was right in the first place.
- ❑ He must know where he has to return to—and how to get there. If someone is going to live righteously before God (as he once did prior to his having sinned against God), he has to know specifically what is required of him, and what must be relinquished in order to accommodate this life.
- ❑ He has to actually *do* whatever is required of him to return to that ideal state of being from which he had originally strayed. No one can accomplish repentance by just talking about it; good intentions cannot replace obedient actions. Mark Buchanan rightly observes: "Confession in itself is only a beginning. It is lifeless if it's not followed by renouncing sin—without repentance. ... Confession is ground clearing, getting the garbage and debris out of the way so that we can build something there. It has zero value unless you actually get on with building."[181]

In effect, the one who repents says, "I know where I should be; I know I have strayed from where I should be; and I know (now) what

I must do to get back to where I should be." This process begins as an act of human will—a personal decision—but ultimately must be demonstrated through visible actions consistent with that decision. Consider what Jesus said to the church in Sardis: "So remember what you have received and heard; and keep it, and repent" (Revelation 3:3a). These Christians had strayed from their original commitment to Christ; they needed to turn their hearts back to the One from whom they had strayed. So it is with us: if we say, "I repent!" then we must demonstrate a genuine *change of attitude* accompanied by appropriate *change of action*. Again, this is not "change" just for the sake of change, but the *right* change in the *right* direction—one that is in compliance with the Word of God, not regardless of it. No one can stumble into repentance (or any other positive change) any more than he can accidentally stumble into heaven.

Good Fruit Comes from Good Trees

Repentance is your responsibility toward the sins that you have committed. You cannot repent for someone else, and you have no need to repent if indeed you have done nothing wrong. If you *have* sinned, however, then you need to take care of that. Having made a change for the worse (by having chosen sin over righteousness), you now need to make a change for the better (by choosing to return to the righteousness that you once had). This means: you need to stop the sinful thinking and/or behavior, and you have to also begin pursuing righteous thinking and/or behavior instead. You cannot just *stop* the one thing without also *pursuing* the other.

In Titus 2:11-12, Paul says that the gospel of grace has instructed us to "deny ungodliness and worldly desires" *and at the same time* "live sensibly, righteously and godly in the present age." The reason for this is clear: we cannot have fellowship with God and fellowship with sin at the same time. Jesus gave Himself as a sacrifice *not* so that we can continue in sin, but to redeem us from our sinful lives *and* to "purify for Himself a people for His own possession, zealous for good deeds" (Titus 2:14b; see also Romans 6:1-3). So then, any sins that you commit against God must be addressed without delay so that your fellowship with Him can continue. A failure to repent indicates a serious breach of covenant, and puts you in a perilous situation (see Hebrews 10:26-31).

In order to put on the "new self," you have to lay aside the *old* self, which was corrupted with sins that you chose to commit (see Ephesians 4:22-24). This "new self" is nothing like the old self; it "has been created in righteousness and holiness of the truth"—not a monstrous conception of wicked lust in the human heart (as described in James 1:14-15). You must cease any participation in satanic deeds of darkness and walk instead in the light of God's truth. Paul then provides a detailed "not that, but this" formula (Ephesians 4:25 – 5:21): not lying, but speaking truth; not brooding in anger, but resolving your differences; not stealing, but being industrious and earning your own wages; etc. C. S. Lewis writes:

> [In dealing with sin,] you must ask for God's help. Even when you have done so, it may seem to you for a long time that no help, or less help than you need, is given. Never mind. After each failure, ask forgiveness, pick yourself up, and try again. Very often what God helps us towards is not the virtue itself but just this power of always trying again. ... This process trains us in habits of the soul which are more important [than the immediate mastery of the virtue of faith itself]. It cures our illusions about ourselves and teaches us to depend on God. We learn, on the one hand, that we cannot trust ourselves even in our best moments, and, on the other, that we need not despair even in our worst, for our failures are forgiven [or, forgivable]. The only fatal thing is to sit down content with anything less than perfection.[182]

It is not enough, however, to put a stop to sinful *action*; you need also to remove yourself from the sinful *environment* in which it is found.

For example, suppose you stop getting drunk every Friday night, but you still sit with your old drinking buddies in the bar. They order beer and whiskey, you order a Coke. Technically, you have stopped the sinful *behavior*, yet you are still immersed in the sinful *environment*. This is not to say that it is a sin merely to sit in a bar, although it may be extremely unwise for you to do so under any circumstance. Rather, you are allowing yourself to be surrounded with what tempts you rather than fleeing from it; you are giving the devil all kinds of opportunity rather than drawing near to God so that he (the devil) will flee from *you* (Ephesians 4:27, James 4:7-8).[183]

Repentance is not simply responding to what you "got caught" doing; it is the process of putting an end to a specific sin altogether. For example, if you catch me in a lie and I say, "I repent of lying to you," but I continue lying to someone else, I have responded to a specific situation but have not really addressed the sin itself. The "sorrow of the world" is all about the regret and disappointment we feel when we get "caught" in our sin. "Godly sorrow," however, seeks to remove the sin altogether and at the same time pursue a godly course of action from that point forward (cf. 2 Corinthians 7:10).

Many people try to pluck "bad fruit" from their lives without addressing how it got there in the first place.[184] Jesus said, "So every good tree bears good fruit, but the bad tree bears bad fruit. A good tree cannot produce bad fruit, nor can a bad tree produce good fruit" (Matthew 7:17-18). If we simply pluck bad fruit (habits, behavior, etc.) but do not change the tree from which it came (our heart), then it will be just a matter of time before bad fruit reappears. In order to produce good fruit, we have to change our heart—the mechanism (so to speak) that is producing the bad fruit. A "good tree" represents a pure heart and a godly character. A pure heart will produce the "fruit of the Spirit"; a corrupted heart will manifest "deeds of the flesh" (cf. Galatians 5:19-23).[185] A godly character is not something you acquire during the course of a sermon, a week, or even a year. "Character is a slowly forming thing. You can no more force character on someone than you can force a tree to produce fruit when it isn't ready to do so. The person has to choose, again and again, to develop the moral muscles and skills which will shape and form the fully flourishing character."[186] Change the tree, and the right kind of fruit will follow. Otherwise, whatever "change" is taking place is superficial and temporary.[187]

The opportunity to change for the better is a gift from God, and repentance is all about change. Many people want the gift of grace, but not necessarily the gift of change (or, spiritual transformation). They want to be with Christ in heaven, but they are not necessarily willing to conform to Christ while they remain here on earth. Nonetheless, there are numerous passages in the New Testament that necessitate holiness (1 Peter 1:16), purity (Titus 2:7), spiritual cleansing (2 Corinthians 7:1), and abstaining from every form of evil while *at the same time* clinging to what is good (1 Thessalonians 5:21-22).

> When holiness becomes more attractive than sin, when knowing God seems more important than finding self, when no cost seems too great to pay for the privilege of intimacy with Christ, then we will find the strength to resist sin meaningfully—not perfectly, but meaningfully. Then our obedience will be sincere rather than manipulative. Then our efforts to live properly will seem more like *going after* something good than *giving up* something good.[188]

"God has not called us for the purpose of impurity, but in sanctification"—and those who reject this message (or ignore it) are rejecting God Himself (1 Thessalonians 4:7-8). On the other hand, "… everyone who has this hope [of Christ's return] fixed on Him purifies himself, just as He is pure" (1 John 3:3, bracketed words are mine). This must be *your* focus as well—to purify yourself for His service. He is worth all the sacrifices you will make to do this, and when you are with Him in glory, you will be very thankful that you made those sacrifices.

What do *you* think?

1.) In Paul's "not that, but this" formula (Ephesians 4:17 – 5:21), please indicate what actions must replace whatever is inconsistent with the "new self" in Christ.

   a. Not lying (falsehood) but *this* instead:
   b. Not sustained anger, but *this* instead:
   c. Not stealing or "mooching" off of others, but *this* instead:
   d. Not speaking unwholesome words, but *this* instead:
   e. Not grieving the Holy Spirit, but *this* instead:
   f. Not filled with bitterness, wrath, anger, etc., but *this* instead:
   g. Not imitating the world, but *this* instead:
   h. Not practicing immorality or covetousness, but *this* instead:
   i. Not engaging in filthy talk, but *this* instead:
   j. Not walking in darkness, but *this* instead:
   k. Not living in ignorance of God's will, but *this* instead:
   l. Not participating in deeds of darkness, but *this* instead:
   m. Not walking as "unwise men," but *this* instead:
   n. Not being foolish, but *this* instead:
   o. Not being filled with intoxicants, but *this* instead:

2.) Please read Hebrews 6:7-8. Can this describe a Christian who readily receives God's generous gifts, but whose heart is not being transformed in the process? Please explain.

3.) Imagine a person—Christian or not—who claims to be very "spiritual" and "close" to God, yet has sin in his (or her) life for which he refuses to take responsibility. What would you say to him? What does *God* say of him?

   a. Can a person repent of his sins without taking personal responsibility for them?

   b. Can a person take personal responsibility for his sins without repenting of them?

4.) What are the differences between "godly sorrow" and worldly sorrow, remorse, or regret (see 2 Corinthians 7:10)?

5.) How important is moral purity in a Christian's life? Who or what *defines* moral purity for the Christian?

Summary Thoughts

Christian Thinking Leads to Christian Living

All the Christian thinking in the world *will not replace* a single demonstration of godly love toward someone. Likewise, logic and reason are necessary in order to understand Scripture—to argue for it as well as refute teachings contrary to it (cf. Titus 1:9)—but no one can be saved through logic and reason alone. These are not equal to and cannot take the place of love, desire for God, devotion to God, or gratitude. They cannot transform the heart or forgive the soul; no one can "draw near to God" simply because he exercises them. "God decided *in His wisdom* that human wisdom would not be the path to knowing God."[189]

Christian thinking is supposed to prepare the mind for action, not merely fill our heads with concepts, words, and verses to remember. "We must come to the Bible with the purpose of self-exposure consciously in mind" rather than trying only to learn more "stuff."[190] For example, we are instructed (1 Peter 1:13-16):

> Therefore, prepare your minds for action, keep sober in spirit, fix your hope completely on the grace to be brought to you at the revelation of Jesus Christ. As obedient children, do not be conformed to the former lusts which were yours in your ignorance, but like the Holy One who called you, be holy yourselves also in all your behavior; because it is written, "You shall be holy, for I am holy."

Now let's break down what Peter said into individual instructions or actions:

- ❏ **"Prepare your minds for action"**: In the context of our present study, this means, "Have an attitude to do the work of a disciple."

Preparation is one of the necessary keys to a successful ministry. But preparedness *by itself* does not equal productivity. Many Christians have been "preparing" for years (or decades!) to fully engage in the work of a disciple, but are still sitting on pews, attending classes, or listening to sermons. While there is a time for such things, these will not actually accomplish God's work that He has planned for you (see Ephesians 2:10, Philippians 2:12-16). "Having potential" to do something is not the same as actually *doing something*. No one ever carried out the will of God with mere "good potential." "It's the thought that counts" may sound appealing to the modern ear, but no one ever carried out God's will with a mere thought.

❑ **"Keep sober in spirit":** This means to *be serious* and *attentive* in what you are doing. One with the right attitude will not allow himself to be distracted, undisciplined, or divided in his heart (see Luke 9:57-62 and 2 Timothy 2:3-7). He will not only be prepared to serve, but he will look vigilantly for opportunities to serve. On the other hand, when Christians are inebriated (drunk) with worldly lusts and intoxicated (poisoned) with ungodly behavior, they are unable to stand before God.

❑ **"Fix your hope completely on the grace...":** Grace is not just something God provides for us; it must also be that which motivates us to act. Because we *are* forgiven people means that we are supposed to *live* like those who have been given a new life with new hope. Thus, we are to be lights to the world, salt of the earth, and instructors to those who are still in the "snare of the devil" (cf. 2 Timothy 2:24-26). In other words, there is a correct response to our salvation, and we must know what this is.

❑ **"As obedient children...":** We cannot just be "children of God" in a nominal or technical sense, but we must also be *obedient* to our Father. According to the Law of Moses, a "worthless son" was to be executed (Deuteronomy 21:18-21) since he failed to honor his parents *and* obey God. God does not think lightly about obedience, and neither should we. Our having been made "sons of God" gives us privileged access to the Father as well as the promise of a spiritual inheritance. We are to take this seriously and do our best to conduct ourselves appropriately.

- **"Do not be conformed to the former lusts..."**: This sounds similar to what Paul wrote: "And do not be conformed to this world, but be transformed by the renewing of your mind..." (Romans 12:2). Our attitude—and its resulting behavior—must not be conformed to the reasoning, selfishness, or conclusions of the godless world, but must instead be based upon God's Word and Christ's personal example.

- **"Be holy yourselves also in all your behavior"**: Notice that *preparing your mind for action* is expected to lead to *holy behavior*. Both the *mental preparation* and the *resulting action* are defined and expounded upon throughout the New Testament. Everything we need to know has been provided; whatever is personally lacking in us is supplied or "equipped" by God Himself (Ephesians 3:14-21, Hebrews 13:20-21). No one will enter into God's glory who has not striven to "...cleanse [himself] from all defilement of flesh and spirit, perfecting holiness in the fear of God" (2 Corinthians 7:1). Yet, those who "seek first His kingdom and His righteousness" (Matthew 6:33) will most certainly find favor with God and be useful to His service. Paul sums up both sides of the situation in Titus 1:15-16: "To the pure, all things are pure; but to those who are defiled and unbelieving, nothing is pure, but both their mind and their conscience are defiled. They profess to know God, but by their deeds they deny Him, being detestable and disobedient and worthless for any good deed."

Conforming to Christ means far more than just accepting what He said as the truth or adopting His practices. We are to conform to the Person of *Christ Himself*, not just go through the mechanics of "conformity." The more we are like Him, the more we will embrace His attitude and manifest His behavior. "[Conformity to the image of Christ] is what we mean when we speak of Christ dwelling in our hearts. His life on earth is not finished yet, for He continues to live in the lives of His followers. Indeed it is wrong to speak of the Christian life: we should speak rather of Christ living in us."[191]

Thinking of Heaven

It seems entirely appropriate to leave you with some of the very best inspiration for Christian thinking that exists: being with God in His heaven. There is an old hymn called "Heaven Will Be Worth It All," and the message of the gospel is that this is certainly true. Once we are standing in the presence of God Himself—His Son at His right hand, His Holy Spirit enveloping us in a fellowship that human words cannot even describe—it will have been worth whatever it took, whatever it cost, or whatever had to be endured to be there in that never-ending moment. When that final trumpet is sounded and the world is brought to an end, we who have trusted in the Savior and striven to enter the narrow gate will not be disappointed by the glory into which we will then be ushered. Standing in the presence of the Lord will be the culmination of our entire existence, having brought together Christ's cross, our faith, and God's promises.

Heaven is something that Christians should always keep close to the surface of their thoughts. While non-Christians may dream of exotic vacations, material wealth, and indulgent lifestyles, Christians dwell upon their future life with God. We long for our "Sabbath rest" that awaits us (Hebrews 4:9) in which we will no longer have to face the difficulties, disappointments, and separations of this present life. We are to be "...looking for and hastening the coming of the day of God..." when He signals the end of the physical world and closes the final chapter of the history of mankind (2 Peter 3:11-12). We are to "...keep seeking the things above, where Christ is, seated at the right hand of God," because when Christ is finally revealed to us, "...then you also will be revealed with Him in glory" (Colossians 3:1-4).

Those who are in heaven will experience happiness unlike anything imagined here on earth. In heaven, there will be no sorrow, no

Summary Thoughts

mourning, no death, and no pain. The sorrows, disappointments, and separations of this life do not exist in God's world. These "first things" will have passed away; "Behold, I am making all things new" (Revelation 21:3-5). Heaven will be a beautiful "place," but it really is not a "place" at all, but a *fellowship* in Christ in the literal *presence* of the Father. The church in glory is described as a beautiful and perfect bride, and simultaneously as a glorious city. It is the home of the river of life, the tree of life, and the crystal sea (Revelation 4:6, 22:1-2). It will be filled with angels—beings of authority, responsibility, and power that defy earthly comprehension—yet these immortals will be our servants as well as our friends. Best of all, we will bask in the "unapproachable light" of the Father (cf. 1 Timothy 6:16) while enjoying the intimate company of the Son of God.

Heaven will not only be defined by the *absence* of sorrow, pain, and death, but also the *overflowing abundance* of joy, health, and life. This will not be momentary or temporary joy like what we might experience here on earth, which is separated by much longer periods of fear, struggles, and disappointment. Instead, we will be immersed in an incomprehensible joy that will never end and that no one can take away from us. Christ will crown those who have "overcome" with a crown of victory—not because we earned it on our own, but because *He* earned it and chooses to share His victory celebration with us (Revelation 2:10). This "crown of life" will be awarded to those who have loved Christ for having appeared in the flesh, His sacrifice on the cross, and His resurrection from the dead (Philippians 3:8-11, 2 Timothy 4:8, and James 1:12). Here, "...we walk by faith, not by sight..." (2 Corinthians 5:7); there, we will no longer need faith, for we will see the Lord as He is in His glory, and we will be glorified with Him.

Those who are in heaven will no longer have to coexist with evil people. For now, we strive to be lights of the world and salt of the earth, even though many do not listen to us, hate our message, or do not care altogether. In heaven, we will no longer have to endure the scoffing, snickering, and contempt of godless men and women—people who think that Christians are idiots but view themselves as wise, intellectual, and reasonable. In heaven, God will vindicate us for the good decision we made to choose Him over all other things.

In heaven, there will be no places where we cannot go at night (because there *is* no night). There will be no dark alleys, bad neighborhoods, crime-infested ghettos, or seedy businesses; there will be no thieves, muggers, liars, cheaters, murderers, or immoral people. Everything that is dark, ugly, frightening, and satanic will be removed forever from us; God's heaven will have none of these things. Those "outside" of the city of God will face darkness, torment, weeping, and gnashing of teeth—not because they were not invited into the city, but because they refused the invitation. Inside the city will be a beautiful society of blood-washed saints who will enjoy forever God's glory and protection. This will be the most wonderful existence that anyone could ever imagine: "They will hunger no longer, nor thirst anymore; nor will the sun beat down on them, nor any heat; for the Lamb in the center of the throne will be their shepherd, and will guide them to springs of the water of life; and God will wipe every tear from their eyes" (Revelation 7:16-17). No one will ever have to work *for* a living, because everyone will already be fully *alive*—more "alive" than was ever possible on earth!

Once we are in heaven, the first will be last, the servant will be crowned as king, the humble will be exalted, and the martyr will become the immortal priest. We will join "...a great multitude, which no one could count, from every nation and tribes and peoples and tongues, standing before the throne and before the Lamb..." (Revelation 7:9)—a pristine, perfect, and permanent society, an ideal family where no one will ever have to say goodbye and everyone is completely happy and thoroughly enjoys one another's fellowship.

Once we are in heaven, we will dwell in the presence of God the Father and Christ the Son. We will enjoy full communion with the Holy Spirit of God. We will be surrounded by beauty, music, singing, and breathtaking scenes.

Once we are in heaven, we will be filled with peace, warmth, love, and endless joy. We will live in eternal security knowing that God will take care of every need, fulfill every longing, and keep us with Him *forever*. Once we are in heaven, "... we shall always be with the Lord. Therefore comfort one another with these words" (1 Thessalonians 4:17-18). This is what Christians should think about often. These are the best thoughts that exist, period.

Endnotes

[1] "The Word" is the Bible, and especially the New Testament (or, gospel of Christ), since this provides the basis for all Christian doctrine, the method for becoming a Christian, and the pattern of Christian worship and behavior. I firmly and unapologetically maintain throughout this book that the Word is most certainly the revealed communication of the Holy Spirit of God, given to us through divine inspiration and preserved for us through divine providence. As such, it is the ultimate and very best authority concerning God's divine nature, the spiritual realm, the nature of sin, the disposition of the human soul, God's plan of redemption through Jesus Christ, Christ's church, and "all the truth" necessary for salvation (John 16:13).

[2] Christians are also referred to in the New Testament as "saints" (1 Corinthians 1:2), "disciples" (Acts 14:21-22), "brethren" (2 Peter 1:10), "believers" (1 Peter 1:21), "sons of God" (Galatians 3:26-27), "children of light" (Ephesians 5:7-10), and other biblical designations.

[3] I have a previously-published book on the subject of baptism: *Being Born of God: The Role and Significance of Baptism in Becoming a Christian* (Summitville, IN: Spiritbuilding Publishing, 2014), available through www.spiritbuilding.com. I strongly recommend that you explore this most important topic even if you *have* been baptized.

[4] If you are interested in receiving this material, it is not available through a publisher at this time. You can request this material by contacting me directly: chad@booksbychad.com.

[5] Dr. Joe Dispenza, *Breaking the Habit of Being Yourself* (New York: Hay House, Inc., 2012), 243.

[6] W. W. Davies, "Attitude," *International Standard Bible Encyclopedia*, or *ISBE* [electronic edition] (database © 2004 WORDsearch Corp.). This is also true with regard to ancient art: the "attitude" of the one being painted or sculpted referred to the sitting or standing posture of that person.

Endnotes

⁷ Dr. Henry Cloud and Dr. John Townsend, *12 "Christian" Beliefs That Can Drive You Crazy* (Grand Rapids: Zondervan, 1994), 168; emphases are theirs.

⁸ I credit Darrell Beane, a fellow preacher who is also a counselor, for his help with some of these ideas.

⁹ James MacDonald, *Lord, Change My Attitude* (Chicago: Moody Publishers, 2008), 36.

¹⁰ The word "attitude" or "mind" in all these verses is from *phroneo* (Strong's #G5426) which has a variety of English translations: "to exercise the mind"; "to have or entertain an opinion"; "to be mentally disposed [toward something]"; "to concern oneself [with something]"; etc. It is the context of Scripture which best identifies which meaning is the most appropriate (*Strong's Talking Greek and Hebrew Dictionary* [electronic edition], database © 2012 WORDsearch Corp.).

¹¹ Adapted from *Merriam-Webster's 11th Collegiate Dictionary* [electronic edition] (© 2003 by Merriam-Webster, Inc., ver. 3.0). "Knowledge strictly is the apprehension by the mind of some fact or truth in accordance with its real nature; in a personal relation the intellectual act is necessarily conjoined with the element of affection and will (choice, love, favor, or, conversely, repugnance, dislike, etc.). Knowledge is distinguished from 'opinion' by its greater certainty" (James Orr, "Know; Knowledge," *ISBE* [electronic edition]).

¹² John Piper, *Think: The Life of the Mind and the Love of God* (Wheaton, IL: Crossway Books, 2010), 128.

¹³ Dispenza, *Breaking the Habit*, 168.

¹⁴ On the heels of 19th century "romanticism" and 20th century "existentialism," author N. T. Wright calls the 21st century mindset the "emotivist movement" in which "all moral discourse could be reduced in any case to statements of likes and dislikes. 'Murder is wrong' simply means 'I don't like murder.' 'Giving to charity is good' means 'I like people giving to charity.' From this point of view, following

moral rules and following your own inclinations both boil down to pretty much the same thing. Often today people who are discussing moral choices will say that this person 'prefers' Option A or that that person 'applauds' Option B, as though moral choices were a matter of personal preference or taste. Sometimes they speak of 'moral attitudes,' as though what a particular person believed about the rights and wrongs of certain actions were simply an 'attitude,' an innate prejudice which they hadn't bothered to think through" (*After You Believe: Why Christian Character Matters* [New York: HarperCollins Publishers, 2010], 50).

[15] Dispenza, *Breaking the Habit*, 90.

[16] Certainly a person can feel a sense of "joy" while entertaining wicked thoughts, such as a man viewing pornography or a jilted woman plotting her revenge. Nonetheless, we are defining "good" (as in "good thoughts") by a godly standard, not a human or worldly standard.

[17] The *reason* why you may forego wicked behavior may not be necessarily for the right reason, however. If you simply want to maintain your good feeling, that is one thing—and it is not a very noble one in itself. You must not choose to make righteous decisions only because of how it makes you feel. Yet, if you want to *please* God and therefore resist those temptations that offend Him, this is quite another thing—and it is a noble decision, since this is the right thing to do.

[18] On this point, Dr. Larry Crabb rightly adds: "We simply must get rid of the idea that the obedient Christian is supposed to feel good all the time" (*Inside Out* [Colorado Springs, CO: Navpress, 1988], 94).

[19] I am including Simon Ponsonby's personal account here, because I feel it is valuable in understanding this point: "When I gave my life to Jesus as Lord and Savior, it did seem I was a totally new creation. The old had gone, and the new had come. It was clear there were many things that I had died to—I stopped smoking instantly, and no foul language came out of my mouth again. Immediately, certain passions

and desires were gone. It seemed as if I was truly dead to sin and alive to God. But other sins did not die. They were still there to haunt me and taunt me. Lusts of the flesh, attitudes of the heart, programs of the mind ... the old sinful Simon, though crucified with Christ, seemed to be present with me. And seeds of sins I didn't even exhibit as a young adult have flowered in my flesh. There is clearly a need to die daily, as Paul said. Daily, weekly, monthly, the Lord reveals latent sins of the flesh that must be brought to the cross and crucified. Yes, I am a new creation, but in my old body with my old mind. The difference is that now, by union with Christ, the power and pattern of sin in body and mind can be overcome" (*The Pursuit of the Holy* [Colorado Springs, CO: David C. Cook, 2010], 183-184).

[20] The Jewish scribes were experts at "[searching] the Scriptures" (cf. John 5:39), but they focused on the meticulous details of a given passage rather than internalize its spiritual meaning and practical application. "The scribes, whose task it was to copy and teach the sacred text, subjected it to the closest scrutiny. They weighed its every syllable. They went so far as to count up the number of words, even the letters, of each book. They performed all this labor, not only for the sake of accurate copying but because they imagined that eternal life consisted in such accurate knowledge. Like some Bible commentators and readers, they became so engrossed in the *words* that they lost sight of the *truth* the words were intended to express" (Daniel H. King, Sr., *At the Feet of the Master: Studies in the Background, Content and Methods of Jesus' Teaching* [Bowling Green, KY: Guardian of Truth Foundation, 1997], 161).

[21] I invite you to study this point further in my book, *The Holy Spirit of God: A Biblical Perspective* (Spiritbuilding Publishing, 2010); go to www.spiritbuilding.com.

[22] Dr. Larry Crabb, *Finding God* (Grand Rapids: Zondervan, 1993), 168.

[23] Ibid., 172; emphases are his.

24 Ponsonby, *The Pursuit of the Holy* (203), with regard to Romans 8:6-9.

25 For a more detailed study on the Epistle to the Philippians, I recommend my *Philippians, Colossians, and Philemon Study Workbook*; go to www.spiritbuilding.com.

26 Personally, I am unable to declare *every* seeming "bad" experience as being devoid of anything good, especially in what those experiences might produce. Certainly something that causes us harm, pain, loss, unwanted separation, etc., seems "bad" enough at the time it happens, but in the long run, it *may* be the best thing that ever happened to us. The "in the long run" perspective must be viewed through the lens of divine providence, however, not just flowery optimism. Christ's crucifixion, for example, most certainly was a *bad experience* for Him while He endured it, but we see how much good came from it "in the long run."

27 Norman Vincent Peale, *The Power of Positive Thinking* (Pawling, NY: Foundation for Christian Living, 1978), 204; bracketed word is mine.

28 Dave Miller, *Piloting the Strait: A Guidebook for Assessing Change in Churches of Christ* (Pulaski, TN: Sain Publications, 1996), 73-74.

29 We are talking here, in essence, of "boundaries." There are two kinds of boundaries for an individual: moral and personal. God is the One who sets the moral boundaries for *every living person* in telling us distinctly what is right and what is wrong. Put another way: He defines for us what is consistent with His holy nature (good) and what is inconsistent with this (evil). God's moral boundaries are universal in nature, that is, they apply to *all* people; they are also changeless, inasmuch as God's own holy nature is immutable. Personal boundaries ideally ought to be based upon God's Word, but are chosen individually regardless. Such boundaries live and die with each person; they cannot be imposed universally and can be changed for various reasons. If you wish to learn about moral boundaries, then the Bible is the first and fi-

nal authority on the matter. If you wish to learn about personal boundaries, then the Bible also is a foremost authority, but others can help provide its practical, everyday application. I found Dr. Henry Cloud and Dr. John Townsend's book *Boundaries* (Grand Rapids: Zondervan, 1992) to be helpful for this, especially in determining when it is best to say "yes" or "no" to whatever it is that is being asked of you.

[30] "God's righteousness is not just his *faithfulness*, it is his *saving faithfulness*" (Jim McGuiggan, *The Dragon Slayer: Reflections on the Saving of the World* [self-published, no date], 137). His is a faithfulness that *does* something for us—that *saves* us.

[31] Dietrich Bonhoeffer, *The Cost of Discipleship* (New York: Simon & Schuster, 1959), 216.

[32] Crabb, *Inside Out*, 132.

[33] Adapted from Crabb, *Inside Out*, 197.

[34] John Piper, as quoted in MacDonald, *Lord, Change My Attitude*, 208; bracketed words are mine.

[35] Greg Sidders, *The Invitation* (Grand Rapids: Revell Books, 2011), 46; see Luke 9:57-62, 14:26.

[36] Dr. Scott Stanley, *The Power of Commitment* (San Francisco: Jossey-Bass, 2005), 55.

[37] Bonhoeffer, *The Cost of Discipleship*, 110; emphases are his.

[38] This "being at peace with God within" must be that which God defines (objectively), not us (subjectively). Just because a person *feels* he is "at peace" does not mean he really is, as far as God is concerned. Peace with God demands unity with Him, which demands obedience to His Word. One who is living in disobedience to God cannot be at peace with Him no matter *how* "peaceful" or "content" he feels within. As Paul said, "If anyone thinks he is something when he is nothing, he deceives himself" (Galatians 6:3).

[39] Robert Jamieson, Andrew Fausset, and David Brown, *New Commentary on the Whole Bible: New Testament Volume* [electronic

edition] (© 1990 Tyndale House Publishers; database © 2012 WORDsearch Corp.), on Philippians 2:5. See also my exposition on this passage (Philippians 2:5-11) in my *Philippians, Colossians, and Philemon Study Workbook*; go to www.spiritbuilding.com.

[40] Jim McGuiggan, *The God of the Towel* (Lubbock, TX: Montex Publications, 1984), 99-100; bracketed words are mine.

[41] Jared Wilson, *Your Jesus Is Too Safe* (Grand Rapids: Kregel Publications, 2009), 94-95.

[42] "If our heart is frozen in grief [over loss, or sins committed], we are unable to feel feelings God has designed for us. Many people experience frozen grief as depression. Grief (sadness and anger) that has not been expressed and resolved leads to depression. ...Sadness and anger need to go somewhere. If we express them, we let go of them and can move toward happiness" (Cloud and Townsend, *12 'Christian' Beliefs*, 104; bracketed words are mine).

[43] "To *choose* to serve Sin when Sin's aims and goals are radically opposed to those of Christ's is not logical. It is a repudiation of the new Master! Such a choice would be a denial of all that has been undergone and all the sacrifices made by this Master, Jesus" (McGuiggan, *The Book of Romans* [Lubbock, TX: Montex Publishing Co., 1982], 202, in comments on Romans 6:16).

[44] This is exactly the error to which Paul refers in Colossians 2:16-23. By focusing on external behavior, ritual practices, and ascetic living, certain Jews (the Essenes and others) thought they could obtain righteousness with God. Yet, these things have only "the appearance of wisdom in self-made religion," and offer no value *by themselves* in the cleansing of the human heart or atonement for one's sins. Nonetheless, many contemporary Christians and churches have succumbed to this same error—all with good intentions, but the wrong approach.

[45] Cloud and Townsend, *12 'Christian' Beliefs*, 89. On the other hand, Crabb warns us against trying to "find God" by absorbing ourselves in our problems. The result: "We get bogged down in them and never go *through* them"; we get "absorbed in them with a selfish

energy that masquerades as a commitment to personal growth" (*Inside Out*, 164).

⁴⁶ The EULA is an analogy, not a perfect illustration. You enter into a covenant with God, not a contractual agreement. In your covenant agreement, both parties—you and God—have certain responsibilities and seek mutually-beneficial objectives. Even so, this covenant is legally binding, and, once a person has initiated it, he cannot renege on it without incurring serious consequences.

⁴⁷ Bonhoeffer, *The Cost of Discipleship*, 231, 256. McGuiggan clarifies: "The 'death' discussed in these verses [Romans 6:3-7] is a once-for-all death that *need not* be repeated. The death of the 'old man' need never be repeated but our present struggle with sin requires that we daily put to death the deeds (sinful) of the body. …The 'old man' was myself 'in Adam.' …[The] 'new man' is myself in relation to Christ. See Colossians 3:9-10. I am a new man in Christ and I am daily being transformed into his image" (*The Book of Romans*, 195; bracketed words are mine).

⁴⁸ *Merriam-Webster's Collegiate Dictionary* [electronic edition] provides some enlightening expositions on this word: "AMUSE suggests that one's attention is engaged lightly or frivolously ('amuse yourselves while I prepare dinner'); DIVERT implies the distracting of the attention from worry or routine occupation especially by something funny ('a light comedy to divert the tired businessman'); ENTERTAIN suggests supplying amusement or diversion by specially prepared or contrived methods ('a magician entertaining children at a party')."

⁴⁹ "Legalism is the loveless submission to commandments" (McGuiggan, *The God of the Towel*, 147). But just because someone *does* submit to God's commandments does not make him a legalist. Jesus upheld *all* of God's commandments, yet He never once succumbed to legalism. It is not "legalism" to uphold God's truth or to preach that truth in its rightful context—no matter whom it offends. Therefore, "Let us not mistake 'legalism' for loving obedience to the will of God in every facet of our lives" (Miller, *Piloting the Strait*, 98).

⁵⁰ In other words, we cannot merely ask the question popular among evangelicals, "What would Jesus do?" (or, WWJD). Instead, we should simultaneously ask, "And *why* would Jesus do it?"

⁵¹ "The goal [of holiness] is not so much 'not doing wrong' or 'must do right'; those actions may be part of the means, but the goal is *being like God*" (Ponsonby, *The Pursuit of the Holy*, 76, regarding Leviticus 19:2; emphases are his, bracketed words are mine). Another author rightly observes that holiness is not just purity or separation, nor the combination of these. Purity and separation are attributes of, not synonyms for, holiness. Real holiness is "to imitate Christ in all we do" (John Bevere, *Extraordinary* [Colorado Springs, CO: Waterbrooke Press, 2009], 90-91).

⁵² William Hendriksen, *New Testament Commentary: Matthew* (Grand Rapids: Baker Book House, 1973), 265.

⁵³ H. Leo Boles, *A Commentary on the Gospel According to Matthew* (Nashville: Gospel Advocate Co., 1936), 120.

⁵⁴ Boles, *Matthew*, 122.

⁵⁵ James B. Coffman, *Commentary on the Gospel of Matthew* (Austin, TX: Firm Foundation, 1968), 52.

⁵⁶ Hendriksen, *Matthew*, 269.

⁵⁷ Ibid., 275.

⁵⁸ Boles, *Matthew*, 124.

⁵⁹ R. C. H. Lenski, *Commentary on the New Testament: Matthew* (Peabody, MA: Hendrickson Publishers, 1998), 193; bracketed words are mine.

⁶⁰ Bonhoeffer, *The Cost of Discipleship*, 66.

⁶¹ Ibid., 83; bracketed words are mine.

⁶² "Enthusiasm" is from a Greek compound: *en*, "with" or "by" + *theos*, "God."

⁶³ MacDonald, *Lord, Change My Attitude*, 80.

⁶⁴ Crabb, *Finding God*, 18.

⁶⁵ "...We manufacture our unhappiness by thinking unhappy thoughts, by the attitudes which we habitually take, such as the negative feeling that everything is going to turn out badly, or that other people are getting what they do not deserve and we are failing to get what we do deserve" (Peale, *Positive Thinking*, 74).

⁶⁶ Cloud and Townsend, *12 'Christian' Beliefs*, 42-43.

⁶⁷ "Their atheism isn't a rational denial of God as much as an attempt to retaliate against him" (Randy Alcorn, *If God Is Good* [Colorado Springs, CO: Multnomah Books, 2009], 136). Dinesh D'Souza refers to many atheists as "wounded theists": "The wounded theist is distinguished from the atheist in that the atheist doesn't believe in God; the wounded theist is angry with God. In some cases, the wounded theist hates God; his atheism is a form of revenge. ...Their atheism becomes a way of spitting in God's face" (*God Forsaken* [Carol Stream, IL: Tyndale House Publishers, 2012], 20, 255).

⁶⁸ C. S. Lewis, *Mere Christianity* (New York: MacMillan Publishing Co., 1952), 54.

⁶⁹ Adapted from McGuiggan, *The Dragon Slayer*, 101-102.

⁷⁰ See Ezekiel 14:1-7, where God rightly accuses some of the elders of Israel (in Babylonian captivity) of having "idols in their hearts," even as they come to inquire of God's prophet. As a result of this, God said that He would not hear their prayers ("Should I be consulted by them at all?"). The same thing is true today: a Christian whose heart houses idols—whether one or many—estranges himself from his God, and hinders that person's prayers from being heard (Proverbs 28:9).

⁷¹ Adapted from *Merriam-Webster's Collegiate Dictionary* [electronic version].

⁷² Dispenza, *Breaking the Habit*, 40, 92.

⁷³ Piper, *Think*, 30.

⁷⁴ *Merriam-Webster's Collegiate Dictionary* [electronic edition].

75 "Liberal" is derived from Old Latin *liber*, meaning "free," from which we get "liberty."

76 Miller, *Piloting the Strait*, 62.

77 Liberalism usually follows the path of pragmatism—i.e., a philosophy that seeks a practical approach or solution to a given situation, without necessarily or directly appealing to a moral standard. Truth is evaluated by the practical results (or, consequences) of one's belief. In a non-philosophical or general sense, it makes sense to be "pragmatic" and "practical"—especially when you are working on your car, painting your house, or bandaging your child's scraped knee. When this approach becomes an "-ism," however, it takes on a life of its own and thus abandons the biblical pattern. "Pragmatism... contains the seeds of its own undoing. It professes to be tolerant of all views, but its concealed intolerance becomes clear when, confronted and seriously challenged by the Christian absolute [the Word of God—MY WORDS], it dogmatically refuses to reconsider any return to universally valid truth and objective principle" (Carl F. H. Henry, *God, Revelation and Authority*, vol. I [Wheaton, IL: Crossway Books, 1999], 41).

78 "Some people choose to suppress the truth rather than live by it. *In fact, we humans have a fatal tendency to try to adjust the truth to fit our desires rather than adjusting our desires to fit the truth*" (Norman L. Geisler and Frank Turek, *I Don't Have Enough Faith to Be an Atheist* [Wheaton, IL: Crossway Books, 2004], 32; emphases are theirs).

79 "Human reason is not a source of infallible truth about ultimate reality. For human intelligence is not infinite, and left to itself man's reasoning all too evidently reflects his finitude. All speculative interpretations of reality and life projected on the basis of human insight and ingenuity—modern no less than ancient—are merely provisional in character. Whether arrived at by sustained scientific inquiry or disciplined philosophical reasoning, they are destined inevitably to revision and replacement. So limited is human life that

no man has time or opportunity to gather all the information relevant to a comprehensive world-life view, and even if he could, volitional or emotional pressures upon the human spirit prejudice every man's interpretation of the data. This best explains the fact that brilliant minds using the same canons of reason interpret reality in amazingly diverse ways, and expound competing views with compelling force" (Henry, *God, Revelation and Authority*, I:91).

[80] "The stench of moral death hovers over a generation that seals itself against enduring concerns of truth and conscience. A culture that welcomes its own glaring inconsistencies as inescapable will inevitably suffocate for lack of spiritual oxygen and find human existence devoid of worth and meaning. It is man who dies, not God, when the truth of truth and the meaning of meaning evaporate" (*Ibid.*, I:29).

[81] *Strong's*, #G1253, as used in Hebrews 5:14: "…The mature… have their senses trained to discern good and evil."

[82] "The Critical Thinking Community" website (http://www.criticalthinking.org/pages/defining-critical-thinking/766), cited April, 2015.

[83] "The Critical Thinking Community" (www.criticalthinking.org/aboutCT/ourConceptCT.shtml), cited November, 2005.

[84] Quoted in Vincent Ryan's *Beyond Feelings: A Guide to Critical Thinking* (Mountain View, CA: Mayfield Publishing Co., 1995), 55.

[85] "'You ought not question someone's religious beliefs' is itself a religious belief for pluralists" (Geisler and Turek, *I Don't Have Enough Faith to Be an Atheist*, 47). "Pluralism" (also known as inclusivism) is the belief that there are many paths to God (or heaven), and that Christianity is simply one of those paths. "Pluralists think all non-pluralist beliefs are wrong. So pluralists are just as dogmatic and close-minded" as they accuse non-pluralists to be (47).

[86] As the author of this book, I admit that I am *heavily biased* toward Jesus Christ and New Testament Christianity. Yet, I am not trying to persuade you to accept my personal bias. I am appealing to

your mental faculties of logic and reason to accept *the truth*, not my religion or private beliefs.

[87] Dr. Charles Stanley writes: "Sin is an agent of decay. Once sin is introduced into anything—a relationship, a community, or an individual—order and productivity begin to diminish. The term *decay* means 'to pass gradually from a sound or perfect state to one of unsoundness and imperfection.' Such is the nature of sin" (*Winning the War Within* [Nashville: Thomas Nelson Publishers, 1988], 26).

[88] Adapted from Ronald B. Adler and George Rodman, *Understanding Human Communication*, 5th ed. (New York: Harcourt Brace College Publishers, 1994), 31.

[89] *Merriam-Webster's Collegiate Dictionary* [electronic edition].

[90] "The specific meaning of 'agape' which we find in the New Testament isn't the result of the early Christians discovering a word which already said exactly what they wanted to say and latching on to it. Rather, they seem to have settled quickly on this word as the best available one, and they then gave it the fresh privilege of carrying a new depth of meaning in which some aspects of its previous career [in classical Greek usage] were highlighted and others were set aside" (Wright, *After You Believe*, 183; bracketed words are mine). This is similar to what the early Christians did with words like "virtue" and "propitiation."

[91] Timothy R. Jennings, MD, *The God-shaped Brain: How Changing Your View of God Transforms Your Life* (Downers Grove, IL: InterVarsity Press, 2013), 22.

[92] MacDonald, *Lord, Change My Attitude,* 201; emphases are his.

[93] Piper, *Think,* 83; emphases are his.

[94] Ibid.; emphases are his.

[95] Crabb, *Inside Out,* 200.

[96] Sidders, *The Invitation,* 50.

[97] Ibid., 52.

⁹⁸ H. A. Ironside (on Luke 14:26) adds: "This does not mean that we are to have ill will toward our loved ones; it does not mean that we are to bear malice toward them. But our consideration for Christ, our love for Him who died for us is to be so great that, in comparison to our interest in our dearest on earth, if they oppose what is right, our attitude will seem almost as hatred. ...Many people have had to leave their homes for Christ's sake, and their names have been cast down as evil, because they loved Him supremely" (*Addresses on the Gospel of Luke* [New York: Loizeaux Brothers, 1947], 477-478).

⁹⁹ "We often use the terms *pain* and *suffering* synonymously, but they are not the same. Pain is physical, whereas suffering is mental. Pain is the sensation of hurting, while suffering is the consciousness of pain. Suffering also involves the anticipation of pain, the ability to feel pain even before it comes, as well as the reflexive capacity to keep pain going even after the actual sensation of hurt passes. Suffering is often worse than pain" (D'Souza, *God Forsaken*, 153).

¹⁰⁰ "From a purely apologetic perspective, more skepticism, agnosticism, and atheism have sprung from an inability to answer various aspects of evil than from any other single issue. What is more, when doubt begins in this area, it moves quickly to other areas" (Norman L. Geisler, *If God, Why Evil?* [Bloomington, MN: Bethany House Publishers, 2011], 10).

¹⁰¹ This is the ultimate conclusion, for example, in Harold Kushner's popular book, *When Bad Things Happen to Good People* (New York: Schoken Books, 1989). "God wants the righteous to live peaceful, happy lives, but sometimes even He can't bring that about. It is too difficult for even God to keep cruelty and chaos from claiming their innocent victims" (43). Despite this, he claims that we are to "learn to love and forgive Him despite His limitations" (148). There are so many things wrong with this unbiblical perspective that it would take another entire book to address them.

¹⁰² But the phrase "good reason" is purely subjective, left to itself; it is profoundly limited and prone to all kinds of errors in

reasoning. The one who maintains this position assumes that he knows confidently, infallibly, and absolutely what is "good"—a moral value without a moral standard!—and then judges the biblical God with his conclusions. D'Souza says of this: "Given our extremely limited perspective, it is premature to leap from 'I can't see the reason' to 'There is no reason.' We cannot condemn what we don't fully understand" (*God Forsaken*, 69).

[103] Geisler, *If God, Why Evil?*, 13.

[104] There is a great deal of writing already devoted to this sad subject. Dinesh D'Souza sums it up nicely: "If the West gives up Christianity, it will also endanger the egalitarian values that Christianity brought into the world. The end of Christianity also means the systematic erosion of values like equal dignity and equal rights that both religious and secular people cherish. …Some of these values seem to have taken on a life of their own, and this gives us the illusion that we can get rid of Christianity and keep the values. …Remove the Christian foundation, and the values must go, too" (*What's So Great about Christianity* [Carol Stream, IL: Tyndale House Publishers, 2007], 69, 80).

[105] Piper, *Think*, 149; emphases are his.

[106] Crabb, *Finding God*, 61; emphases are his.

[107] Adapted from Crabb, *Inside Out*, 197. Pain in this world must be something that we learn to *accept*, not seek to *solve* or *eliminate*. "There are unnecessary problems that develop when we insist that necessary pain be eliminated. …The idea that peace and joy might merely *support* us during times of struggle and sorrow rather than *eliminate* those times is not appealing. We want to do away with the necessary pain of living in a disappointing world as imperfect people. We insist on experiencing neither pain nor failure, so when the inevitable happens, it becomes reason for discouragement" (204).

[108] "New" here is from *kainos*, meaning "fresh," "unprecedented," and "superior to what preceded it." This is different than another Greek word for "new" (*neos*) which means only newer with respect

to age. To compare the two different meanings: a "new" creature in Christ (2 Corinthians 5:17) is from *kainos*; "younger" men (1 Peter 5:5) is from *neos* (*Strong's*, #G2537 and G3501).

[109] "The kind of love meant [in Matthew 5:44-45] is the love manifested by God himself in that he sends rain on the just and unjust, etc. The implication is that the Christian shall treat his enemies with fairness and equity, doing unto them as he would desire men should do unto himself [Matthew 7:12]" (Coffman, *Matthew*, 70; bracketed words are mine).

[110] Quoted in Peale, *Positive Thinking*, 79.

[111] Kyle Idleman, *Not a Fan* (Grand Rapids: Zondervan, 2011), 24-25.

[112] "Disciple" (from Greek, *mathetes*) in the New Testament (after Acts 2) almost invariably meant *Christian*, although "disciple" is predominantly used to define those who believed upon the Christian faith. In this study, any use of "disciple(s) of Christ" has absolutely no reference to the specific organization of churches referred to as "Disciples of Christ" (or "Christian Church") which was first formally recognized by the U.S. Religious Census in 1906.

[113] McGuiggan, *The God of the Towel*, 129; emphasis is his.

[114] Some Christians may be bothered by my reference to being "filled with the Holy Spirit," as though I am referring to some miraculous visible demonstration of this. Instead, I am merely referring to the indwelling *of* the Holy Spirit and the Spirit-led life (Romans 8:9, Galatians 5:16, et al). For a fuller explanation of what this actually means, I recommend my book, *The Holy Spirit of God*; go to www.spiritbuilding.com.

[115] "What he is really saying, therefore, is that simple trust in him and obedience to his commands out of gratitude for the salvation already imparted by him is delightful. It brings peace and joy. The person who lives this kind of life is no longer a slave. He has become free. He serves the Lord spontaneously, eagerly, enthusiastically. He

is doing what he (the 'new man' in him) wants to do" (Hendriksen, *Matthew*, 505).

[116] "Denominationalism" refers to the distinct separation of a group of churches under one name, one central government, and one particular belief system. The very concept of denominationalism defies the unity and singular gospel teaching that pervades the entire New Testament. Simply put, this system of doctrine and church organization is impossible to defend biblically: anyone who reads the New Testament sincerely and objectively will be taught to become a *Christian*—nothing more, but nothing less, either. He will never be taught to become a certain *kind* or *brand* of Christian who follows a different "faith" or belief system than every other Christian is taught to follow.

[117] "Conviction" can be described as a strong personal belief strong that demands action. "Moral excellence" (or "virtue"; see 2 Peter 1:5) refers to the courage to do what is right simply *because* it is right, regardless of opposition, personal feelings, or consequences.

[118] Certainly some go to the other extreme as well. We have all seen the militant, irrational, and often "in-your-face" person who mistakes his fanaticism for loyalty and a love for Christ. This is neither appropriate nor profitable for the cause of Christ, and whatever is said in the following paragraphs of this book is not in support of it.

[119] The *act* of calling is not the same thing as the group into which those who are called are identified (i.e., the "called" or "chosen"), but with regard to salvation in Christ the two ideas are certainly related. Nonetheless, a distinction needs to be made between those who are called into fellowship with God but refuse it ("Many are called, but few are chosen"—Matthew 22:14) and those who are called and accept the invitation (those "chosen of God" who are "holy and beloved"—Colossians 3:12). The word translated "church" (and, in some cases, "assembly") in the New Testament is from *ekklesia*, a compound word that literally means "the called out" (*Strong's*, #G1577). This is the

group of those who were not only *called* by the gospel (2 Thessalonians 2:13-14) but also *responded* in faithful obedience to that calling.

[120] I am *not* suggesting that these activities are useless or expendable. Each of them serves a purpose, and ideally it is a good one. At the same time, none of these activities can equal or replace the allegiance of one's heart to the Master. One who is a disciple indeed will likely be involved with such activities; yet mere participation by itself does not make one a disciple.

[121] For a deeper study on the subject of God's (Christ's) sacredness, I recommend my book, *Seeking the Sacred* (Summitville, IN: Spiritbuilding Publishing, 2009); go to www.spiritbuilding.com.

[122] Wilson, *Your Jesus Is Too Safe*, 12-13.

[123] The relationship between Christ and His church is always described differently than His relationship between Himself and His kingdom. (The church is the sanctuary of believers *within* the kingdom of God; the realm of the kingdom, however, far exceeds the boundaries of the church.) With regard to His church, Christ is called Head, Shepherd, Bridegroom (or Husband), and Savior; with regard to His kingdom, Christ is called King, Lord, "David" of prophecy, and Son of God.

[124] This is not far from atheism itself: "The atheist objection is not to morality but to absolute morality. Rather than deriving morality from an external code of divine commandments, atheists think of morality as man-made, something forged through individual and group experience" (D'Souza, *What's So Great about Christianity*, 230).

[125] William Hendriksen, *New Testament Commentary: Luke* (Grand Rapids: Baker Book House, 1978), 365.

[126] "The thought is overwhelming: Christ, carrying his cross, leads, and all his disciples, each bearing his own cross, follow in one immense procession like men being led away to be crucified. Paul carries the figure farther: they that are Christ's have crucified the flesh (Gal. 5:24);

and Paul himself is crucified with Christ (Gal. 2:20). The earthly prospects of a disciple are not alluring. [Yet] however heavy your cross may be, he [Christ] helps you to bear it after him" (Lenski, *Matthew*, 644; bracketed words are mine).

[127] McGuiggan, *The God of the Towel*, 210; emphasis is his.

[128] "Throughout the whole of His ministry, and notably in the Sermon on the Mount, He [Christ] bears Himself with a kingly grandeur, dispensing the rewards and punishments of the world to come; opening the Kingdom of Heaven to those only who fulfill His requirements; and resting the future prospects of men on the reception they give His words" (Dr. Cunningham Geikie, *The Life and Words of Christ* [New York: Appleton and Company, 1894], II:54; bracketed word is mine).

[129] King, *At the Feet of the Master*, 85.

[130] Alfred Edersheim, *The Life and Times of Jesus the Messiah* (Peabody, MA: Hendrickson Publishers, 1993), 365. This is similar to what John means in 1 John 1:1-3 and 5:20.

[131] King, *At the Feet of the Master*, 86.

[132] Ibid., 88; bracketed words are mine.

[133] "Jesus forbade his disciples to seek such titles of distinction. The reason which he gave was that he was himself their Master and Teacher. They were on a level; they were to be equal in authority; they were brethren; and they should neither covet nor receive a title which implied either an elevation of one above another, or which appeared to infringe on the absolute right of the Saviour [sic] to be their only Teacher and Master" (Alfred Barnes, "The Gospels: Matthew," *Barnes' Notes*, vol. 9 [Grand Rapids: Baker Book House, no date], 242).

[134] This distinction between forbearance and forgiveness is an important yet often overlooked one. For further reading, I recommend my book, *The Gospel of Forgiveness* (Summitville, IN: Spiritbuilding Publishing, 2011); go to www.spiritbuilding.com.

¹³⁵ This is a radical message: "People are messy, so forgiveness is messy. People are radically broken, so grace is radically healing" (Wilson, *Your Jesus Is Too Safe*, 60).

¹³⁶ Geikie, *The Life and Words of Christ*, I:453-454.

¹³⁷ This is a most interesting statement: "things which I have seen with My Father." This necessarily implies not just the transmission of information ("things I have heard" or "things He has taught Me"), but a very *personal fellowship* with the One who provides the information. We are made to picture Jesus—as the incarnate Son of God—as being in the visual and intimate presence of His Father, receiving instruction as to what to say or do next in His earthly ministry. Jesus alone has come *from* the Father, and has therefore "heard His voice" and "seen His form." He alone, therefore, is able to "explain" Him to us who have never seen, heard, or experienced the literal presence of God the Father (John 1:18, 5:37-38).

¹³⁸ C. S. Lewis, *The Problem of Pain* (New York: Simon & Schuster, 1996), 112. The full quote is: "To enter heaven is to become more human than you ever succeeded in being on earth; to enter hell, is to be banished from humanity." In heaven, we become *fully* human; whatever is thrown into hell is merely a shriveled and empty shell of what we were meant to be. We are *meant* to dwell forever in the presence of our Creator; those who are lost forever in hell have forfeited that opportunity and thus, for all intents and purposes, cease to be human.

¹³⁹ King, *At the Feet of the Master*, 91.

¹⁴⁰ *Merriam-Webster's Collegiate Dictionary* [electronic edition].

¹⁴¹ *Thayer's Greek-English Lexicon* [electronic edition] (database © 2005 by WORDsearch Corp.), #G1249.

¹⁴² Idleman, *Not a Fan*, 151.

¹⁴³ There are several examples in the New Testament of "priestly" language with regard to our service to God (e.g., Romans 12:1-2,

Ephesians 5:1-2, Philippians 2:17, Hebrews 12:28, 13:15 and 1 Peter 2:5).

144 McGuiggan, *The God of the Towel*, 163-164.

145 "God loves...unforgiven people as much as He loves the forgiven. It is His love for the unforgiven which resulted in their being forgiven. [Furthermore,] it is *God* who urged us to love those who don't love us" rather than, say, our own decision or church policy (McGuiggan, *The God of the Towel*, 206-207; bracketed word is mine).

146 To clarify, we cannot "accept" into *spiritual fellowship* those who remain alienated from God, since these have no connection to us in that context (cf. 2 Corinthians 6:14-18). But we can accept *all* people as fellow human beings and thus treat them with kindness, dignity, and respect—just as we would want to be treated (Matthew 7:12, Galatians 6:10).

147 Not only may Christians be "strangers" to one another, with regard to personal acquaintance, but we are also "strangers" to the world (1 Peter 2:11). In the first sense, our spiritual fellowship exists regardless of any previous communication with such believers; in the second sense, however, we have no spiritual fellowship with unbelievers, regardless of whatever history of earthly acquaintance we might have with them.

148 Stanley, *The Power of Commitment*, 254.

149 John's words in this passage cannot be limited to mere figures of speech, but include literal expectations. Just as Jesus literally died for the sake of His "friends," so we are to give up our lives—figuratively *and* literally—for our fellow believers (John 15:12-14).

150 Unlike love, however, forgiveness is *not* unconditional, but is contingent upon the one who has committed the offense to take responsibility for his (or her) actions. He must do his part in restoring that which his offense has corrupted and reconciling that which his offense has severed. For a detailed understanding of this subject,

I recommend my book, *The Gospel of Forgiveness*; go to www.spiritbuilding.com.

[151] Idleman, *Not a Fan*, 74.

[152] Mark Buchanan, *Your God Is Too Safe* (Sisters, OR: Multnomah Publishers, 2001), 133; all emphases are his; bracketed words are mine.

[153] *Strong's*, #G2169.

[154] Alcorn, *If God Is Good*, 414.

[155] A good illustration of this can be found in the holy anointing oil used for the consecration of the Levitical priests and the holy furniture of the tabernacle (Exodus 30:22-33). This oil was special, unique, and superior to all other concoctions of perfumes; it was never to be used for anything other than what it was intended; it was a physical characteristic of the holy worship of Jehovah.

[156] William Hendriksen, on Colossians 2:7, *New Testament Commentary: Colossians* (Grand Rapids: Baker Book House, 1964), 108.

[157] "God knows my heart!" is often offered in defense of one's otherwise inexplicable actions. Allegedly, God knowing "your heart" overrides any need for outward demonstration of respect or reverence—and such a person is allegedly above being challenged. But God knows *everyone's* heart, even the hearts of unbelievers, hypocrites, and those who have fallen away—so what is the point being made, exactly? Jesus told the scoffing, money-loving Jews that "God knows your hearts," but this did nothing to exonerate them (Luke 16:15). The real point is: reverence must not be something confined to one's "heart"; it must be visibly demonstrated in one's outward actions. Just as love, gratitude, obedience, mercy, and forgiveness mean nothing without actual demonstration, so reverence means nothing until it is acted out rather than being only cited as a heartfelt experience.

[158] James Denney, "St. Paul's Epistle to the Romans," *The Expositor's Greek Testament*, as quoted in JFB's commentary on Romans 1:24.

¹⁵⁹ In fact, an excess of "favorable circumstances" tends to make people unfocused, overconfident, spoiled, and lazy. This does not mean that a steady diet of bad experiences will automatically make a person more noble or faithful, however. The point here is not to assume that good or bad experiences will always bring about a predictable result, but that whether one's experiences *are* good or bad, they are not to be used as a determination of our contentment in Christ.

¹⁶⁰ Crabb, *Finding God*, 38; emphases are his.

¹⁶¹ All the passages cited here deal with suffering *as a Christian*—i.e., for our faith in Christ—rather than simply enduring the hardships that all people face in the world. We must not confuse the two contexts. Unbelievers suffer bad experiences in this life; believers also may suffer many of these same bad experiences *as well as* those brought upon them because of their spiritual convictions. "Indeed," Paul says, "all who desire to live godly in Christ Jesus will be persecuted" for that decision (2 Timothy 3:12).

¹⁶² Jim Harrell (while dying from ALS), wrote: "Suffering is the icy splash that wakes us up from the complacency of living this life. We truly don't see God and his purpose and strength without suffering, because we just become too comfortable" (quoted in Alcorn, *If God Is Good*, 417).

¹⁶³ Bonhoeffer, *The Cost of Discipleship*, 91.

¹⁶⁴ Alcorn, *If God Is Good*, 487.

¹⁶⁵ Crabb says that those living in a "Fool's Paradise" are "running from the hard facts of life by insisting that Christianity offers a simple formula for making life work" (*Finding God*, 79).

¹⁶⁶ Crabb, *Inside Out*, 36.

¹⁶⁷ Someone might object to this, saying, "Give the guy some credit! At least he's made a step in the right direction." And in principle, I agree. It is better to do something *good* than it is to do nothing at all. But the point I am making goes beyond this. The *reason* for the positive changes we make in our lives must be addressed even before

the actual changes themselves. All the churchgoing in the world will not *by itself* bring a person one step closer to God. But one whose heart belongs to the Lord will do far more than attend church services: he will strive to conform to the Master in *all* respects.

[168] Lewis, *Mere Christianity*, 142.

[169] Crabb, *Inside Out*, 211. He also says that "the urge to trust in ourselves is addictive—and it is the root of all other addictions" (*Finding God*, 128). It is also possible to become chemically addicted to our problems. We are self-injected, in a manner of speaking, with a powerful shot of emotion-stimulating endorphins when we recreate those experiences that originally gave us pleasure, power, control, etc. (adapted from Dispenza, *Breaking the Habit*, 104).

[170] The word "improved" here necessarily implies at least two things. First, it implies a moral standard by which an action can be measured, since nothing can "improve" without comparing it to a fixed point of reference. Second, it implies a closer conformity to that fixed standard than before, since no one can "improve" morally until he leaves behind his inferior thinking and/or behavior and adopts a superior one instead. In other words, improvement requires that one is moving *toward* the standard, not away from it, and not remaining still.

[171] "The righteousness of 'the scribes and Pharisees' was in general artificial, outward, and unreal; they professed to be exceedingly righteous, but were hypocrites. Jesus does not mean to say that they were as righteous as they professed to be; he knew them to be hypocrites" (Boles, *Matthew*, 133). Dr. Geikie, in his concluding comments on Jesus' sermon on the mount, says this: "They [i.e., the multitude of listeners] had been accustomed to the tame and slavish servility of the Rabbis—with their dread of varying a word from precedent and authority; their cobwebbery of endless sophistries and verbal trifling; their laborious dissertations on the infinitely little; their unconscious oversight of all that could affect the heart; their industrious trackings through the jungle of tradition and prescription—and felt that in the preaching of Jesus, they, for the first time, had something that

stirred their souls and came home to their consciences" (*The Life and Words of Christ*, 84; bracketed words are mine).

172 Lenski has insightful things to say on this passage: "These illustrations have often been misapplied. Because Christ's teaching is now old, modernistic thinkers have compared it to the old, dried-out wineskins and state that it is no longer to be combined with the new religious concepts that they advance. So they call for new moral codes and standards, new 'categories of thought,' new conceptions of sin and righteousness, new visions of God, etc. They are wrong in two respects: their new ideas are not new, and the teaching of Christ is still as new, true, and glorious as it was in the days when he walked on earth. ... Jesus' teaching and morals are not old and worn-out, but modernism has for many a century been outworn" (*Commentary on the New Testament: Luke* [Peabody, MA: Hendrickson Publishers, 1998], 319).

173 Quoted in Ponsonby, *The Pursuit of the Holy*, 218.

174 This doctrine is called universalism, which assumes that all people are (eventually) saved from condemnation and ushered into a heavenly existence. "Pastor" Rob Bell promotes this old view in a contemporary packaging in his very popular book, *Love Wins* (New York: HarperOne, 2011). In what he calls the "ultimate reconciliation," Bell writes: "[After physical death,] there will be endless opportunities in an endless amount of time for people [who rejected God in this life] to say yes to God. As long as it takes, in other words. At the heart of this perspective is the belief that, given enough time, everybody will turn to God and find themselves in the joy and peace of God's presence. The love of God will melt every hard heart, and even the most 'depraved sinners' will eventually give up their resistance and turn to God" (106-107, bracketed words are mine). While this may sound comforting to some, it is a completely contrived theology that has been plucked out of thin air. There is nothing in the Bible to support it. Nonetheless, it is exactly what many people want to hear—which is why such a book is so popular (see 2 Timothy 4:3-4).

175 On the other hand: "One of the marks of a certain type of bad

man is that he cannot give up a thing himself without wanting everyone else to give it up. That is not the Christian way. An individual Christian may see fit to give up all sorts of things for special reasons... but the moment he starts saying the things are bad in themselves, or looking down his nose at other people who do use them, he has taken a wrong turn" (Lewis, *Mere Christianity*, 76).

[176] Randy Alcorn, *If God Is Good*, 79.

[177] With reference to Matthew 23:26, Dr. Larry Crabb asks rhetorically, "What is the dirt on the inside of the cup and dish that must be exposed and scoured off?" (*Inside Out*, 186). After all, it is not God's "dirt" that needs to be addressed, but our own. The dirt, Crabb says, is the sin that is in our heart, which always boils down to a failure to *love* and *trust* God as we were intended to do (195). "The sole value of an inside look is measured by its helpfulness in moving us toward greater love, both for God and for others" (165).

[178] Peter preached, "Repent, and each of you be baptized in the name of Jesus Christ for the forgiveness of your sins..." (Acts 2:38). Those who *were* baptized were also *converted* to a new life in Christ—something they never had before—but in the process they had to *repent* of their abandonment of what they knew to be right (i.e., a lifestyle consistent with God's holy nature). Paul's preaching also necessarily included repentance, since Christ's gospel requires this (Luke 24:45-47). His message to both Jews and Gentiles was that "...they should repent and turn to God, performing deeds appropriate to repentance" (Acts 26:20). Both actions—conversion ("turn to God" through Jesus Christ) and repentance—are mentioned here. One is a turn to something they never had before; the other is a return to that which they had left behind. Both are necessary in becoming a Christian.

[179] Calvinism (a.k.a. Doctrine of Predestination, or Reformed Theology) is one of the most misleading and destructive heresies against the gospel of Christ. It is unbiblical, illogical, and therefore indefensible; yet, it is the backbone of several major denominations, and has poisoned the minds of millions of people. The definition—and

refutation—of these teachings occupies far more space than this present study will accommodate. I have covered these subjects in sufficient detail in my book, *Being Born of God: The Role and Significance of Baptism in Becoming a Christian*; go to www.spiritbuilding.com.

[180] I recommend reading chapter 14 ("The Ministry of Reconciliation") in my book, *The Gospel of Forgiveness*; go to www.spiritbuilding.com.

[181] Buchanan, *Your God Is Too Safe*, 172.

[182] Lewis, *Mere Christianity*, 94; bracketed words are mine.

[183] The word translated "opportunity" (in the NASB) in Ephesians 4:27 means literally a "place" or "foothold" (*Thayer's Greek-English Lexicon*, #G5117). In essence, Paul says: "Do not even crack the door to temptation, because Satan will stick his foot in the door and force it open."

[184] "So much more is involved in changing from the inside out than pulling rotten fruit off the tree" (Crabb, *Inside Out*, 124).

[185] "'The flesh' stands for many things in the New Testament but it certainly stands for all that is weak and creaturely that has set itself up against God and suffered loss as a consequence" (McGuiggan, *The Dragon Slayer*, 169).

[186] Wright, *After You Believe*, 35.

[187] In my opinion, one of the best books I have read that discusses the *process* of changing one's heart is Dr. Larry Crabb's *Inside Out* (see Sources). This is not to suggest that you cannot change without Dr. Crabb's help; his book is simply a tool that offers insights and details that you may not have considered. In reality, the Bible provides all the essential information for the right kind of change; and God Himself will be the actual transforming Power that you need to overcome whatever obstacles to change you may face.

[188] Crabb, *Finding God*, 170.

[189] Piper, *Think*, 144; emphases are his.

[190] Crabb, *Inside Out*, 174.

[191] Bonhoeffer, *The Cost of Discipleship*, 303; bracketed words are mine.

Sources Used

Adler, Ronald B. and George Rodman. *Understanding Human Communication*, 5th ed. New York: Harcourt Brace College Publishers, 1994.

Alcorn, Randy. *If God Is Good*. Colorado Springs, CO: Multnomah Books, 2009.

Barnes, Alfred. "Matthew." *Barnes' Notes*, vol. 9. Grand Rapids: Baker Book House, no date.

Bell, Rob. *Love Wins: A Book about Heaven, Hell, and the Fate of Every Person Who Ever Lived*. New York: HarperOne, 2011.

Bevere, John. *Extraordinary*. Colorado Springs, CO: Waterbrooke Press, 2009.

Boles, H. Leo. *A Commentary on the Gospel According to Matthew*. Nashville: Gospel Advocate Co., 1936.

Bonhoeffer, Dietrich. *The Cost of Discipleship* (trans. by R. H. Fuller). New York: Simon & Schuster, 1959.

Buchanan, Mark. *Your God Is Too Safe*. Sisters, OR: Multnomah Publishers, 2001.

Coffman, James Burton. *Commentary on the Gospel of Matthew*. Austin, TX: Firm Foundation, 1968.

Cloud, Dr. Henry, and Dr. John Townsend. *12 "Christian" Beliefs That Can Drive You Crazy*. Grand Rapids: Zondervan, 1994.

_____. *Boundaries*. Grand Rapids: Zondervan, 1992.

Crabb, Dr. Larry. *Finding God*. Grand Rapids: Zondervan, 1993.

_____. *Inside Out*. Colorado Springs, CO: Navpress, 1988.

"The Critical Thinking Community" (website). www.criticalthinking.org/... (2005).

Dispenza, Dr. Joe. *Breaking the Habit of Being Yourself: How to Lose Your Mind and Create a New One*. New York: Hay House, Inc., 2012.

Sources Used

D'Souza, Dinesh. *God Forsaken*. Carol Stream, IL: Tyndale House Publishers, 2012.

_____. *What's So Great about Christianity*. Carol Stream, IL: Tyndale House Publishers, 2007.

Edersheim, Alfred. *The Life and Times of Jesus the Messiah*. Peabody, MA: Hendrickson Publishers, 1993.

Geikie, Dr. Cunningham. *The Life and Words of Christ*. New York: Appleton and Company, 1894.

Geisler, Norman L. *If God, Why Evil?* Bloomington, MN: Bethany House Publishers, 2011.

Geisler, Norman L. and Frank Turek. *I Don't Have Enough Faith to Be an Atheist*. Wheaton, IL: Crossway Books, 2004.

Hendriksen, William. *New Testament Commentary: Luke*. Grand Rapids: Baker Book House, 1978.

_____. *New Testament Commentary: Matthew*. Grand Rapids: Baker Book House, 1973.

_____. *New Testament Commentary: Colossians*. Grand Rapids: Baker Book House, 1964.

Henry, Carl F. H. *God, Revelation and Authority*, vol. 1. Wheaton, IL: Crossway Books, 1999.

Idleman, Kyle. *Not a Fan*. Grand Rapids: Zondervan, 2011.

International Standard Bible Encyclopedia (electronic edition). James Orr, gen. ed. Database © 2004 WORDsearch Corp.

Ironside, H. A. *Addresses on the Gospel of Luke*. New York: Loizeaux Brothers, 1947.

Jamieson, Robert, Andrew Fausset, and David Brown. *New Commentary on the Whole Bible: New Testament Volume* (electronic edition). © 1990 Tyndale House Publishers; database © 2012 WORDsearch Corp.

Jennings, Dr. Timothy R. *The God-shaped Brain: How Changing Your View of God Transforms Your Life*. Downers Grove, IL: InterVarsity Press, 2013.

King, Sr., Daniel H. *At the Feet of the Master: Studies in the Background, Content and Methods of Jesus' Teaching.* Bowling Green, KY: Guardian of Truth Foundation, 1997.

Kushner, Harold. *When Bad Things Happen to Good People.* New York: Schoken Books, 1989.

Lenski, R. C. H. *Commentary on the New Testament: Matthew.* Peabody, MA: Hendrickson Publishers, 1998.

_____. *Commentary on the New Testament: Luke.* Peabody, MA: Hendrickson Publishers, 1998.

Lewis, C. S. *Mere Christianity.* New York: MacMillan Publishing Co., 1952.

_____. *The Problem of Pain.* New York: Simon & Schuster, 1996.

MacDonald, James. *Lord, Change My Attitude.* Chicago: Moody Publishers, 2008.

McGuiggan, Jim. *The Book of Romans.* Lubbock, TX: Montex Publishing Co., 1982.

_____. *The God of the Towel.* Lubbock, TX: Montex Publishin Co., 1984.

_____. *The Dragon Slayer: Reflections on the Saving of the World.* Self-published, no date.

Merriam-Webster's 11th Collegiate Dictionary (electronic edition), ver. 3.0. © 2003 by Merriam-Webster, Inc.

Miller, Dave. *Piloting the Strait: A Guidebook for Assessing Change in Churches of Christ.* Pulaski, TN: Sain Publications, 1996.

Orr, James (gen. ed.). *International Standard Bible Encyclopedia* (electronic edition). Database © 2004 WORDsearch Corp.

Peale, Norman Vincent. *The Power of Positive Thinking.* Pawling, NY: Foundation for Christian Living, 1978.

Piper, John. *Think: The Life of the Mind and the Love of God.* Wheaton, IL: Crossway Books, 2010.

Ponsonby, Simon. *The Pursuit of the Holy*. Colorado Springs, CO: David C. Cook, 2010.

Ryan, Vincent. *Beyond Feelings: A Guide to Critical Thinking*. Mountain View, CA: Mayfield Publishing Co., 1995.

Sidders, Greg. *The Invitation*. Grand Rapids: Revell Books, 2011.

Stanley, Dr. Charles. *Winning the War Within*. Nashville: Thomas Nelson Publishers, 1988.

Stanley, Dr. Scott. *The Power of Commitment*. San Francisco: Jossey-Bass, 2005.

Strong, James. *Strong's Talking Greek and Hebrew Dictionary* (electronic edition). Database © 2012 by WORDsearch Corp.

Sychtysz, Chad. *Being Born of God: The Role and Significance of Baptism in Becoming a Christian*. Summitville, IN: Spiritbuilding Publishing, 2014.

_____. *The Gospel of Forgiveness*. Summitville, IN: Spiritbuilding Publishing, 2011.

_____. *The Holy Spirit of God: A Biblical Perspective*. Summitville, IN: Spiritbuilding Publishing, 2010.

Thayer, Joseph. *Thayer's Greek-English Lexicon* (electronic edition). Database © 2005 by WORDsearch Corp.

Wilson, Jared C. *Your Jesus Is Too Safe*. Grand Rapids: Kregel Publications, 2009.

Wright, N. T. *After You Believe: Why Christian Character Matters*. New York: HarperCollins Publishers, 2010.

Scripture (unless otherwise noted) taken from the NEW AMERICAN STANDARD BIBLE ®, Copyright © 1960, 1962, 1963, 1968, 1971, 1972, 1973, 1975, 1977, 1995 by The Lockman Foundation. Used by permission.

More Bible Study workbooks that you can order from Spiritbuilding.com or your favorite Christian bookstore.

Inside Out (Carl McMurray)
Studying spiritual growth in bite-sized pieces
Night and Day (Andrew Roberts)
Comparing New Testament Christianity and Islam
Church Discipline (Royce DeBerry)
A study on an important responsibility for the Lord's church
Exercising Authority (John Baughn)
How we use and understand authority on a daily basis
Compass Points (Carl McMurray)
22 foundation lessons for home studies, prospects, or new Christians
We're Different Because... (Carl McMurray)
A workbook on authority and recent church history
Communing with the Lord (Matthew Allen)
A study of the Lord's Supper & issues surrounding it
Parenting Through the Ages (Royce & Cindy DeBerry)
Bible principles tested & explained by successful parents
Marriage Through the Ages (Royce & Cindy DeBerry)
A quarter's study of God's design for this part of our life
What Should I Do? (Dennis Tucker)
A study that seeks Bible answers to life's important questions
How To Study the Bible (Jeff Archer)
25 lessons on how to study & understand the Bible
From Fear to Faith (Matthew Allen)
Coming to grips with the doctrine of grace
The Messiah's Misfits (Bryan Nash)
A study of the apostles of Jesus Christ
Living a Spirit Filled Life (Matthew Allen)
A study of Galatians & Ephesians with practical applications
The Lion Is the Lamb (Andrew Roberts)
A study of the King of Kings, His glorious kingdom, & His promised return
When Opportunity Knocks (Matthew Allen)
Lessons on how to meet the J.W./Mormon who knocks on your door
The Last Mile of the Way (Kipp Campbell)
A workbook study of the last week of the Messiah's life
Ancient Choices for Modern Dilemmas (John Baughn)
Biblical view of the modern family, current culture, and American politics
In Search of Christian Confidence (John Baughn)
A study to help one find the confidence God intended for His people

Textual Studies

The Parables, Taking a Deeper Look (Kipp Campbell)
A detailed look at our Lord's teaching stories
That I May Know Him (Aaron Kemple) Vol. 1 & 2
A chronological study of the life of Christ in a harmony of the gospels
1st Corinthians study guide (Chad Sychtysz)
Studies to take the student through this important letter
2nd Corinthians study guide (Chad Sychtysz)
Studies to take the student through this important letter
Hebrews study guide (Chad Sychtysz)
Studies to take the student through this important letter
Romans study guide (Chad Sychtysz)
Studies to take the student through this important letter
Galatians study guide (Chad Sychtysz)
Studies to take the student through this important letter
Ephesian study guide (Chad Sychtysz)
Studies to take the student through this important letter
Philippian, Colossians, Philemon study guide (Chad Sychtysz)
Studies to take the student through these important letters
1 & 2 Timothy and Titus (Matthew Allen)
A commentary workbook on these letters from Paul
Faith in Action: Studies in James (Mike Wilson)
Bible class workbook and commentary on James
From Beneath the Altar (Carl McMurray)
A workbook commentary on the Book of Revelation
1 Samuel (Matthew Allen)
Studying the life and times of this prophet, priest, & judge
Proverbs, Wisdom for Dummies (Carl McMurray)
A workbook study including every verse in Proverbs, divided into topics
An Overview of Isaiah (Chad Sychtysz)
A workbook study of this messianic prophet
An Overview of Jeremiah (Chad Sychtysz)
A workbook study of this prophet
Esteemed of God, Studying the Book of Daniel (Carl McMurray)
Covering the man as well as the time between the testaments
The Minor Prophets, Vol. 1 & 2 (Matthew Allen)
Old lessons that speak directly to us today

Special Interest

The AD 70 Doctrine (Morris Bowers)
The truth about Realized Eschatology

The Holy Spirit of God (Chad Sychtysz)
A diligent, thorough study of this important subject

The Gospel of Forgiveness (Chad Sychtysz)
A presentation of this subject from different biblical angles

Letters to Young Preachers (Warren Berkley)
Letters from older preachers to younger on what they face

Behind the Preacher's Door (Warren Berkley and Mark Roberts)
Issues that preachers will have to deal with

Seeking the Sacred (Chad Sychtysz)
How to know God the way that HE wants us to know Him

Will You Wipe My Tears? (Joyce Jamerson)
Wisdom & resources to teach us how to help others through sorrow

Do Things Well (Warren Berkley and Mark Roberts)
Encouraging and teaching churches to worship with passion

Studies for Women

I Will NOT Be Lukewarm (Dana Burk)
A ladies study on defeating mediocrity

Reveal in Me... (Jeanne Sullivan)
A study to assist ladies in discovering and developing their talents

Will You Wipe My Tears? (Joyce Jamerson)
Wisdom & resources to teach us how to help others through sorrow

Bridges or Barriers (Cindy DeBerry & Angie Kmitta)
Study encouraging harmony with younger/older sisters-in-Christ

Learning to Sing at Midnight (Joanne Beckley)
A study book about spiritual growth benefiting women of all ages

Re-charging Your Prayer Life (Lonnie Cruse)
Workbook for any woman wanting a richer prayer life

Does This Armor Make Me Look Fat? (Lonnie Cruse)
A study of the Christian armor and how it fits women

Heading for Harvest (Joyce Jamerson)
A study of the fruit of the Spirit

Behind Every Good Man (Joyce Jamerson)
Studying the women that stand behind faithful men of today

Forgotten Womanhood (Joanne Beckley)
Studying the traits of godly womanhood

Look Into Your Heart (Joyce Jamerson)
Studying how to calm one's heart, to develop one that is God approved

Studies for Young People

The Purity Pursuit (Andrew Roberts)
Helping teens achieve purity in all aspects of life

Paul's Letter to the Romans (Matthew Allen)
Putting righteousness by faith on a young person's level

Snapshots, Defining Moments in a Girl's Life (Nicole Sardinas)
How to make godly decisions when it really matters

The Path of Peace (Cassondra Givans)
Relevant and important topics of study for teens

Transitions (Ken Weliever)
A relevant life study for twenty-somethings

A Christian's Approach to... (Cougan Collins)
Studies that deal with the issues of life

God's Plan for Dating and Marriage (Dennis Tucker)
Considering God's directions in this vital area

Back to the Beginning (Cougan Collins)
Studying the book of Genesis

Compass Points (Carl McMurray)
22 foundation lessons for youth, home studies, or new Christians

Eye to Eye with Women of the Bible (Joanne Beckley)
Studies for girls of biblical women, good and bad

The Gospel and You (Andrew Roberts)
Helping teens achieve and possess their own saving faith

We're Different Because... (Carl McMurray)
A workbook on authority and recent church history

**Try any of these study workbooks in the
LIVING LETTER SERIES by Frank Jamerson**

The Gospel of Mark / The Gospel of John / Acts
The Letter to the Romans / 1 Corinthians / 2 Corinthians
The Letter to the Galatians / The Letter to the Ephesians
Philippians and Colossians / 1 & 2 Timothy & Titus
1 & 2 Thessalonians / The Letter to the Hebrews
The Letter of James /1 Peter / 2 Peter and Jude / 1-2-3 John

Other Bible Study Workbooks by Frank Jamerson
The Godhead / Lord, Please Teach Us to Give!
A Study of the New Testament Church
Bible Authority, How Established How Applied

www.ingramcontent.com/pod-product-compliance
Lightning Source LLC
Chambersburg PA
CBHW022354040426
42450CB00005B/172